DEVELOPMENT CENTRE SEMINARS

FISCAL DECENTRALISATION IN EMERGING ECONOMIES

Governance Issues

Edited by
Kiichiro Fukusaku *and* Luiz R. de Mello Jr.

DEVELOPPEMENT CENTRE
OF THE ORGANISATION FOR ECONOMIC CO-OPERATION AND DEVELOPMENT

ORGANISATION FOR ECONOMIC CO-OPERATION AND DEVELOPMENT

Pursuant to Article 1 of the Convention signed in Paris on 14th December 1960, and which came into force on 30th September 1961, the Organisation for Economic Co-operation and Development (OECD) shall promote policies designed:

- to achieve the highest sustainable economic growth and employment and a rising standard of living in Member countries, while maintaining financial stability, and thus to contribute to the development of the world economy;
- to contribute to sound economic expansion in Member as well as non-member countries in the process of economic development; and
- to contribute to the expansion of world trade on a multilateral, non-discriminatory basis in accordance with international obligations.

The original Member countries of the OECD are Austria, Belgium, Canada, Denmark, France, Germany, Greece, Iceland, Ireland, Italy, Luxembourg, the Netherlands, Norway, Portugal, Spain, Sweden, Switzerland, Turkey, the United Kingdom and the United States. The following countries became Members subsequently through accession at the dates indicated hereafter: Japan (28th April 1964), Finland (28th January 1969), Australia (7th June 1971), New Zealand (29th May 1973), Mexico (18th May 1994), the Czech Republic (21st December 1995), Hungary (7th May 1996), Poland (22nd November 1996) and Korea (12th December 1996). The Commission of the European Communities takes part in the work of the OECD (Article 13 of the OECD Convention).

The Development Centre of the Organisation for Economic Co-operation and Development was established by decision of the OECD Council on 23rd October 1962 and comprises twenty-three Member countries of the OECD: Austria, Belgium, Canada, the Czech Republic, Denmark, Finland, France, Germany, Greece, Iceland, Ireland, Italy, Japan, Korea, Luxembourg, Mexico, the Netherlands, Norway, Poland, Portugal, Spain, Sweden and Switzerland, as well as Argentina and Brazil from March 1994, and Chile since November 1998. The Commission of the European Communities also takes part in the Centre's Advisory Board.

The purpose of the Centre is to bring together the knowledge and experience available in Member countries of both economic development and the formulation and execution of general economic policies; to adapt such knowledge and experience to the actual needs of countries or regions in the process of development and to put the results at the disposal of the countries by appropriate means.

The Centre has a special and autonomous position within the OECD which enables it to enjoy scientific independence in the execution of its task. Nevertheless, the Centre can draw upon the experience and knowledge available in the OECD in the development field.

Publié en français sous le titre :

LA DÉCENTRALISATION BUDGÉTAIRE DANS LES ÉCONOMIES ÉMERGENTES

Problèmes de gestion des affaires publiques

Foreword

This volume contains contributions from participants in the conference on "Decentralisation, Intergovernmental Fiscal Relations and Macroeconomic Governance", organised jointly by the OECD Development Centre and ESAF, the School of Tax Administration of the Brazilian Ministry of Finance. The conference was held in Brasilia, on 16–17 June 1997, in the context of the Development Centre's research on the reform and growth of large developing countries.

Table of Contents

PART TWO
CASE STUDIES: LATIN AMERICAN PERSPECTIVES

PART THREE
CASE STUDIES: ASIAN PERSPECTIVES

Preface

Putting public finance in order is one of the most important policy challenges facing large decentralised countries. The reform of public finance aims to achieve two main goals: consolidate the fiscal position of the government, and improve efficiency in allocating public funds. Fiscal consolidation plays a pivotal role in maintaining macroeconomic stability, especially in the context of financial market liberalisation and growing capital mobility. Moreover, designing efficient institutions which foster strong intergovernmental fiscal relations is an integral part of overall fiscal reform. Many OECD countries have made significant efforts and improved their fiscal performance during the past decade with possible lessons for other countries.

This book is the outcome of a June 1997 International Conference organised by the OECD Development Centre and the ESAF/Ministry of Finance of Brazil in Brasilia to examine the relationship between fiscal decentralisation and macroeconomic stability in emerging economies, particularly those in Latin America. Brazilian Finance Minister Pedro Malan, who inaugurated the conference, highlighted the importance of continuing fiscal reform efforts for the more than 200 participants, including top–ranking officials of the Brazilian Government, senior staff from national and international organisations and experts from both developing and OECD countries.

Fiscal decentralisation poses a particular challenge to policy makers in Latin America. This book examines how public finance regimes differ across countries and distinguishes specific country characteristics. Given the gap between theory and practice, the country case studies provide valuable insights into the real relationships between macroeconomic stability, fiscal policy and public finance.

This unique comparative analysis, covering countries in Latin America, Asia and the OECD area, helps to identify future directions in the fiscal role of governments world–wide and will make a significant contribution to public finance reform in emerging economies.

Jean Bonvin
President
OECD Development Centre
Paris

Maria de Fátima Cartaxo
Director General
Escola de Administração Fazendária (ESAF)
Brasilia

March 1999

7

Contributors

Vito Tanzi	Director of the Fiscal Affairs Division of the International Monetary Fund
Anwar Shah	Principal Evaluation Officer, Operations Evaluation Department, World Bank
Teresa Ter-Minassian	Deputy Director, Western Hemisphere Division, International Monetary Fund
Jon Blondal	Administrator, Public Management Service, OECD
Gabriel Aghón	Head of Division, Regional Project of Fiscal Decentralisation, ECLAC
Carlos Casas	Professor of Economics, Universidad del Pacífico, Peru
Ernesto Rezk	Professor of Economics, Universidad de Córdoba, Argentina
Ricardo López Murphy	Chief Economist at FIEL, Argentina
Luiz R. de Mello Jr	Lecturer in Economics, University of Kent at Canterbury, United Kingdom
Rafael Gamboa	Administrator, Banco de Mexico
Kiichiro Fukasaku	Head, Research Division, OECD Development Centre
Parthasarathi Shome	Advisor, Fiscal Affairs Department, International Monetary Fund, formerly Director, National Institute of Public Finance and Policy, India
Fan Gang	Director, China Reform Foundation, National Economic Research Institute, People's Republic of China

Commentators

Rakesh Mohan	Director, National Council of Applied Economic Research, India
Kathryn Gordon	Administrator, Economics Division, OECD
José Roberto Afonso	Head, Fiscal Affairs Division of BNDES, Brazil
Rui Affonso	Director of FUNDAP, Brazil
Fábio Giambiagi	Economist, BNDES, Brazil
Isaías Coelho	Economist, International Monetary Fund
Bert Hofman	Economist, World Bank

Introduction and Overview

Kiichiro Fukasaku and Luiz R. de Mello, Jr

Fiscal decentralisation — the devolution of taxing and spending powers to lower levels of government — has become an important element of fiscal reform in both OECD and non–OECD countries. Countries have differing motivations for reform, and their experience and its consequences for macroeconomic stability and growth have varied significantly from one country to another.

The large and growing literature on public finance, social choice and fiscal federalism highlights the expected benefits and costs of fiscal decentralisation and the role intergovernmental relations play in overall fiscal outcomes. Decentralisation is advocated on the ground that the central government cannot adequately meet the growing local demand for public goods and services. The centre often fails to improve fiscal efficiency, as it tends to ignore local differences in culture, environment and natural resource endowments as well as economic and social factors, all important determinants of public–sector performance. Bringing government closer to the public should enhance accountability in service delivery and allocative efficiency by closing the gap between expenditure assignments and revenue sources. With significant efficiency gains, fiscal decentralisation will enhance growth as well. At the same time, it can reduce operational and information costs in service delivery and streamline public sector activities, hence facilitating fiscal consolidation and improving overall macroeconomic performance.

Decentralisation is not without pitfalls. Its expected benefits must be properly weighed against the risks involved in the devolution of taxing and spending powers to subnational governments (SNGs). There is growing recognition that it may aggravate fiscal imbalances by creating a deficit bias in fiscal policy making and consequently endanger overall macroeconomic stability. For many developing countries, the key policy challenge will be to design and develop appropriate systems of public finance to provide local public services effectively and efficiently, while at the same time maintaining macroeconomic stability. The issues related to decentralisation, including intergovernmental fiscal relations, thus have direct relevance for public sector reform.

A central question involves whether decentralisation leads to a deterioration of subnational finances and whether that negatively affects the fiscal position of the central government. This likely will happen when the transfer of spending assignments to SNGs is not matched by a proportional reduction in the spending mandate of the central government. Similarly, the transfer of revenue sources to SNGs, following the devolution of expenditure functions, may deprive the central government of important ones, particularly those most efficiently used by higher tiers of government. Moreover, the system of revenue sharing across government levels, based mainly on intergovernmental transfers, may not encourage local revenue mobilisation.

When fiscal decentralisation leads to a deterioration of the central government's fiscal position, it is also likely to affect monetary policy, depending on how fiscal imbalances are financed — i.e. when the financing occurs through money creation and the assignment of public sector functions to different levels of government does not ensure arm's length transactions between the public sector and the banking system, including the central bank. Under such circumstances, fiscal decentralisation may be incompatible with monetary discipline.

An additional pitfall of fiscal decentralisation is that its benefits might be smaller than expected because SNGs might assign resources to expenditure functions not likely, in principle, to generate economy–wide, growth–enhancing externalities. Any significant mismatch between national and subnational policy objectives and priorities may affect negatively a country's growth potential and the scope of short–term demand management.

Prerequisites for Successful Decentralisation

The fiscal decentralisation literature at large and the papers presented in this volume emphasise some general prerequisites for successful decentralisation. *First,* decentralisation programmes that give new budgetary rights and responsibilities to SNGs will promote institutional clarity and transparency in budgeting only if spending matches resources at the subnational level and SNGs are committed to fiscal discipline. A successful decentralisation programme must include incentives for prudence in debt and expenditure management at lower tiers of government, impose stringent, credible constraints on subnational indebtedness, and create effective instruments to monitor subnational fiscal positions. Institutions that allow effective monitoring of subnational positions should be complemented by a credible commitment to fiscal discipline at the central government level.

Second, a successful decentralisation programme also depends largely on the availability of expertise at the subnational level, without which those governments cannot handle increased resources and ensure effective expenditure management. Moreover, the matching of revenue sources and expenditure functions at that level involves encouraging local revenue mobilisation. By boosting subnational spending, fiscal decentralisation may put further strains on the finances of higher levels of government if it drives a wedge between resources mobilised locally and those transferred from higher levels, between local spending and local resources, or between the costs and benefits of providing local public goods and services.

The case studies presented in this volume reveal a number of important elements common to fiscal decentralisation in emerging economies[1]. *First,* the devolution of expenditure functions and revenue sources to lower levels of government has been unbalanced in many, notably at the expense of revenue sources controlled by the central government. *Second,* revenue–sharing arrangements have relied excessively on intergovernmental transfers without encouraging significant local revenue mobilisation. *Third* and most important, the design of institutional arrangements often allows the loss of central government control over subnational finances, leading to a deterioration of its fiscal position. In the absence of arm's–length relationships between fiscal and monetary authorities, the overall fiscal imbalances resulting from decentralisation do not encourage good macroeconomic governance.

The country experiences surveyed here also suggest that OECD Member countries have generally had more success in implementing fiscal decentralisation programmes than most of the emerging economies in the sample. Stringent control of subnational finances apparently has prevented national and subnational fiscal positions from deteriorating. One may argue that the gains of fiscal decentralisation may be overestimated for those emerging economies in which the costs of decentralisation may be too high to ignore because of the difficulty of removing institutional hurdles that prevent effective and efficient decentralisation.

Overview

Part One of this book, which deals with general topics in fiscal decentralisation, public finance and intergovernmental fiscal relations, opens with Vito Tanzi's paper. It examines the role of the state from an historical perspective and highlights the reasons for the increase in the size of the public sector in most developed countries in the 20th century. They include the need for effective demand management in the Keynesian tradition, for equity in income distribution in the Marxist tradition and, more recently, to correct market failures and promote social welfare. Comparing and contrasting the economic roles of the state in developing and developed countries, the author argues that interventionism and distortionary regulations increased that role in developing countries, as measured by expenditure/GDP ratios. Since the 1980s, deterioration in the quality of public sector service delivery and the aggravation of fiscal imbalances in both developed and developing countries have generated renewed confidence in the allocative role of the market, and hence justified limiting the scope of government intervention.

Against this historical background, Anwar Shah and Teresa Ter–Minassian discuss fiscal federalism issues and their implications for macroeconomic governance. Anwar Shah's paper devotes particular attention to the impact of decentralisation on monetary policy. It argues that decentralisation is likely to promote central bank independence and highlights the institutional setting for policy making in the course of decentralisation.

As for fiscal policy, the author argues that decentralisation reduces the ability of the central government to perform stabilisation and demand management functions, a point also raised by Teresa Ter–Minassian and a number of others. The paper stresses the need to strengthen policy co–ordination across different levels of government and to control subnational fiscal positions in order to make decentralisation successful.

Teresa Ter–Minassian draws attention to the risks for macroeconomic governance and fiscal discipline involved in the process of fiscal decentralisation. She argues that in developing countries fiscal decentralisation is likely to generate fiscal imbalances at the subnational level, which may lead to a fiscal deterioration at the centre. As does Anwar Shah's paper, this study makes a strong case for increased surveillance and institutional control of subnational finances, particularly in decentralised federations. The paper also highlights the pitfalls of decentralisation for the central government's ability to implement macroeconomic adjustment and demand management policies.

Jon Blondal examines the OECD experience with intergovernmental fiscal relations, looking at the political–economy aspects of budget reform with special reference to budget institutions and expenditure management. He discusses the mechanisms through which market forces rather than institutional restrictions can control subnational indebtedness, as illustrated by US subnational debts, which have remained stable as a share of GDP. The paper also examines New Zealand's successful reform of budget institutions.

Gabriel Aghón and Carlos Casas place special emphasis on financing urban development in the context of fiscal federalism. They provide a detailed discussion of local government finances in Latin America, focusing on the municipalities of La Paz, Bolivia, and Bogota, Colombia. They highlight a potential shortage of municipal expertise and the inability of local governments to finance their expenditure assignments locally as important constraints to successful decentralisation. Their case studies suggest that fiscal decentralisation programmes do not often encourage local revenue mobilisation and fiscal discipline from the institutional point of view.

Part Two focuses on five case studies that illustrate the issues raised in Part One. They cover three countries in Latin America (Argentina, Brazil, and Mexico) and two in Asia (China and India). The selection of case studies was based on the scope and depth of reform, contrasting macroeconomic indicators, institutional features and overall economic performance. In most Latin American countries, the return to democracy in the 1980s prompted to a considerable extent the decentralisation of fiscal decision making and public sector administration. In the 1960s and 1970s, growth based on import substitution had furnished the main driving force for increasing the economic role of the state and centralisation in economic decision making. In Asia, with the exception of India, unitary fiscal systems are widespread. The case studies fall broadly in line with the arguments raised in the papers in Part One and contain insightful empirical validation of those arguments. They also provide valuable information for international comparisons of fiscal federalism regimes in different parts of the developing world.

Ernesto Rezk examines the Latin American experience with fiscal decentralisation. He highlights important differences across several countries in the scope and depth of fiscal decentralisation policy packages and their repercussions on macroeconomic stability, given the region's history of chronic inflation and erratic growth. The paper emphasises the institutional aspects of multilevel government structures and intergovernmental fiscal relations.

Ricardo López Murphy and Cynthia Moskovits describe Argentina as a relatively centralised federation in which a system of revenue sharing has particular importance because subnational governments have relatively little taxing power. The authors highlight the risks of decentralisation when control over subnational finances is lost, particularly if financial rescue from the central government is expected in the event of default. They also share the views of others in this volume that the process of decentralisation must strengthen budget control in lower tiers of government and that arm's–length relationships between the government and banking and financial institutions are necessary to preserve monetary discipline in a more decentralised environment.

Luiz de Mello's paper shows that Brazil has gone a long way in fiscal decentralisation by raising subnational spending ratios substantially, devolving revenue sources and expenditure functions to subnational jurisdictions and granting significant autonomy in policy making to SNGs. In fact, the country is among the most decentralised federations in the world in terms of subnational fiscal autonomy and spending as a share of total government spending. Yet, the author argues, the country's system of intergovernmental transfers has not encouraged local revenue mobilisation, even though controlling subnational indebtedness stands as an important prerequisite for overall fiscal restraint and the consolidation of macroeconomic stability.

According to Rafael Gamboa, the Mexican experience provides another illustration of the channels through which fiscal decentralisation may generate significant fiscal and monetary imbalances at the centre. He describes in detail the institutional aspects of fiscal federalism in Mexico, including the assignment of expenditure functions and revenue sources across different government levels, and the country's system of intergovernmental transfers. This system makes it difficult to promote policy co–ordination across different levels of government despite the relative centralisation of Mexican federalism. The paper shows how the Mexican revenue–sharing system discourages local revenue mobilisation by increasing the dependency of subnational governments on transfers from the central government. As in other federations, closing the gap between local revenues and service delivery costs tends to improve governance in countries with loose central control over subnational finances and significant financial autonomy enjoyed by lower tiers of government.

Part Three continues with case studies, turning to Asia. Kiichiro Fukasaku provides an overview of fiscal performance and the main characteristics of fiscal systems in Asian developing countries. His paper highlights, in sharp contrast with Latin America, the relative centralism of most Asian countries and efforts in pursuit of fiscal consolidation in a number of them, notably in Southeast Asia. India and China stand out as noteworthy cases where fiscal consolidation has not been pursued with the vigour of other Asian governments. The author emphasises the importance of fiscal conservatism as a link between openness and macroeconomic stability in the region.

According to Parthasarathi Shome, India has a long tradition of fiscal decentralisation. He describes the institutional features of Indian centre–state fiscal relations for revenue–sharing agreements and the assignment of expenditure functions. As in other federations, he advocates reform in the system of intergovernmental transfers as a prerequisite for sound macroeconomic governance. Excessive subnational borrowing adversely affects growth prospects for the economy, pushing interest rates up and depressing private investment. Shome argues that the efficiency gains associated with fiscal decentralisation may be overestimated in developing countries, given the risks it involves.

Fan Gang's paper reviews China's fiscal decentralisation and again highlights the risks of excessive decentralisation in a reforming economy. The Chinese experience offers particular insights as the only case study in this volume devoted to a reforming centrally planned economy. The core element in the ongoing reform involves the redefinition of intergovernmental fiscal relations in a new environment of increasingly decentralised, market–based resource allocation. Fan points out reform of the Chinese tax–sharing system as a key ingredient of the post–1994 fiscal reform package, although the budget–making process remains problematic and institutionally complex. China needs to strike a balance between decentralising and recentralising forces in the years to come.

Note

1.   During the conference, Grzegorz W. Kolodko, former Deputy Prime Minister of Poland, presented his country's recent experience of reforms which enhanced the fiscal position of local governments. See Kolodko, G.W. (1996), *Poland 2000: the New Economic Strategy*, Poltext, Warsaw.

PART ONE

HISTORY, THEORY AND POLITICAL ECONOMY

Chapter 1

The Changing Role of the State in the Economy: An Historical Perspective

Vito Tanzi

Positive and Normative Roles of the State

The French poet, Paul Valéry, has been reported to believe that, "If the state is strong, it will crush us; if it is weak, we will perish."[1] Its ideal powers must therefore lie between these two extremes. Governments play many roles, some political, some social, and some economic. This paper will focus on the economic one. In its pursuit, government uses many policy instruments and by so doing allocates resources, redistributes income, and influences the level of activity.

At least since Richard Musgrave wrote his influential *Theory of Public Finance* in 1959, public finance economists have found useful the distinction between the *normative* and the *positive* roles of the state. The normative role determines guidelines, principles, or norms for welfare–enhancing public sector intervention in the economy. Based on fundamental economic principles, it attempts to define what government should do to correct market imperfections and otherwise complement the market to promote and maximise social welfare.

Although economists do not explicitly recognise it, the political constitution of a country affects the normative role. Western, market–oriented democracies, from which much modern economic thinking has originated, implicitly tie the state's normative function to the individualistic political process that assumes no goals or needs outside those of individual citizens or voters. They thus see the public interest as the summation of the interests of individual citizens or voters[2]. In a way, this explains why many see a close relationship between a market economy and a democratic process. In a market individuals vote with their dollars, while in a democratic process they use ballots to promote their political goals. The state cannot have objectives different from those of its citizens. One could assume an alternative concept of the state — for example, a Hegelian notion of an organic or a totalitarian state that exists outside the individuals living at a given time and thus has a life of its own. This view would not be popular, especially among Western–oriented economists[3].

While the normative role attempts to define what the government should do to maximise economic welfare, the positive one analyses what the government actually does. In an ideal world, the two would merge: the ideal and the actual would become the same in the sense that the state would do exactly what it is expected to do and all the reforms needed to maximise social welfare would be carried out. In the real world, the two roles tend to diverge, at times by a great deal, implying that many needed reforms have not occurred. The divergence has several reasons, ranging from differences between the interests of those who govern and those who are governed, to policy makers' mistakes and misconceptions, to inadequate controls by policy makers over policy instruments and to the residual effects of past decisions.

Even when political leaders would like to achieve welfare–promoting social objectives, their economic training may not be adequate for the task. Some of them come from disciplines other than economics and are thus unsophisticated in economic matters. Some may have simplistic notions of how economies operate or, in Keynes's terms, be slaves of the theories of defunct economists[4]. Still others, trained or not, may confuse their own personal interests with the public interest; they would pursue policies that help them, their friends, their families or their political allies, but are not optimal for the country. Unfortunately, examples of official rent seeking or even corruption are far from rare.

Officials who make the basic policy decisions promote the role of the state, but wide differences can emerge between expectations based on those policies and final outcomes. The decisions made upstream by policy makers must be implemented downstream by the public administration or other institutions. Principal–agent problems are common, especially when those who must implement policies have objectives of their own or fear harm from those policies. Therefore, the process of implementation may change or distort the policies, and the final results may differ from the anticipated results[5]. This outcome also occurs when public administration is incompetent or corrupt; public employees in a way privatise the use of some of the policy instruments.

Because many policies have consequences that last, the role of the state at a given moment is much influenced by *past* policies in addition to the theories of defunct economists. Policy decisions made by previous governments heavily determine the current economic role of the state and constrain current government actions. They often create a role for the state different from that which current policy makers might prefer. Legal, political, or administrative constraints may limit the power of an incumbent government to change economic policies. This is an important reason why ministers often agree with the need for some reform, but argue that it would be difficult or impossible to implement.

Examples of decisions with long–term consequences include those related to the size of the civil service, to whether enterprises are public or private, to the level of public sector salaries, to pension rights, to tenure in public jobs, to tax incentives and subsidies to particular groups or sectors, and so on[6]. These past decisions create legal or implicit entitlements or other claims that a current government may find difficult or impossible to change, especially in the short run. In some countries, interest on the public debt and other hard–to–reduce spending, such as entitlements, account for three–fourths of total spending[7]. In reality, no government has the freedom to start with a *tabula rasa*, so to speak, unaffected by past commitments.

Current economic policy is thus to varying degrees a slave of past governments' decisions. Those who benefit from them will oppose reforms, even those in the public interest. This in part explains why some economists have argued that authoritarian governments may be needed to pursue policies favourable to growth[8]. Current governments often receive blame for economic problems created largely by the policies of previous ones. In short, the current economic role of the state must be seen as the outcome of both past and present economic policy decisions.

Thus historical developments matter. Many industrial countries, for example, reflect the influence of their experience with the Great Depression, major wars and the threat of communism, all of which forced particular policies on past governments. In many developing countries, the state's economic role felt the influence of their backgrounds as colonies of foreign powers. Nationalisation of enterprises, for example, often occurred because at independence many of them had been in the hands of individuals from the colonial powers.

Other important factors may include: *a)* social attitudes, which may stem from cultural heritage or religion; *b)* levels of economic development that, depending on the sophistication of the market and private institutions, may call for more or less state intervention; *c)* the degree of openness of the economy[9]; *d)* technological developments that may create or destroy natural monopolies or govern the need to regulate new activities, such as financial markets, communication or transportation; and, finally, *e)* the quality of public administration, which may impose limits on the scope of effective governmental intervention[10].

A priori, it would appear that the less developed a country, the more it could benefit from a larger government role to supplement the market and correct its many imperfections, the consequence of informational deficiencies, limited mobility of resources and excessive individual economic power in local markets. It is also true, however, that generally, although not always, the less developed a country, the less able is its public administration. One of the unpleasant realities of economic development is that the very countries that have the greatest need for an expanded public sector role may be the same ones where the public sector is least prepared efficiently to play such a part. In these circumstances, when policy makers attempt to pursue an ambitious public sector role, as they often do, the results tend to be disappointing[11]. Yet as markets develop, they become more efficient, and for this reason they require a less active normative role for the state; at the same time, the ability of policy makers and of the public administration to deal with market deficiencies (and other problems that, at least in theory, government could solve), should rise — just as new markets that need regulation come into existence.

Economists and political scientists customarily assess the state's part in the economy by measuring the ratio of tax revenue or government spending to gross domestic product. On this criterion, the role of the state is much larger (on average, twice as large) in industrial countries than in developing countries. Sweden's ratio, for example, is almost five times as large as China's. Knowledgeable observers would recognise that the reality often differs. They would be aware that, in recent decades, the public sectors of many developing countries, through regulatory policies, have acted much more than the governments of the industrial countries to allocate investment, credit, foreign exchange, and economic resources in general.

Many of these countries require permits or authorisations to engage in most economic activities[12]. As a consequence, private enterprise managers in some countries spend a large proportion of their time negotiating with officials[13]. This often gives government bureaucrats the power to delay or stop economic decisions by private individuals and enterprises, and thus the opportunity to demand payments for these permits or authorisations. The state has also played an extensive role in the direct production of goods and services.

Expansion of Government's Role in the 20th Century

The classical economists, from Adam Smith onward, favoured a minimal role for the public sector. They generally preferred one limited to the provision of essential public works, the maintenance of law and order and the defence of the country. In their view, the government should guarantee property rights and the sanctity of contracts and protect the economic and political liberties of individuals, as the core activities of the public sector. This conservative attitude arose partly in reaction to the widespread interference of governments with the working of the market in 18th century Europe. The classical economists considered such interference as damaging to economic activity and an obstacle to growth. Perhaps as a consequence, in the 19th century the economic role of the government tended to be much more limited. In most of the industrial countries, public spending was around 10 per cent of GDP and *laissez–faire* the dominant economic philosophy[14].

The 20th century saw a gradual but large expansion of the state into the economy, particularly evident from data on the growth of public spending as a share of GDP. For the newly industrialised countries that share grew on average from about 12 per cent in 1913 to about 45 per cent in 1995[15]. Both political and ideological factors contributed. Aside from the historical and political factors (such as wars and depressions)

20

changes in prevalent attitudes *vis–à–vis* what the state was expected to do were important and created the climate that made possible much of the government activism of recent decades.

Marxist and socialist thinking (which emphasised income equality among individuals) created strong pressures on the governments of countries with market economies to play a significant part in redistributing income — a function not even contemplated by the classical economists with their focus on the allocative function of the state. The advent of communism in the Soviet Union and later other Eastern European countries, and the attraction of central planning for many intellectuals in the rest of the world, pushed countries toward a "mixed" economy with more government intervention. Income redistribution came to be seen as a major, legitimate policy objective[16], which called for policies to reduce the income of the rich and increase that of the poor. Income taxation, with high progressive rates, subsidies to basic commodities and welfare payments — policies rare or non–existent in the past — became common. Higher public spending on education and health also often was justified by its impact on income distribution[17].

Keynesian thinking also created pressures to stabilise the economy by helping to sustain the disposable income of individuals during cyclical fluctuations. It justified public works programmes and unemployment compensation, together with public sector expansion and taxes with high built–in flexibility. Many countries introduced public pension schemes, often with redistributive features, and various forms of assistance to those with incomes below certain levels. Public enterprises were used to maximise public employment. The goal was to build an economy with characteristics that reduced its exposure to fluctuations, because countries with large public sectors were believed to be less subject to business cycles.

In addition to the impact of socialist and, more generally, Keynesian thinking, technical developments in economics, especially after World War II, provided additional justifications for public sector intervention. For example, the concept of public goods, made popular by influential economists like Paul Samuelson and Richard Musgrave, justified government provision of many goods with public–good characteristics because it implied that without such intervention the market would undersupply them; the private sector would have no incentive to produce them due to the difficulty of excluding from their consumption individuals who would not contribute to the cost of their production (i.e. free riders)[18].

Closely related to public goods was the concept of externality. The recognition that the consumption or production of some goods may generate positive or negative externalities not reflected in their prices created a further case for market failure requiring governmental intervention[19]. The government was expected to increase the private cost of producing or consuming goods with undesirable externalities and to decrease the cost of goods with desirable ones. Externalities became often–cited and politically exploited justifications for expanding the role of the public sector into health, education, research, transportation, training and many other areas. Some authors even argued that welfare payments to the poor could be justified in terms of externalities such as the reduction of crime. The argument was familiar: without governmental intervention, the market would underproduce or overproduce such goods depending on whether the externalities were good or bad. Government could play its part through subsidies to the private sector (either directly or by tax incentives), through public production as in health or education, or by regulation[20].

In addition to ideological factors which influenced government behaviour in all countries, some arguments had particular importance for developing countries. The early literature on economic development often assumed that governments had abilities lacking in the private sector. One of the arguments used to justify the government's role in direct production activities (through public enterprises) held that managerial skills absent in the private sector were somehow available in the public sector. Another stressed that some large–scale activities or projects required amounts of capital or degrees of expertise that only the public sector could generate or assemble. Still another asserted that information essential for the successful conduct of some activities was more available, or only available, to the public sector. This might result from rational ignorance when, for individuals, the cost of getting information exceeds the benefit from it.

In the 1950s and 1960s, especially in developing countries, people often assumed that the government was the best judge in deciding which goods were "essential" or "necessary" and which were not. Its judgement replaced that of the market[21]. Incentive legislation accorded favourable treatment (in taxation, the provision of credit, access to foreign exchange) to investments aimed at producing "essential" or "necessary" goods. It penalised or even prohibited the use of some resources (credit or foreign exchange) for the provision of "nonessential" or luxury goods. Many countries provided high protection to domestic production of "necessary" goods.

Paternalistic policies that replace the preferences of consumers with those of policy makers remain common in many countries as, for example, in industrial policy. The assumption is that the government has more knowledge than the private sector of how the market and the economy operate or what the citizens need most. Thus, the government can pursue an industrial policy that picks future winners and provides them with "temporary" protection or assistance as the expected giants of tomorrow.

The 1950s and 1960s, the golden age of public sector intervention, were influenced by some naive political perceptions or assumptions of how governments operate. For example:

—   the objective of promoting social welfare drives public sector actions; rent seeking by those who formulate policies is insignificant or non–existent. The literature on rent seeking appeared only in the 1970s[22] and that on corruption and governance has come mainly in the 1990s;

—   the public sector is monolithic, with a clear nerve centre that makes all the important economic decisions in a rational and transparent way. Thus, policies cannot be inconsistent among themselves. For example, those pursued by public enterprises or other decentralised entities (local governments, stabilisation boards, social security institutions and so on) cannot be at odds with those of the central government; and within the central government, of course, all the ministries promote consistent policies[23]. It is puzzling how little interest existed until the 1990s in issues of fiscal federalism and policy co–ordination *within* countries[24];

— policies are consistent not just in space but also in time. Governments have political horizons long enough so that current policies will not be allowed to conflict with future ones, either by mistake or out of political considerations (such as winning the next elections) that may lead governments to choose in the short run policies inconsistent with long–run goals. Again, the literature on the time–inconsistency of economic policy is recent[25];

— policy decisions are reversible. Government employees can be dismissed when no longer needed; incentives can be removed when their objectives have been met or their implementation time has expired; entitlements can be ended; and so on. Recently governments have had to face the unpleasant reality that it is far easier to increase benefits (such as pensions) than to reduce them, or to hire civil servants than to fire them;

— policy makers have full control over the policy instruments. They can rely on honest and efficient public sector employees to implement efficiently and objectively policies decided at the top. The literature on corruption, principal–agent problems, and rent seeking is relevant here and is once again a product of recent years.

Experience has shown that such romantic or idealised views of how policy gets made and carried out often lie far from reality[26]. In fact, public sectors *i)* are not monolithic but have several, even many policy making centres which may not all be guided by the same concept of the public interest; *ii)* may not make policies consistent in space or time; *iii)* may be influenced by rent seeking and by pressure groups; *iv)* may contain decision makers ignorant of how the economy really works; *v)* may suffer from principal–agent problems; *vi)* may not be able to reverse their actions; and *vii)* may harbour bureaucracies that are inefficient or corrupt or both. Intellectual developments in these areas — a frontal attack on the thinking of earlier years[27] — have made many people wary or more sceptical about the expanded role of the government and have set the stage for greater reliance on the market.

The view that the government could solve most problems is no longer as widely accepted as two or three decades ago. After several decades of expanded state intervention, expectations can be compared against the results, disappointing in many countries and especially in developing ones. Ample evidence now shows that heavy state intervention has not improved the allocation of resources, promoted faster growth, achieved a better distribution of income or provided a more stable economic environment. Resources continue to be seriously misallocated, often as a direct result of government policies. Gini coefficients and other measures of income inequality have not improved over time and are not much better in countries with heavy state intervention than in those with more limited and more focused public sectors. Inflation, unemployment and macroeconomic disequilibria continue to affect many countries, especially those with extensive state intervention. In fact, those which have limited and better focused the role of the state — Chile, New Zealand and the countries of Southeast Asia, for example — have performed better.

The Return to the Market

Recent years have seen the beginning of a realisation that the growth of governmental intervention in the market occurred in parallel with a deflection of attention from the core activities of the state[28]. Given the limited time and resources available to policy makers, and as they became distracted and overwhelmed by the many responsibilities they had assumed, they lost capacity to dedicate to the core activities the resources, time, energy and attention that these activities required. Notwithstanding appeals to equity goals to justify unproductive or questionable use of public resources, the quality of the basic services provided by the state deteriorated. The state did more and more but did it less and less well. This has had negative implications for the working of the markets, which depends greatly on how well the state performs its core activities. The state shifted over the years from supporting or augmenting the markets to competing with and thus replacing them.

In many countries, law and order, the quintessential core activity, suffered, thus imposing large pecuniary or psychic costs on the population. Crime became a big problem because governments allowed police and court services to deteriorate from lack of resources or attention, often amidst attempts to explain or justify crime on the basis of social conditions. Disputes among citizens or between citizens and the state in many countries could not be solved expeditiously because access to justice became very expensive and the judicial system was on the verge of collapse. Much–delayed judicial decisions (sometimes for many years), when they finally came, were seen by the relevant parties as capricious or unfair and lost much of their deterrent effect. Their implementation was also capricious and very slow. All these factors made access to the law highly unequal and, inevitably, legal rights, including those related to property and contracts, became uncertain. The judicial systems of many countries were not immune from corruption.

In many countries, obtaining basic documents or permits, such as passports, drivers' licenses and authorisations to open shops or to import, may take months and/or the payment of some "speed money"[29]. Governments often do not enforce contracts, thus creating doubts or uncertainties about property rights and encouraging some to ignore the terms of contracts. This has destroyed or at least hurt some markets. In some countries, the threshold costs of getting access to the justice system are so high as to discourage all but the better–off, thus creating unequal justice. A kind of bureaucratic cholesterol has thus clogged the arteries which energise market economies.

In health, the provision of basic services, such as vaccination and preventive services, suffered when the state extended its role into more complex and expensive areas like curative services provided in large urban hospitals. Elementary education (a core activity) flagged when the state expanded into far more expensive higher education. The maintenance of basic physical infrastructure lagged when the state became distracted by large investments and gave priority to investment over expenditure for operation and maintenance[30].

Recent years have witnessed a universal rediscovery of the market, or at least a greater appreciation among policy makers and the public of the role that the market can play in the economy. This has led to a gradual reduction in governmental intervention and greater reliance on the allocative function of the market. Government has slowly moved from competing with the market to augmenting and improving its operation. In a growing number of countries:

—   public enterprises are being privatised;

—   quantitative restrictions on trade are being reduced or removed and import duties lowered, in some cases to very low levels, making trade more responsive to changes in relative prices;

—   restrictions on the allocation of credit and controls on interest rates are being reduced or removed, thus, restoring to the credit market its important allocative function;

—   price controls have become less popular and many other constraints on economic activities are being reduced.

All these actions increase the role of market forces and, *mutatis mutandis*, limit the scope of governmental intervention. Policy makers are slowly realising that government should not replace the market in allocating resources, but rather take actions that make it work better. It is perhaps no distortion of the truth to say that the governments of many countries, although not all, would now like to see the state play a smaller role. Yet they confront the legacy of past decisions and the special interests of groups that benefit from past decisions, groups often powerful enough to prevent or slow reform. As a consequence, it may take several years before the role of the state can be brought in line with current thinking.

What main changes should take place? A full answer to this question would require far more pages and time than can be used here. Yet one can suggest a broad sketch, fully realising that often the devil is in the details and that some points could benefit from much more nuance.

The classical economists, even those who strongly believed in *laissez–faire* and the sovereignty of the market, wanted the state to play a significant role focused on the core activities, such as essential public works, law and order including the guarantee of property rights and the enforcement of contracts, and defence of the country. In these areas, the state has simply not performed well. In some cases, it has been the main violator of property rights and contracts[31]. Thus, a reallocation of attention by policy makers to these core activities would greatly benefit the market.

Privatisation of public enterprises must continue and in many countries accelerate. In a market economy, the state has little reason for involvement in production activities. If, through privatisation, it can reduce the public sector wage bill and the subsidies it often pays to public enterprises, as well as improve the efficiency of the economy, then privatisation is a good policy. When interest rates on public sector debt are high and some debt can be repaid with the proceeds from privatisation, then from a fiscal point of view it becomes an excellent policy[32]. Privatisation, accompanied by the opening of the market, which in many sectors introduces competition, and accompanied by rules that prevent monopolies, will usually increase the efficiency of the economy. In time it will also reduce corruption, although the process can also lead to a situation where corruption becomes a major issue.

The government must stop controlling prices of traded goods, domestic goods, or those in specialised markets such as financial markets. Price controls always distort markets and create inefficiencies and rent seeking. The government must also stop subsidising basic commodities; in several cases, subsidies have reduced the prices of some commodities or services to such an extent as to lead to excess demand and waste. Some of the most extreme examples of government–induced misallocation of resources have been reported in this area.

The government must reduce its role in allocating investment and economic activities through incentives or regulations. It should focus on improving the efficiency of the market *a)* by opening it to foreign competition; *b)* by eliminating unnecessary or inefficient economic regulations (whether of the government itself or of private groups such as unions or professional associations)[33]; *c)* through better provision and diffusion of information; and *d)* through the establishment of efficient regulatory bodies that provide needed information to consumers and establish transparent rules of the game, known and applied objectively to all. The government can promote competitive behaviour by levelling the playing field for all market participants, removing monopolies and monopolistic practices and eliminating obstacles to entry.

It may seem a bit odd to advocate the elimination of many existing regulations while calling for the establishment of regulatory bodies to establish rules of the game. The economies of many countries are overburdened with useless and damaging regulations[34], yet suffer from a dearth of controls or rules over some, especially new activities. Governments need to regulate particular sectors, such as credit and capital markets, and certain industries, such as communication, transportation, health, and energy. A market economy needs established rules of the game and essential consumer information, but no need exists to replace it in allocative decisions, except in extreme cases.

A brief digression on the use of regulations to pursue the objectives of public policy may help clarify the point made above. To varying degrees, regulations may be damaging and useless, or useful and essential, for a modern economy. A few examples of both include:

— some regulations have no other purpose than to give power to the government and the bureaucrats charged with enforcing them. They include the myriad of authorisations often required by local governments for entry into legitimate activities such as shops and factories;

— some regulations aim at achieving social objectives that could be achieved more efficiently in other ways. One example is rent control, presumably to subsidise housing for those with low incomes by implicitly taxing those who own houses[35];

— some regulations have purely social and somewhat debatable objectives, such as controls on working hours, minimum wages, and length of the work week;

— some regulations, like traffic regulations, are necessary to allow activities to operate smoothly;

— some regulations try to deal with externalities until better and more flexible tools are available. For example, they find frequent use in environmental policies when theoretically more efficient tools, such as taxes, are not yet feasible;

— finally, and of most interest, some regulations aim to protect the public in a market economy, especially when it cannot get the information it needs to make rational choices. In a modern economy that produces many products or services of which most consumers have little knowledge, reasons exist for an expansion of this type of regulation. When individuals step into a plane, they want certainty that the airline is as airworthy as possible so that the probability of a crash is very low. Because plane crashes are rare events and have many causes, crashes cannot provide *ex ante* information to travellers about the objective probability that the plane might crash. When individuals entrust their savings to a bank, they want certainty that it follows sound investment practices. Because bank failures are rare events, bank failures cannot provide a guide for depositors. When individuals buy a medicine, they want no dangerous side effects; if it does have them, they want to be informed. When they buy a product like meat, they want to be sure that it does not carry a disease. When individuals buy shares in a publicly traded company, they want assurance that the value of the shares has not been manipulated and that the available information on the company is reliable.

In all the above examples, it would not be rational, because of the costs, for individuals to acquire on their own enough knowledge to make rational decisions. That knowledge also has a public good element, because once available it can be shared at zero cost. Thus, the government has a fundamental duty both to regulate the activities and to provide the necessary information to the public[36].

Regulations to protect individuals raise a more general issue about the role of government in protecting individuals from various risks. In a recent paper, Devarajan and Hammer (1997) have argued that much of the difference in spending between developed and developing countries (a difference mostly explained by transfer payments) may arise from attempts by the governments of developed countries to protect citizens from various risks such as unemployment, loss of income due to old age, sickness and risks inherent in some economic activities. Why cannot markets, even in developed countries, provide the institutions (insurance, etc.) that would make it unnecessary for the government to enter this area?

Market failure in dealing with risk often arises for two reasons: adverse selection and moral hazard. Adverse selection results from asymmetric information between those who buy insurance and those who sell it. Normally, those who buy it have more information than those who sell it, making it difficult to establish the ideal price for each individual. As a consequence, markets do not develop fully and the government is expected to intervene. Moral hazard arises because insured individuals tend to be less careful than those not insured or may even precipitate the event for which they are insured, as with fire insurance.

Government protects individuals from risk in three ways: spending, regulation, and guarantees. In some cases, as with pensions, regulation may offer an alternative to spending, as the Chilean pension reform has shown[37]. In this approach, endorsed by the staff of the World Bank and various economists, the government regulates that individuals must allocate a given share of their income to pensions bought from highly controlled private managers. The regulation replaces government spending. Regulations do not seem to work well in health care, however, where, within a country, the amounts that individuals spend for it cannot be related to their incomes. Medical procedures cost the same whether one is rich or poor, so that an insurance scheme would generate highly differentiated health care. This is why governments remain heavily involved through public spending in the health sector.

Government guarantees have replaced government spending in areas such as banking and increasingly in infrastructure, which in recent years has seen a trend towards privatisation, at times accompanied by guarantees for investors. In this way governments reduce their current spending and fiscal deficits but at the cost of exposing themselves to potentially large costs in the future. As the guarantees are not shown as expenditures, they may at times create the illusion that intervention and spending have fallen more than they actually have.

Major economists, including Arrow, Samuelson, Stiglitz and others, have made important contributions to the extremely difficult analysis of the general role of government in dealing with risks. The extent to which improvements in the private sector plus government regulations can replace government spending remains an important development to watch. It will largely determine whether public spending as a share of GDP, especially in industrial countries, will fall in the future.

The government should rethink its role in income distribution. Broad and vague policies (such as general subsidies, price controls and higher spending for activities such as education and health), justified on grounds that they benefit the poor, should be questioned. These policies do not necessarily benefit the poor. Redistribution should occur through well focused and targeted policies on both the expenditure and revenue sides of the budget[38]. Their design should avoid significant disincentive effects or high administrative costs.

Finally, most countries have a great need for public administration reform. One finds within public administrations the most extreme cases of unproductive spending, sometimes reminiscent of the Russian joke that during central planning workers pretended to work and the government pretended to pay them. An efficient public administration must expect *all* workers to give a full day's work and must pay them a good wage. Too many public institutions give realism to an observation attributed to Pareto: that in public institutions 20 per cent of the work force performs 80 per cent of the useful work. The employment policies of governments in past decades, often justified on income–distribution grounds, produced large civil services with too many poorly paid workers. The efficient, core function of the public sector can best be promoted by a small, well paid civil service, fully aware of its responsibilities and penalised when it does not perform.

Concluding Remarks

This paper has discussed the changing economic role of the state. It has described the forces that over much of this century led to its expansion and then a reaction against it, which started a few years ago and continues. That reaction results less from ideology than from the realisation that not much welfare was gained under intrusive governments in recent decades. At the same time, scholars have identified many shortcomings associated with the expanded state; their work inevitably has affected the way we now feel about government. A danger exists that the pendulum might swing too far, from the view that assigned the solution of most problems to the state to one that identifies the state as the problem. Government has clear, important functions; as Paul Valéry said, if the state is weak, we may perish.

Many economists and political scientists now think about the state in a world where technology makes major strides and economies are getting more integrated. We know that in this world the state will have to act differently from in the past, when economies were less developed and less open, technology was less advanced and information was difficult to obtain. It will have to take more intelligent regulatory action while the private sector carries a greater burden in areas hitherto under the responsibility of governments, such as the provision of infrastructure and services like utilities, pensions, education and health.

Given recent technological advances, even the traditional "natural monopolies" may be exposed to some competition and no longer provide an obvious justification for governmental intervention. For several of them (railroads, power, and communication), their genuine monopoly activities can be separated from their other operations. For example, the generation and distribution of electricity can be detached from transmission, with competition introduced in the former while monopoly remains in the latter[39]. In some countries, private investment now plays a major part in several of these traditional monopolies.

In this brave new world, strict but intelligent public supervision of economic activity and clear rules of the game will be necessary. It remains to be seen whether governments will be able to rise to this new challenge and how national governments will behave in a world where many economic decisions may be pushed down to local governments or up to international organisations.

Globalisation and tax competition will likely reduce the scope for redistributive policies, especially those promoted through progressive taxation. Tax competition will reduce the revenue of central governments much more than that of local governments, which generally rely on tax sources, such as property and business tax, less exposed to tax competition. Globalisation will reduce the scope for stabilisation and redistributive policies by reducing the resources available to national governments at the same time as their regulatory activities will increase.

A final comment is in order on the state's role in income redistribution and providing safety nets, an issue only touched upon so far with the mention that *a)* classical economists did not recognise income redistribution as a legitimate governmental function; and *b)* many inefficient policies arose in recent decades under the justification of redistributing income[40]. Under proper conditions, markets allocate resources very well, but they are not very good at generating an income distribution that reflects the conscience or the prevalent view of society. Therefore, government cannot abdicate this difficult role, which will become more difficult with globalisation and tax competition. Yet it must operate differently from in the past, learning how to seek equity with efficient and well targeted policies. It also must not forget that growth offers the best way to escape from absolute poverty and provide productive jobs.

Notes

1. Cited in Bardhan (1996), p. 11.

2. Whether such a summation is theoretically feasible is an open question. See on this the seminal work by Arrow (1963), and subsequent related literature.

3. Problems may arise also when the nature of the issue requires paying attention to different generations. This is the case with environment, public debt, and public pensions. How should the interests of future generations be taken into account? Different but related issues also arise in connection with individuals who are not citizens of the countries in which they live. Should the state reflect only the views of the citizens or, even, of the voters?

4. It is not necessary for political leaders to have advanced economic training themselves. However, they need to have the sophistication to choose competent economic advisors and to distinguish between good and bad economic advice.

5. A common example is tax reform where the actual drafting of the laws (that is supposed to just give concrete content to the decision made) can bring many surprises. Sometimes the basic intent of the legislation may be largely neutralised by some innocent–looking clause. At other times the drafting is fine but the tax administration renders the law ineffective by not making the administrative changes necessary to effectively implement the law. For a discussion of some of these issues, see Tanzi (1994a).

6. The current difficulties that many industrial countries, such as Brazil, are having in reforming pension laws and in scaling down the welfare state are good examples of such decisions.

7. See especially the three chapters in the "Yoke of Prior Commitments" in Part Two of Steuerle and Kawai (1996).

8. Chile, under General Pinochet, China in the past two decades, and some Southeast Asian countries are assumed to provide examples of economies that have prospered under authoritarian governments able to push growth–promoting policies.

9. In a recent paper, Dani Rodrik has argued that more open economies need and have larger public sectors because they are inherently more unstable. See Rodrik (1996).

10. The normative role of the state requires and assumes that public administrations exhibit ideal Weberian characteristics. See Tanzi (1994a).

11. For example, in poor countries, not only the public administration is less skilled, but the government's ability to raise taxes is much more limited. In these countries, the government's more ambitious role is normally played through a greater use of quasi–fiscal regulations. See Tanzi (1995*a*). These quasi–fiscal regulations replace taxing and spending and often give rise to problems of governance and corruption.

12. De Soto (1989) has reported that 11 basic steps were required in Peru in the 1980 to set up a small industry. It has been reported that in Tanzania it took 28 essential steps to get approval for a medium–sized and large investment project.

13. According to a World Bank study (1995): in Morocco, it takes as many as 20 documents to register a business; in Egypt 90 per cent of an entrepreneur's time is spent resolving problems with regulatory agencies; in Lebanon it takes 18 signatures to clear goods from customs. In Ecuador, at one time, it took no less than 30 documents to apply for a tax incentive. See Tanzi (1969). For the time spent by managers negotiating with public officials, see World Bank (1997), p. 43, Fig. 3.2.

14. See Tanzi and Schuknecht (1997).

15. It is likely that there was also a gradual growth in economic regulations although there are no statistics to back this view.

16. In some ways it became the dominating objective in many countries.

17. Here one should make a distinction between the rhetoric and the reality of income redistribution. Often the impact of governmental action in redistributing income towards the poor was much more modest than one would assume from the rhetoric. The reason was that social spending was often largely appropriated by the middle classes. See Tanzi (1974); Alesina (1997).

18. See Samuelson (1954); Musgrave (1959).

19. Externalities had been recognised for a long time, as for example by Pigou. However, it was only in the post World War II era that they became a major justification for public sector intervention. James Buchanan has often argued that externalities were politicised to justify larger government intervention.

20. In more recent years, this argument has come under attack in part as a consequence of the work of Ronald Coase, who received the Noble Prize for it. See Coase (1960). Coase argued that in a market economy free arrangements among individuals would internalise the effects of externalities and thus lead to an optimum without the need for governmental intervention. Public choice literature has emphasized that while externalities create market failures, governmental intervention is often characterised by political failure which results from rent seeking. Thus, market failure does not necessarily justify governmental intervention.

21. This was a departure from the individualistic view of public interest as mentioned earlier. When the government assigns to itself the right to judge the merit of goods, it is behaving in an authoritarian fashion. The concept of *merit good* proposed by Musgrave reflects, in some way, the same assumption although Musgrave would never support an authoritarian government.

22. See Tullock (1967); Krueger (1974). See also Tullock (1989).

23. For examples of inconsistent policies within the United States government, see Krueger (1993). An extreme example for the United States is provided by the subsidies given to the production of tobacco at the same time that the government is trying to discourage smoking.

24. For examples of inconsistent policies between the central government and the local governments, see Tanzi (1995*b*).

25. See Calvo (1978).

26. The extreme version of this romantic view is implicit in the work of Tinbergen (1952) and Johansen (1965). Tinbergen's work was very influential in the 1950s and 1960s.

27. The role of the public sector in stabilising the economy was also subjected to sharp criticism especially in the 1970s by Robert Lucas, Robert Barro, and economists associated with the rational expectation school.

28. The 1997 World Development Report of the World Bank elaborates on this theme.

29. In some countries, individuals who act as "facilitators" or go–betweens have come into existence, adding to the transaction costs of operating in certain areas.

30. In many countries, a larger public sector workforce has been bought at the cost of low wages. This in turn is likely to have stimulated corruption on the part of the civil service. For empirical support to this intuitive conclusion, see van Rijckeghem and Weder (1977).

31. For example, rent control laws have violated the property rights of owners of houses. Government arrears in payments have violated the sanctity of contractual obligations.

32. In fact, in many cases this is the best use of the proceeds from privatisation. In the process of privatisation, a problem has been present. To set the highest price from the privatisation of a public enterprise, the government should let the enterprise retain some monopoly power. However, this would reduce the efficiency of the economy. A government that is much interested in maximising present revenue is likely to allow the privatised enterprises to retain some monopoly power.

33. Restrictions to competition through regulations imposed by professional associations are common. They have not received the attention they deserve. They create rents for those who are already members of these associations and unemployment for those who are not.

34. Many of these damaging regulations are imposed by labor unions, local governments, or even private associations.

35. In many cases, this policy discourages the building of new houses and the renting of existing houses and, when maintained over the long run, it ends up taxing some poor people, while subsidising some richer ones.

36. Whether the government should also provide guarantees (as for example for bank deposits) is a difficult issue that cannot be addressed here. Issues of moral hazard become relevant in this context.

37. For an analysis of Chile's pension reform, see Holzmann (1997).

38. Some conservative writers, such as James Buchanan, argue that the government should pursue only policies that affect everyone equally. They rule out selective or targeted policies and thus active, redistributive policies. See Buchanan (1997).

39. In the past, natural monopolies often played some redistributive or nation–building role by providing some of their services at reduced prices to poorer families and to far away places. For example, the privatisation of the railroad in Argentina has left some rural and far away places without the services of the trains. With privatisation, a decision must be made whether to preserve this role through the use of other policy instruments.

40. Because of their inefficient policies, it can be argued that the limited redistribution that has taken place has been achieved at a very high cost.

Bibliography

ALESINA, A. (1997), "The Political Economy of Macroeconomic Stabilisation and Income Inequality: Myths and Reality", in V. TANZI AND KE–YOUNG CHU (eds.), *Income Distribution and High Quality Growth*, MIT Press, Cambridge, MA.

ARROW, K. (1963), *Social Choice and Individual Values*, 2nd ed., John Wiley and Sons, Inc., New York.

BARDHAN, P. (1996), "The Nature of Institutional Impediments to Economic Development", *Working Paper No. C96–066*, Center for International and Development Economics Research, University of California, Berkeley.

BUCHANAN, J. (1997), "The Fiscal Crises in Welfare Democracies with some Implications for Public Investment", paper presented at the IIPF Congress, Kyoto, Japan, August.

CALVO, G. (1978), "On the Time Consistency of Optimal Policy in a Monetary Economy", *Econometrica*, 46.

COASE, R. (1960), "The Problem of Social Cost", *The Journal of Law and Economics*, October.

DEVARAJAN, S. AND J.S. HAMMER (1997), "Public Expenditure and Risk Reduction", paper presented at the IIPF Congress, Kyoto, Japan, August.

HOLZMANN, R. (1997), "Pension Reform, Financial Market Development, and Economic Growth: Preliminary Evidence from Chile", IMF *Staff Papers*, Vol. 44, No. 2, International Monetary Fund, Washington, D.C., June.

JOHANSEN, L. (1965), *Public Economics,* North–Holland, Amsterdam.

KRUEGER, A.O. (1974), "The Political Economy of the Rent–Seeking Society," *The American Economic Review*, Vol. 64, No. 3, June.

KRUEGER, A.O. (1993), *Economic Policies at Cross Purpose: The United States in Developing Countries,* The Brookings Institution, Washington, D.C.

MUSGRAVE, R.A. (1959), *The Theory of Public Finance,* McGraw Hill, New York.

VAN RIJCKEGHEM, C. AND B. WEDER (1997), "Corruption and the Rate of Temptation: Do Low Wages in the Civil Service Cause Corruption?", IMF Working Paper WP/97/73, International Monetary Fund, Washington, D.C., June.

RODRIK, D. (1996), "Why Do More Open Economies Have Bigger Governments?" Discussion Paper Series, No. 1386, London Centre for Economic Policy Research, London, May.

SAMUELSON, P. (1954), "The Pure Theory of Public Expenditure," *The Review of Economics and Statistics,* November.

DE SOTO, H. (1989), *The Other Path: The Invisible Revolution in the Third World*, Harper & Row, New York.

STEUERLE, C.E. AND M. KAWAI (eds.) (1996), *The New World Fiscal Order,* The Urban Institute, Washington, D.C.

TANZI, V. (1969), "Tax Incentives and Economic Development: The Ecuadorian Experience", *Finanzarchiv,* March.

TANZI, V. (1974), "Redistributing Income through the Budget in Latin America" in Banca Nazionale del Lavoro *Quarterly Review*, No. 108, March.

TANZI, V. (1994*a*), "The Political Economy of Fiscal Deficit Reduction", in W. EASTERLY, C.A. RODRIGUEZ ET K. SCHMIDT–HEBBEL (eds.), *Public Sector Deficits and Macroeconomic Performance*, Oxford University Press for the World Bank, New York.

TANZI, V. (1994*b*), "Corruption, Governmental Activities, and Markets," IMF Working Paper WP/94/99, Washington, D.C., IMF, August; Published as "Corruption, Arm's Length Relationships and Markets" in G. FIORENTINI AND S. PELTZMAN (eds.) (1995), *The Economics of Organised Crime*, Cambridge University Press, Cambridge.

TANZI, V. (1995*a*), "Government Role and the Efficiency of Policy Instrument", IMF Working Paper WP/95/100, IMF, Washington, D.C., October, and in P.B. SORENSEN (ed.), *Public Finance in a Changing World*, MacMillan Press, London and New York.

TANZI, V. (1995*b*), "Fiscal Federalism and Decentralisation: A Review of Some Efficiency and Macroeconomic Aspects," in M. BRUNO AND B. PLESKOVIC (eds.), *Annual World Bank Conference on Development Economics.*

TANZI, V. AND L. SCHUKNECHT (1997), "Reconsidering the Fiscal Role of Government: The International Perspective", *American Economic Review*, May.

TINBERGEN, J. (1952), *On the Theory of Economic Policy,* North–Holland, Amsterdam.

TULLOCK, G. (1967), "The Welfare Costs of Tariffs, Monopolies, and Theft", *Western Economic Journal*, No. 5.

TULLOCK, G. (1989), *The Economics of Special Privilege and Rent–Seeking,* Kluwer Academic Publishers, Boston.

WORLD BANK (1995), *Claiming the Future: Choosing Prosperity in the Middle East and North Africa,* Washington, D.C.

WORLD BANK (1997), *World Development Report: The Stage in a Changing World,* Oxford University Press for the World Bank, New York.

Chapter 2

Fiscal Federalism and Macroeconomic Governance: for Better or for Worse?

*Anwar Shah**

Introduction

With a view to creating governments that work and serve their people, many countries are re–examining the various levels of government and their partnerships with the private sector and the civil society (Shah, 1997, for motivations for a change). This rethinking has led to a resurgence of interest in fiscal federalism principles and practices but also invited much controversy and debate. A perceived potential for macroeconomic mismanagement and instability in federal systems has excited the most intense interest and led to a common conclusion that decentralised governance is incompatible with prudent fiscal management (e.g. Prud'homme 1995; Tanzi, 1996). This paper reflects upon the "dangers of decentralisation" for macroeconomic management by providing a synthesis of theoretical and empirical literature as well as new evidence. An overall conclusion is that the application of fiscal federalism principles to the design of economic constitutions offers a significant potential for improving the institutional framework for macroeconomic policy, provided that careful attention is paid to the design of institutions vital for the success of decentralisation policies.

Institutional Environment for Macroeconomic Management

Using Musgrave's trilogy of public functions, namely allocation, redistribution and stabilisation, the fiscal federalism literature has reached a broad consensus that while allocation can be assigned to lower levels of government, the latter two remain more appropriate for the national government. Thus macroeconomic management — especially stabilisation policy — is seen as clearly a central function (e.g. Musgrave, 1983; Oates, 1972). The stabilisation function is inappropriate for subnational assignment, as *a)* raising debt at the local level would entail higher regional costs while the benefits would spill beyond regional borders, and too little stabilisation would be provided as a result; *b)* the monetisation of local debt will create inflationary pressures and pose a threat for price stability; *c)* currency stability requires that both monetary and fiscal policy functions belong to the centre alone; and *d)* cyclical shocks are usually national in scope (symmetric across all regions) and therefore require a national response. Several writers have challenged these views on theoretical and empirical grounds (e.g. Scott, 1964; Dafflon, 1977; Sheikh and Winer, 1977; Gramlich, 1987; Walsh, 1992; Biehl, 1994; Shah, 1994; Mihaljek, 1995; Sewell, 1996; Huther and Shah, 1996), yet they continue to command a considerable following. An implication often drawn is that public sector decentralisation, especially in developing countries, poses significant risks for the "aggravation of macroeconomic problems" (Tanzi, 1996). A perspective on this issue requires reflection on the theoretical and empirical underpinnings of the institutional framework required for monetary and fiscal policies.

Institutional Setting for Monetary Policy

Monetary policy tries to control the levels and rates of change of nominal variables such as prices, monetary aggregates, exchange rates and nominal GDP, to provide a stable macro environment. All nation states, federal and unitary alike, centralise monetary policy. Nevertheless, occasional arguments propose adding a regional dimension to monetary policy design and implementation. For example, Mundell (1961) argues that an optimal currency area may be smaller than the nation state in federations like Canada and the United States; such circumstances may make the differential impact of exchange–rate policies inconsistent with the constitutional requirement of fair treatment of regions. Further complications arise when the federal government raises debt domestically but provincial governments borrow from abroad — as in Canada, when federal exchange–rate policies affect provincial debt servicing. Buchanan (1997) argues against establishing confederate central banks like the European Central Bank, as it negates the spirit of competitive federalism.

Barro (1996) has cautioned that a stable macro environment may not be achievable without a strong commitment to price stability by the monetary authority; if people anticipate money supply growth to counteract a recession, the lack of such a response will deepen it. A credibly strong commitment to price stability can be established by consistent adherence to formal rules, such as a fixed exchange rate or monetary rules. Guaranteeing independence from all levels of government for a central bank whose principal mission is price stability could do the same (Barro, 1996; Shah, 1994). Barro considers the focus on price stability so vital that he regards an ideal central banker as not necessarily a good macroeconomist but unshakeably committed to price stability: "The ideal central banker should always appear sombre in public, never tell any jokes, and complain continually about the dangers of inflation" (1996).

Empirical studies show that the three most independent central banks (the National Bank of Switzerland, Germany's Bundesbank and the US Federal Reserve) had average inflation rates of 4.4 per cent over the period 1955–88, with less volatility, compared to 7.8 per cent for the three least independent (New Zealand until 1989, Spain and Italy). The same studies also show the degree of central bank independence as unrelated to the average rates of growth and unemployment. Thus Barro argues that a "more independent central bank appears to be all gain and no pain" (1996). The European Union has recognised this principle by establishing an independent European Central Bank. The critical question then is whether or not a decentralised fiscal system compromises central bank independence. One would expect, a priori, that the central bank would have greater stakes and independence under a decentralised system, which requires clarification of the rules under which the bank operates, its functions and its relationships with various governments.

To examine this question systematically, Huther and Shah (1996) relate the evidence presented in Cukierman et al. (1992) on central bank independence for 80 countries to their indices of fiscal decentralisation. Cukierman et al. assess central bank independence based upon an examination of 16 statutory aspects of central bank operations including the terms of office of the chief executive officer, the formal structure of policy formulation, the bank's objectives as stated in its charter, and limitations on lending to the government. The correlation coefficient in Table 2.1 shows a weak but positive association, confirming an a priori judgement that independence strengthens under decentralised systems. Increases in the monetary base, caused by a central bank's bailout of failing state and non–state banks, occasionally represent an important source of monetary instability and a significant obstacle to macroeconomic management. Thus a central bank's role in ensuring arm's–length transactions between governments and the banking sector would enhance monetary stability regardless of the degree of decentralisation of the fiscal system.

Available empirical evidence suggests that such arm's–length transactions are more difficult to achieve in countries with centralised government structures than under decentralised structures with larger sets of players. Decentralisation requires greater clarity in the roles of various public players, including the central bank. No wonder one finds that the four central banks most widely acknowledged to be independent (in Switzerland, Germany, Austria and the United States) all operate within highly decentralised federal fiscal systems. The German Constitution does not assure the independence of the Bundesbank, and the Bundesbank Law which does provide it also stipulates the Bundesbank's obligation to support the economic policy of the federal government. In practice, the Bundesbank has sought to establish its independence primarily by focusing on price stability — as demonstrated most recently by its decision to raise interest rates to finance German unification despite the adverse impacts on federal debt obligations (Biehl, 1994).

Table 2.1. Correlation of the Decentralisation Index with Governance Quality Indicators

(sample size: 80 countries)

	Pearson Correlation Coefficients
Citizen Participation	
Political Freedom	0.599[b]
Political Stability	0.604[b]
Government Orientation	
Judicial Efficiency	0.544[b]
Bureaucratic Efficiency	0.540[b]
Absence of Corruption	0.532[b]
Social Development	
Human Development Index	0.369[a]
Egalitarianism in Income Distribution	0.373[a]
(inverse of Gini coefficient)	
Economic Management	
Central Bank Independence	0.327[a]
Debt Management Discipline	0.263[a]
Openness of the Economy	0.523[b]
Governance Quality Index	0.617[b]

a.   Significant at the 0.05 per cent level (2–tailed test).
b.   Significant at the 0.01 per cent level (2–tailed test).
Source: Huther and Shah (1996).

The Swiss Federal Constitution (article 39) assigns monetary policy to the federal government, which has delegated the conduct of monetary policy to the Swiss National Bank, a private, limited company regulated by a special law. The National Bank Act of 1953 granted it independence in the conduct of monetary policy although it is required to conduct policy in the general interest of the country. It allocates a portion of its profits to cantons, to infuse a sense of regional ownership and participation in the conduct of monetary policy (Gygi, 1991).

Institutional Setting for Fiscal Policy

In a unitary country, the central government assumes exclusive responsibility for fiscal policy. In federal countries, fiscal policy becomes a responsibility shared by all levels of government; the federal government uses its powers of the purse (transfers) and moral suasion, through joint meetings, to induce a co–ordinated fiscal–policy approach. The allocation of responsibilities under a federal system also pays some attention to stabilisation policies, often by assigning stable and cyclically less sensitive revenue sources and expenditure responsibilities to subnational governments. This attempts to insulate local governments from economic cycles and give the national government prominence in the conduct of stabilisation policy. In large federal countries, such insulation usually works only for the lowest tier of government, as the intermediate tier (states and provinces) shares responsibilities in providing cyclically sensitive services such as social assistance. These intermediate–tier governments have access to cyclically sensitive revenue bases that act as built–in (automatic) stabilisers.

Several writers (Tanzi, 1996; Wonnacott, 1972) have argued that the financing of subnational governments (SNGs) will likely create concern within open federal systems because SNGs may circumvent federal fiscal policy objectives. Tanzi (1994) is also concerned with deficit creation and debt management by junior governments. Available theoretical and empirical work does not support the validity of these concerns. On the first point, at the theoretical level, Sheikh and Winer (1977) demonstrate that relatively extreme and unrealistic assumptions about discretionary non–co–operation by junior jurisdictions are needed to conclude that stabilisation by the central authorities would not work at all simply because of a lack of co–operation. These untenable assumptions include regionally symmetric shocks, a closed economy, segmented capital markets, lack of supply side–effects of local fiscal policy, non–availability of built–in stabilisers in the tax–transfer systems of SNGs and in inter–regional trade, constraints on the use of federal spending power (such as conditional grants intended to influence subnational behaviour), unconstrained and undisciplined local borrowing and extremely non–co–operative, collusive behaviour by SNGs (see also Gramlich, 1987; Spahn, 1997). The empirical simulations of Sheikh and Winer for Canada further suggest that the failure of federal fiscal policy in most instances cannot be attributed to non–co–operative behaviour by junior governments. Saknini, James and Sheikh (1996) demonstrate that, in a decentralised federation having markedly differentiated subnational economies with incomplete markets and non–traded goods, federal fiscal policy acts as insurance against region–specific risks and therefore decentralised fiscal structures do not compromise any of the goals sought under a centralised fiscal policy (see also CEPR, 1993).

Gramlich (1987) points out that, in open economies, exposure to international competition would benefit some regions at the expense of others. He argues that regional stabilisation policies can more effectively deal with the resulting asymmetric shocks with the better information and instruments available at regional/local levels. This conclusion, however, needs qualification because errant fiscal behaviour by powerful members of a federation can have an important constraining influence on the conduct of federal macroeconomic policies. For example, the inflationary pressures arising from Ontario's increases in social spending during the boom years of late 1980s made achievement of the Bank of Canada's price–stability goal more difficult. Such difficulties stress the need for fiscal policy co–ordination under a decentralised federal system.

On the potential for fiscal mismanagement noted by Tanzi, empirical evidence from a number of countries suggests that, while national/central/federal fiscal policies typically do not adhere to the European Union (EU) guidelines that deficits should not exceed 3 per cent of GDP and debt should not exceed 60 per cent of GDP, junior governments' policies typically do. This is true both in decentralised federal countries such as Argentina, Brazil, Canada and Germany, and centralised federal countries such as Australia, India and Pakistan. Centralised unitary countries do even worse on the basis of these indicators. For example, Greece, Turkey, Portugal and many developing countries do not satisfy the EU standards. National governments also typically do not adhere to EU requirements that central banks should not act as lenders of last resort. The failure of collective action in forcing fiscal discipline at the national level arises from the "norm of universalism" or "pork barrel politics"; to avoid deadlocks legislators trade votes and support each other's projects by implicitly agreeing that "I'll favour your best project if you favour mine" (Inman and Rubinfeld, 1992). Such behaviour leads to overspending and higher debt overhang at the national level. It also generates regionally differentiated bases for federal corporate income taxation and thereby loss of federal revenues through these tax expenditures. Such tax expenditures accentuate fiscal deficits at the national level.

Solutions proposed to overcome these national fiscal policy difficulties include "gatekeeper" committees (Wiengast and Marshall, 1988) to impose party discipline within legislatures, constitutionally imposed fiscal rules (Niskanen, 1992), executive agenda setting (Ingberman and Yao, 1991) and decentralising when the potential inefficiencies of centralised democratic choice outweigh the economic gains from centralisation. Observing a similar situation in Latin American countries prompted Eichengreen, Hausmann and von Hagen (1996) to propose an independent "gatekeeper" in the form of a national fiscal council to set periodically maximum allowable increases in general government debt. Fiscal stabilisation failed under centralised structures in Argentina and Brazil, but they achieved major successes in this arena later under decentralised fiscal systems. Table 2.1 provides further confirmation of these observations, showing that debt management discipline had a positive association with the degree of fiscal decentralisation for a sample of 80 countries.

Because the potential exists for errant fiscal behaviour by national and subnational governments to complicate the conduct of monetary policy, institutional arrangements must safeguard against it. Industrial countries place much emphasis on intergovernmental co–ordination of policies at different levels. Developing countries, on the other hand, have traditionally emphasised centralisation or direct central controls, which typically have failed to achieve co–ordinated responses due to intergovernmental gaming. Moreover, the national government completely escapes any scrutiny except when it seeks international help from external sources such as the IMF — and that creates a moral hazard in bureaucratic incentives on both sides to ensure that such assistance is always demanded and used.

Fiscal Policy Co–ordination in Mature Federations

As noted above, the EU, in creating a monetary union under the Maastricht treaty, has established ceilings on national deficits and debts, with supporting provisions prohibiting bailouts of governments by member central banks or by the European Central Bank. The EU also may not provide unconditional guarantees for the public debt of its member states (Pisani–Ferry, 1991). Most mature federations also specify no bailout by their central banks, with the notable exceptions of Australia until 1992 and Brazil. With an explicit or even implicit bailout guarantee, and preferential loans from the banking sector as for the Brazilian states, subnational governments can print money and thereby fuel inflation. The EU guidelines provide a useful framework for macro co–ordination in federal systems, but such guidelines may not ensure monetary stability; they may restrain smaller countries, like Greece, with little influence on monetary stability, but not superpowers like Germany (Courchene, 1996). Thus a proper enforcement of guidelines may require a fiscal co–ordination council.

Fiscal policy co–ordination mechanisms in mature federations vary greatly. The United States has no overall federal–state co–ordination and no constitutional restraints on state borrowing, but states' own constitutions prohibit operating deficits. Intergovernmental co–ordination often comes through fiscal rules legislated by Congress such as the Gramm–Rudman Act. Fiscal discipline arises from three distinct incentives in the political and market cultures. *First,* the conservative electorates vote for candidates with a commitment to keep public spending in check. *Second,* the pursuit of fiscal policies perceived as imprudent lowers property values and thus public revenues. *Third,* capital markets discipline governments that live beyond their means (Inman and Rubinfeld, 1992).

To sum up, fiscal policy co–ordination represents an important challenge for federal systems. The Maastricht guidelines provide a useful framework but not necessarily a solution. Industrialised countries' experience shows that federally imposed controls and constraints typically do not work. Instead, societal norms based on fiscal conservatism, such as the Swiss referenda, and political activism of the electorate play important roles. Ultimately, capital markets and bond rating agencies provide more effective discipline on fiscal policy. They make it important not to backstop state and local debt and not to allow ownership of the banks by any level of government. Transparent budgetary processes and institutions, accountability to the electorate and general availability of information also encourage fiscal discipline.

Subnational Borrowing

The World Bank currently estimates the capital needs of developing and transition countries as exceeding $100 billion a year. Most of these requirements cover local public infrastructure; water and sewage projects account for half of them. Local governments typically command the lion's share of public sector investments, from a low of 30 per cent in developing countries to 70 per cent in industrialised countries. Financing comes from taxes, charges, reserves, capital grants, borrowing and private equity and debt in concessions or build–operate–transfer (BOT) projects. Borrowing has traditionally served as the most important source in industrial countries because it enhances intergenerational equity; these long–lived projects yield returns through several generations, over which the costs should be shared equally. Such burden sharing among generations enables small local governments to undertake these large and lumpy investments — and to tailor projects for consistency with local needs without the constraints of design choices made by higher–level governments. Developing countries typically finance such projects with capital grants and on–lending from higher–level governments, because local governments usually do not have direct access to credit markets. Because the traditional sources of finance cannot meet the large capital finance needs of developing countries, subnational credit market access represents a major challenge.

Credit market access at intermediate levels of government (states and provinces) in decentralised federal countries usually faces few restraints. Domestic and foreign borrowing by states/provinces in the United States and Canada encounter no federally imposed strictures. Indeed, income from state bonds is exempt from US federal income taxes. The fiscal conservatism of these governments in tapping capital markets arises primarily from limitations imposed by state constitutions and credit market discipline. In contrast, credit market access is closely controlled for both state and local governments in unitary (China, France, Indonesia, the United Kingdom and Japan) and centralised federal countries (e.g. India, Pakistan and Australia until 1993) and only for local governments in decentralised federal countries (Canada, the United States, and Germany).

Passive controls on subnational borrowing take many forms, from broad guidelines on allowable ranges for debt/revenue and debt charges/own–source revenue ratios, to more specific rules such as the "golden rule" for local debt commonly adopted in most federations. The golden rule permits borrowing only for capital projects; local governments cannot finance current deficits from this source except to smooth fluctuations in revenue inflows and outflows within a given fiscal year. Canada, the United States, Germany and Switzerland use it. The EU guidelines on deficit and debt limits and its no–bailout rule also apply here. In Brazil, Senate Resolution 11 (1993) restricted new state borrowing by two formal rules: *a)* total debt service cannot exceed the state operating surplus during the past year or 15 per cent of its revenues, whichever is less; and *b)* new borrowing within any 12–month period cannot exceed the level of existing debt service or 27 per cent of revenues, whichever is less.

More active controls on such borrowing include centrally specified limits on capital spending by each municipality as in the United Kingdom; project submission and approval as in the province of Ontario, Canada; approval for bond finance as in Japan; approval of borrowing amounts and rates as in Denmark (usually restricted to energy and urban renewal projects only) and France; and seeking community mandates on borrowing plans through popular referenda, as done infrequently in the United States and Canada and routinely in Switzerland. Developing countries have even more extensive and crude central controls; most of them do not allow local governments to access credit markets. In India and Pakistan, even borrowing at state/provincial levels requires central approval if the borrowers owe any debt to the federal government. Net federal lending to states in India and provinces in Pakistan in 1996–97 was close to zero or negative as their debt service payments equalled or exceeded new loans.

Local borrowing in most industrial countries comes primarily from domestic markets and higher–level governments. In developing countries, state and local debt obligations are primarily owed to the central government. A significant degree of tax decentralisation and secured sources of revenues through formula–based transfers are, however, opening up possibilities of global market access to subnational governments, especially in Latin America.

In a decentralised fiscal environment, SNG access to credit markets poses significant risks for macroeconomic stabilisation, because the constitutional division of powers significantly constrains imposing credit rationing and direct controls. These risks become disproportionately higher if SNGs depend heavily on central revenue sources. In those circumstances, bailout risks are much higher but the market fails to capitalise them due to its anticipation of central government bailout. Decentralised fiscal systems rely on a combination of credit market discipline, moral suasion and agreed rules to impose financial discipline on SNGs. Which system works better is an empirical question worthy of further research. The available evidence nevertheless points to a superior performance of decentralised systems in restraining subnational debt. Central controls in France, Spain, the United Kingdom, India, Pakistan and Australia (until 1992 under the old Australian Loan Council) failed to keep subnational debt in check, as intergovernmental gaming led to weaker discipline and central bailout possibilities encouraged less rigorous scrutiny by the financial sector. Once again, the cornerstone of financial discipline under a decentralised fiscal system is the market discipline enhanced by a public policy environment that stresses central bank independence, no government ownership of commercial banks, no bailouts, and public dissemination of information on public finances. Societal conservatism as in Switzerland introduces an added discipline.

Facilitating Local Access to Credit

Local access to credit requires well functioning financial markets and credit–worthy local governments. Although industrial countries easily meet these prerequisites, well established traditions for assisting local governments from above persist. The exemption from US federal taxation of interest income on state and local bonds constitutes an interest subsidy with many distortionary effects: it favours richer jurisdictions and higher–income individuals; it discriminates against non–debt sources of finance such as reserves and equity; it favours investment by local governments rather than autonomous bodies and discourages private sector participation in the form of concessions and BOT alternatives.

In Canada, most provinces assist local governments with the engineering, financial and economic analysis of projects. Local governments in Alberta, British Columbia and Nova Scotia get help from provincial finance corporations which use the higher credit ratings of the province to lower costs of funds for local governments. Some provinces, notably Manitoba and Quebec, assist in the preparation and marketing of local debt. Canadian provincial governments have also given occasional debt relief to their local governments. Autonomous agencies, run on commercial principles to assist local borrowing, exist in western Europe and Japan. In Denmark, local governments have collectively established a co–operative municipal bank. The UK Public Works Loan Board channels central financing to local public works. An important lesson from the industrial countries is that municipal finance corporations operate well when they run on commercial principles and compete for capital and borrowers. They allow pooling of risk, realise economies of scale and bring to bear their knowledge of local governments and their financing potentials to obtain access to commercial credit on more favourable terms (McMillan, 1995).

In developing countries, undeveloped markets for long–term credit and weak municipal creditworthiness limit municipal access to credit. Nevertheless, most central governments emphasise central policy controls and pay less attention to assistance for borrowing. A few countries make help available through specialised institutions and central guarantees to jump–start municipal access to credit. Ecuador, Indonesia, Jordan, Morocco, the Philippines and Tunisia have established municipal development banks/ funds/facilities for local borrowing. These institutions are quite fragile, not likely to be sustainable and open to political influences. Interest rate subsidies provided through them impede emerging capital market alternatives. Colombia and the Czech Republic provide a rediscount facility to facilitate local access to commercial credit. Thailand has a guarantee fund to assist local governments and the private sector in financing infrastructure investments (Gouarne, 1996).

In conclusion, the choices available to local governments for financing capital projects remain limited, with available alternatives not conducive to a sustainable institutional environment for such finance. Macroeconomic instability and lack of fiscal discipline and appropriate regulatory regimes have impeded the development of financial and capital markets. Tax centralisation limits revenue capacity at the local level. A first, transitory step to provide limited credit market access to local governments may be to establish municipal finance corporations run on commercial principles and to encourage the development of municipal rating agencies. Tax decentralisation is also important to establish private sector confidence in lending to local governments and in sharing its risks and rewards.

Securing An Economic Union

Five dimensions of securing economic union in a federal system have relevance for macroeconomic governance: preservation of the internal common market; tax harmonisation; transfers and social insurance; intergovernmental fiscal transfers; and regional fiscal equity.

Preservation of the Internal Common Market

Preservation of an internal common market remains an important concern to most nations undertaking decentralisation. SNGs may indulge in beggar–thy–neighbour policies to attract labour and capital and in the process erect barriers to goods and factor mobility. Regulatory decentralisation creates a potential for disharmonious economic relations among subnational units; accordingly, regulation of activities like trade and investment is generally best left at the national level, provided that central governments themselves do not pursue policies detrimental to the internal common market. As suggested by Boadway (1992), constitutional guarantees for free domestic flows of goods and services may have to accompany regulatory responsibilities at the centre.

The constitutions of mature federations typically provide a free trade clause (as in Australia, Canada and Switzerland); federal regulatory power over interstate commerce (as in Australia, Canada, Germany, the United States and Switzerland) and individual mobility rights (as in most federations). The Indonesian Constitution embodies a free trade and mobility clause. Yet in most developing countries, an internal common market is impeded both by SNG policies supported by the centre and by formal and informal obstructions of labour and capital mobility. In India and Pakistan, local governments rely on a tax on intermunicipal trade (*octroi* tax) as the predominant source of revenues. China severely constrains individual mobility rights under the "hukou" system of household registration used to determine eligibility for grain rations, employment, housing and health care.

Tax Harmonisation and Co–ordination

Tax competition among jurisdictions can encourage cost–effectiveness and fiscal accountability in state governments and by itself lead to a certain amount of tax harmonisation. At the same time, decentralised tax policies can cause inefficiencies and inequities in a federation, and lead to excessive administrative costs. Tax harmonisation should preserve the best features of tax decentralisation while avoiding its disadvantages.

Inefficiencies from decentralised decision making can occur in a variety of ways. States may implement policies which discriminate in favour of their own residents and businesses. They may engage in beggar–thy–neighbour policies intended to attract economic activity from other states. Inefficiency may also arise simply through the distortions from different tax structures chosen independently by state governments with no collective strategic objective, or if state tax systems adopt different conventions for dealing with businesses (and residents) who operate in more than one jurisdiction at the same time; this can lead to double taxation of some forms of income and non–taxation of others. State tax systems may also introduce inequities, as personal mobility encourages them to abandon progressivity. Administration costs can be excessive in an unco–ordinated tax system (Boadway, Roberts and Shah, 1994). Thus tax harmonisation and co–ordination contribute to internal common market efficiency, reduce collection and compliance costs and help achieve national equity standards.

Transfer Payments and Social Insurance

Along with the provision of public goods and services, transfer payments to persons and businesses account for most government expenditures, especially in industrialised countries. Some transfers serve redistributive purposes in the ordinary sense, and some support industrial policy or regional development. Some foster redistribution in the social insurance sense (unemployment and health insurance, public pensions). Several factors bear on the assignment of responsibility for transfers. Many economists would argue that transfers to businesses should not occur in the first place, but given that they do, they will likely be more distortionary at the provincial than at the federal level because subsidies typically try to increase capital investment by firms, which is mobile across provinces. Because most transfers to individuals (economically just negative direct taxes) have redistributive goals, their assignment revolves around which level of government assumes primary responsibility for equity. One can argue that transfers should be controlled by the level of government that controls direct taxes so that they can be integrated for equity and harmonised across the nation for efficiency. The case for integration at the centre is enhanced because several types of transfers may address different dimensions of equity or social insurance; advantages accrue to co–ordinating unemployment insurance with the income tax system, or pensions with payments to the poor. Decentralising to the provinces will likely lead to inefficiencies in the internal common market, fiscal inequities and inter–jurisdictional, beggar–thy–neighbour policies.

Intergovernmental Fiscal Transfers

Federal–state transfers in a federal system serve important objectives: alleviating structural imbalances, correcting fiscal inefficiencies and inequities, providing compensation for benefit spillouts and achieving fiscal harmonisation. The most important critical consideration is that the grant design must be consistent with grant objectives.

In industrialised countries, two types of transfers dominate: conditional transfers to achieve national standards and equalisation transfers to deal with regional equity. In developing countries, with a handful of exceptions, conditional transfers are of the pork–barrel variety and equalisation transfers with explicit standards do not exist.

Instead, passing–the–buck (PB) transfers in the form of tax–by–tax sharing and revenue sharing with multiple factors are used. With limited or no tax decentralisation, PB transfers finance most subnational expenditures. They build transfer dependencies and discourage responsive and accountable governance (Shah, 1997). Ehdaie (1994) provides empirical support for this proposition. He concludes that simultaneous decentralisation of the national government's taxing and spending powers, by directly linking the costs and benefits of public provision, tends to reduce the size of the public sector. Expenditure decentralisation accompanied by revenue sharing delinks responsibility and accountability and thereby fails to achieve this result. In general, PB transfers create incentives for SNGs to undertake decisions contrary to their long–run economic interests in the absence of such transfers. Thus they impede natural adjustment responses leading to a vicious cycle of perpetual deprivation for less developed regions (see also Courchene, 1996 and Shah, 1996 for a further discussion).

Industrial country experience shows that successful decentralisation cannot occur in the absence of a well designed fiscal transfer programme. The design of transfers must be simple, transparent and consistent with their objectives. Properly structured transfers can enhance competition for the supply of public services, accountability of the fiscal system and fiscal co–ordination, just as general revenue sharing has the potential to undermine it.

The role of fiscal transfers in enhancing competition for the supply of public goods also should not be overlooked. Transfers for basic health and primary education could be made available to both the public and not–for–profit private sectors on an equal basis, using as criteria the demographics of the population served, school age population and student enrolments, etc. This would promote competition and innovation, as both public and private institutions would compete for public funding.

Regional Fiscal Equity

While a paucity of data prevents addressing the regional equity issue, a few casual observations may be in order. As noted earlier, regional inequity is a concern for decentralised fiscal systems, and most attempt to deal with it through the spending powers of the national government or fraternal programmes. Mature federations such as Australia, Canada and Germany have formal equalisation programmes. This important feature of decentralisation has not received adequate attention in the design of institutions in developing countries. Despite serious horizontal fiscal imbalances in many developing countries, explicit equalisation programmes remain untried, although their objectives are implicit in the general revenue–sharing mechanisms of Brazil, Colombia, India, Mexico, Nigeria and Pakistan. These mechanisms typically combine diverse and conflicting objectives into the same formula and fall significantly short on individual objectives. Because the formulas lack explicit equalisation standards, they fail to address regional equity satisfactorily.

Some Lessons for Developing Countries

The following important lessons for reform of fiscal systems in developing countries can be distilled from the foregoing review.

— *Monetary policy is best entrusted to an independent central bank with a mandate for price stability*. Its political feasibility improves under federal (decentralised) fiscal systems.

— *Fiscal rules accompanied by "gatekeeper" intergovernmental councils/committees provide a useful framework for fiscal discipline and fiscal policy co–ordination.* One can draw upon industrial countries' experiences with golden rules, Maastricht–type guidelines and "common budget directives" to develop country–specific guidelines. To ensure voluntary compliance, an appropriate institutional framework must be developed. Transparency of budgetary processes and institutions, accountability to electorates and general availability of comparative data on fiscal positions of all levels of government further strengthen fiscal discipline.

— *The integrity and independence of the financial sector contribute to fiscal prudence in the public sector.* To ensure them, ownership and preferential access to the financial sector should not be available to any level of government. In such an environment, capital markets and bond rating agencies would provide effective fiscal policy discipline.

— *To ensure fiscal discipline, governments at all levels must face the financial consequences of their decisions.* This is possible if the central government does not backstop state and local debt, and the central bank does not act as a lender of last resort to the central government.

— *Societal norms and consensus on the roles of various levels of government and limits to their authorities are vital for the success of decentralised decision making.* In their absence, direct central controls do not work and intergovernmental gaming leads to dysfunctional constitutions.

— *Tax decentralisation is a prerequisite for subnational credit market access.* In countries with highly centralised tax bases, unrestrained credit market access by SNGs poses a risk for macroeconomic stabilisation policies of the national government, as the private sector anticipates bailout in the event of default and does not discount the risks of such lending properly.

— *Higher–level institutional assistance may be needed for financing local capital projects.* This assistance can take the form of municipal finance corporations run on commercial principles, to lower the cost of borrowing by using the superior credit rating of the higher–level government and municipal rating agencies to determine credit worthiness.

—   *An internal common market is best preserved by constitutional guarantees.* National governments in developing countries have typically failed in this role.

—   *Intergovernmental transfers in developing countries undermine fiscal discipline and accountability while building transfer dependencies that cause a slow economic strangulation of fiscally disadvantaged regions.* Properly designed intergovernmental transfers, on the other hand, can enhance competition for the supply of public goods, fiscal harmonisation, SNG accountability and regional equity. Substantial theoretical and empirical guidance on the design of these transfers is readily available.

—   *Periodic review of jurisdictional assignments is essential to realign responsibilities with changing economic and political realities.* With globalisation and localisation, national government's direct role in stabilisation and macroeconomic control is likely to diminish over time, but its role in co–ordination and oversight will increase as subnational governments assume enhanced roles in these areas. Constitutional and legal systems and institutions must be amenable to timely adjustments to adapt to changing circumstances.

—   *Finally, contrary to a common misconception, decentralised fiscal systems offer a greater potential for improved macroeconomic governance than centralised fiscal systems.* This is to be expected, as decentralised fiscal systems require greater clarity in the roles of various players (centres of decision making) and transparency in rules that govern their interactions, to ensure fair play.

*   The author is grateful to Kiichiro Fukasaku for suggesting this topic and to João do Carmo Oliveira, Thomas Courchene, David Sewell, Kathryn Gordon and Bernd Spahn for helpful discussions.

Bibliography

BARRO, R.J. (1996), Getting *It Right: Markets and Choices in a Free Society*, MIT Press, Cambridge, MA.

BIEHL, D. (1994), "Inter–governmental Fiscal Relations and Macroeconomic Management — Possible Lessons from a Federal Case: Germany", in S.P. GUPTA *et al.*

BOADWAY, R. (1992), *The Constitutional Division of Powers: An Economic Perspective*, Economic Council of Canada, Ottawa.

BOADWAY, R., S. ROBERTS AND A. SHAH (1994), "The Reform of Fiscal Systems in Developing and Emerging Market Economies: A Federalism Perspective", Policy Research Working Paper Series No.1259. World Bank, Washington, D.C.

BUCHANAN, J. (1997), "Economic Freedom and Federalism: Prospects for the New Century", paper presented at the World Bank Seminar on Fiscal Decentralisation, 6–7 May.

CENTRE FOR ECONOMIC POLICY RESEARCH (CEPR) (1993), *Making Sense of Subsidiarity: How Much Centralisation for Europe?*, CEPR, London.

COURCHENE, T. (1996), "Macrofederalism", in A. SHAH, *Macrofederalism,* mimeo, World Bank, Washington, D.C.

CUKIERMAN, A., S. WEBB AND B. NEYAPTI (1992), "Measuring the Independence of Central Banks and Its Effect on Policy Outcomes", *The World Bank Economic Review* 6(3).

DAFFLON, B. (1977), *Federal Finance in Theory and Practice With Special Reference to Switzerland,* Verlag Paul Haupt, Berne.

EHDAIE, J. (1994), "Fiscal Decentralisation and the Size of Government", Policy Research Working Paper Series No. 1387, World Bank, Washington, D.C.

EICHENGREEN, B., R. HAUSMANN AND J. VON HAGEN (1996), "Reforming Budgetary Institutions in Latin America: The Case for a National Finance Council", processed.

GOUARNE, V. (1996), "Investing in Urban Infrastructure: Roles and Instruments", processed.

GRAMLICH, E. (1987), "Sub–national Fiscal Policy", in *Perspectives on Local Public Finance and Public Policy: A Research Annual*, Vol. 3.

GUPTA, S.P., P. KNIGHT, R. WAXMAN AND Y.–K. WEN (1994), *Intergovernmental Fiscal Relations and Macroeconomic Management in Large Countries*, World Bank and Indian Council for Research on International Economic Relations, EDI, New Delhi

GYGI, U. (1991). *Maintaining a Coherent Macroeconomic Policy in a Highly Decentralized Federal State: The Experience of Switzerland*, OECD, processed.

CUKIERMAN, A., J. HUTHER AND A. SHAH (1996), "A Simple Measure of Good Governance and its Application to the Debate on the Appropriate Level of Fiscal Decentralisation", processed, World Bank, Washington, D.C.

INGBERMAN, D. AND D. YAO (1991), "Presidential Commitment and the Veto", *American Journal of Political Science*, 35.

INMAN, R. AND D. RUBINFELD (1992), "Fiscal Federalism in Europe: Lessons from the American Experience", processed.

MCMILLAN, M. (1995), "A Local Perspective on Fiscal Federalism: Practices, Experiences and Lessons from Developed Countries", in A. SHAH *Fiscal Federalism: Principles and Practices*, World Bank, Washington, D.C.

MIHALJEK, D. (1995), "Theory and Practice of Confederate Finances", processed.

MUNDELL, R. (1961), "A Theory of Optimum Currency Areas", *American Economic Review*, 51.

MUSGRAVE, R. (1983), "Who Should Tax, Where, What?", in C. MCLURE, JR (ed.), *Tax Assignment in Federal Countries,* Centre for Research on Federal Financial Relations, ANU, Canberra.

NISKANEN, W. (1992), "The Case for a New Fiscal Constitution", *Journal of Economic Perspectives*, 6(2).

OATES, W. (1972), *Fiscal Federalism,* Harcourt, Brace, Jovanovich, New York.

PISANI–FERRY, J. (1991), "Maintaining a Coherent Macro–economic Policy in a Highly Decentralised Federal State: The Experience of the EC", OECD Seminar on Fiscal Federalism in Economies in Transition, 2–3 April.

PRUD'HOMME, R. (1995), "On the Dangers of Decentralisation", *The World Bank Research Observer*, August.

SAKNINI, H., S. JAMES AND M. SHEIKH (1996) "Stabilisation, Insurance, and Risk Sharing in Federal Fiscal Policy", processed, Department of Finance, Ottawa.

SCOTT, A. (1964), "The Economic Goals of Federal Finance", *Public Finance*, 19.

SEWELL, D. (1996), 'The Dangers of Decentralisation' According to Prud'homme: Some Further Aspects", *The World Bank Research Observer*, Vol. 11, No. 1, February.

SHAH, A. (1997). "Fostering Responsive and Accountable Governance: Lessons From Decentralisation Experience", presented at the World Bank Conference on Evaluation and Development, 1–2 April, Washington, D.C.

SHAH, A. (1996), "A Fiscal Need Approach to Equalisation", *Canadian Public Policy*, XXII:2.

SHAH, A. (ed.) (1996), *Macrofederalism,* mimeo, World Bank, Washington, D.C.

SHAH, A.(1994), *The Reform of Inter–governmental Fiscal Relations in Developing and Emerging Market Economies*, World Bank, Washington, D.C.

SHEIKH, M.A. AND S.L. WINER (1977), "Stabilisation and Non–Federal Behaviour in an Open Federal State: An Econometric Study of the Fixed Exchange Rate, Canadian Case", *Empirical Economics*, Vol. 2, No. 3.

SPAHN, P.B. (1997), "Decentralised Government and Macroeconomic Control", processed.

TANZI, V. (1996), "Fiscal Federalism and Decentralisation: A Review of Some Efficiency and Macroeconomic Aspects", *Annual World Bank Conference on Development Economics, 1995*, World Bank, Washington, D.C.

TANZI, V. (1994), *Taxation in an Integrating World*, Brookings Institution, Washington, D.C.

WIENGAST, B. AND W. MARSHALL (1988), "The Industrial Organisation of Congress: Why Legislatures, Like Firms; are not Organised Like Markets", *Journal of Political Economy,* Vol. 96.

WALSH, C. (1992), "Fiscal Federalism: An Overview of Issues and a Discussion of Their Relevance to the European Community", Federalism Research Centre Discussion Paper No. 12, ANU, Canberra.

WONNACOTT, P. (1972), *The Floating Canadian Dollar,* American Enterprise Institute for Public Policy Research, Washington, D.C.

Chapter 3

Decentralisation and Macroeconomic Management

Teresa Ter–Minassian

Introduction

Decentralisation, a growing worldwide trend, reflects a more democratic and participatory approach to government even in countries traditionally characterised by pronounced centralism. The fiscal federalism literature has amply discussed the potential efficiency and welfare gains from decentralisation, and practical experience generally reveals them, especially in countries which have made efforts to strengthen institutions at the subnational level, promote transparency in the operations of subnational governments (SNGs), and increase their responsiveness to local needs and priorities.

The literature also highlights the potential trade–offs between decentralisation and income redistribution, especially in countries with wide regional disparities in resource endowments and levels of development. Country experiences provide examples of equalisation mechanisms designed to attenuate if not eliminate these trade–offs (Ahmad, 1997).

By contrast, writers have given relatively little emphasis to the effects of decentralisation on macroeconomic management, although policy makers worldwide increasingly have to grapple with them. They furnish the focus of this paper, which draws on a range of country experiences[1].

The analysis begins with a discussion of how a substantial devolution of revenues and spending responsibilities to the subnational level can affect the central government's ability to carry out stabilisation and macroeconomic adjustment through the budget, a function which the public finance literature as well as historical practice traditionally attribute to the centre. This section also discusses briefly the potential macroeconomic effects of SNG operations under a balanced budget. The following section focuses on the effects of SNG deficits from the perspectives of both short–run macroeconomic management and intergenerational equity. A look at possible approaches to the control of SNG borrowing follows, focusing in particular on the conditions under which financial markets can be expected to impose adequate discipline on such borrowing, and on alternative methods to ensure discipline if these conditions cannot be fulfilled in practice.

Macroeconomic Effects of Fiscal Decentralisation

On a general level, the degree of devolution of spending and revenue–raising responsibilities has significant implications for the central government's ability to conduct macroeconomic policies through the budget. A loss of major tax instruments or of control over a large share of public expenditures can severely constrain the centre's room for manoeuvre in, e.g. raising taxes or cutting spending to curb overheated domestic demand — especially if the expenditures it is left with are relatively rigid in the short run, such as interest payments on the public debt or entitlement programmes like pensions. Moreover, in a highly decentralised budget setting, the fiscal operations of SNGs can have important macroeconomic effects which, in the absence of effective co–ordination mechanisms, can run counter to the stabilisation efforts of the central government. A balanced–budget expenditure increase by the SNGs can boost aggregate demand and affect the balance of payments unfavourably if the average multiplier for subnational expenditures significantly exceeds that for their revenues. Even if the overall level of SNG expenditures is effectively constrained by limits on their taxing and borrowing powers, changes in their composition — e.g. in favour of items with relatively large multiplier effects, such as public works or transfers to individuals with a high propensity to consume — can boost aggregate demand at a time when the central government is trying to contain it.

Not only the degree but also the sequencing of decentralisation can have important implications for macroeconomic stability and adjustment. Patterns of decentralisation have varied from country to country, often shaped more by political and institutional factors than economic ones. In many countries, the decentralisation of spending responsibilities, reflecting political pressures or an expectation of efficiency gains, has tended to precede the devolution of revenue–raising responsibilities. In countries facing severe fiscal stress — such as the economies in transition — central governments have simply "pushed down" spending responsibilities without transferring to the SNGs adequate resources to meet these responsibilities. In other countries — such as a number of Latin American ones — a transfer of resources to the SNGs has been mandated by laws or even by the constitution before a corresponding transfer of spending responsibilities could be clearly defined and effected.

Neither of these patterns of decentralisation is likely to promote fiscal discipline. Large vertical imbalances in favour of the central government tend to lead to a recourse to *ex–post*, gap–filling transfers from the centre to the SNGs, or to deficit financing and excessive debt accumulation by the latter. Substantial vertical imbalances in favour of the SNGs, on the other hand, tend to promote excessive spending on the functions initially assigned to them, e.g. through overmanning or too–generous wage increases for their employees. The rigidity of these expenditures makes it difficult for the SNGs to accommodate within their budgets the additional spending responsibilities that may subsequently be transferred to them.

Thus, fiscal discipline at all levels of government is best promoted by a broad *ex–ante* matching of revenues with spending responsibilities for each level. Adequate vertical balance needs to be complemented by carefully designed and transparent equalisation mechanisms, to address horizontal imbalances among SNGs, a common problem worldwide.

The design of intergovernmental fiscal relations needs to take into account that increasingly the degree of spending decentralisation called for by efficiency considerations and/or political pressures tends to exceed the degree of devolution of revenue–raising responsibilities consistent with optimal tax assignment. Efficiency and administrative considerations continue to argue for the centre to keep the major taxes, especially the corporate income tax, multistage sales taxes such as the VAT, and taxes on foreign trade. The bases of the personal income tax and of general or selective single–stage taxes can be shared between the central and the regional governments, while the property tax remains the best choice for local government taxation. In conditions of substantial expenditure decentralisation, these generally accepted principles are unlikely to lead to vertical balance.

In such circumstances, a systematic resort to intergovernmental transfers will likely be required. Promoting fiscal responsibility at the subnational level calls for implementation of a stable and transparent system of transfers from the central government to the SNGs, geared to filling any *ex–ante* gap between the assigned spending and revenue–raising responsibilities of the latter. The definition of such a system is far from easy, especially given the need to preserve adequate incentives for tax effort and cost effectiveness in spending by the SNGs.

Stability and transparency considerations call for formula–based revenue–sharing (and other general–purpose transfer) systems. Such mechanisms, however, tend to impart considerable rigidity to the central government budget and to constrain its ability to carry out active macroeconomic management. Specifically, an increase in the rates of shared taxes, or successful efforts to improve their administration, aimed at reducing the central government deficit or at curbing excessive growth of domestic demand, automatically increase the resources available for spending by the SNGs. Unless mechanisms in place ensure that these additional resources are saved, the intended macroeconomic effects of the tax increase can be partly (or even largely, depending on the sharing coefficients) frustrated by the revenue–sharing provisions. Recent history, including that in various Latin American countries, provides examples of more or less successful attempts by central governments to enact such mechanisms. A possible approach would stipulate in the revenue–sharing law that the portion of the revenue transferred to the SNGs would be determined by applying a constant tax rate to the shared tax base[2].

Rigid revenue–sharing arrangements can amplify cyclical fluctuations in output. Cyclically induced booms in national taxes tend to boost the SNG's spending capacity, while cyclical declines in those taxes force the SNGs to cut back their spending (at least if they operate under a hard budget constraint). Thus, swings in SNGs' expenditures tend to exacerbate cyclical swings in output. To address this problem, elements of flexibility could be introduced in revenue–sharing arrangements, e.g. by relating the SNGs' shares in national taxes to a moving average of those taxes, or by requiring the SNGs to maintain revenue stabilisation funds (such as the "rainy day funds" mandated by some state constitutions in the United States). On the spending side, as long as responsibility for macroeconomic stabilisation continues to rest with the central government, it is important that the latter retain responsibility for items of expenditure especially sensitive to economic cycles, such as unemployment benefits. This is indeed the practice in most countries.

The Case for Control of SNG Borrowing

The previous section has highlighted that the operations of SNGs, even under balanced–budget conditions, can have significant macroeconomic effects that may run counter to the stabilisation efforts of the central government and constrain its ability to pursue certain macroeconomic objectives. The destabilising potential of SNGs' operations is much greater when they face no hard budget constraint. Substantial deficits of SNGs — especially the larger states and cities — if financed from abroad or by domestic bank credit, can undermine monetary policy and, even if not financed monetarily, "crowd out" the private sector.

Thus, short–run macroeconomic management considerations call for effective limits on SNGs' deficits, consistent with national objectives for growth, inflation and the balance of payments. The mechanisms for defining and enforcing such limits vary across countries, reflecting the institutional framework for intergovernmental relations and political power balances in each country. Naturally, unitary countries tend to attribute greater powers to the central government than federations. In most unitary countries, where typically SNGs have limited own sources of revenue and are therefore heavily dependent on transfers from the centre, the centre exerts extensive influence on the SNGs' budgets, providing more or less binding guidelines for their preparation and monitoring and controlling their execution. The effectiveness of these controls can be substantially enhanced by the adoption at all levels of modern, comprehensive, standardised and transparent budgetary and accounting procedures and information systems. The creation of institutional forums to ensure a regular and frequent dialogue between the central and subnational authorities on current and prospective budget trends can help much in this respect. Examples of such an approach can be found in a number of European countries (e.g. the United Kingdom, Belgium and the Scandinavian countries).

In federal countries where the states frequently have constitutionally guaranteed status as sovereign entities, or at least much greater autonomy than in unitary countries, the central government may not have the legal authority to impose limits on the SNGs' budget deficits. Attempts by the central government to curb the growth of SNGs' spending by cutting back discretionary transfers to them may be frustrated by stepped–up SNG borrowing.

It is no surprise, then, that a number of federations have moved toward more co–operative approaches to macroeconomic management, which involve SNGs actively in the process of formulating the national macroeconomic objectives and the key fiscal parameters underpinning them, making the SNGs, so to speak, co–responsible for their achievement. A multilateral negotiation process in which the central government generally takes a leading role, produces agreement on an overall balance target for general government as well as on guidelines for growth of the main items of revenue and expenditure. Specific limits are then agreed for the financing requirements of individual subnational jurisdictions. Mechanisms are also agreed for multilateral monitoring of compliance with these limits and for their revision when necessary. Australia, through its Loan Council, has a well developed example of this approach (Craig, 1997); Germany has another variant (Spahn and Föttinger, 1997).

The co–operative approach has the clear advantage of promoting dialogue and exchange of information among the various levels of government. It also raises consciousness among subnational policy makers of the macroeconomic implications of their budgetary choices. It works best, however, in countries with well established cultures of fiscal conservatism and discipline. It may not be effective in preventing a build–up of SNG debt in conditions where either market discipline or the leadership of the central government is weak.

SNGs' deficits can affect adversely not only macroeconomic management and performance in the short run, but also intergenerational equity over the longer term. The running up of substantial debt by the SNGs — not unlike the accumulation of debt by the central government — can impose a heavy debt–service burden on future taxpayers not represented in today's electoral processes (McKinnon and Nachyba, 1997). A quick review of recent developments in major countries — especially, but not exclusively federal ones — shows that indeed the debt of SNGs has risen rapidly over the last few decades, reaching in some instances over a quarter of the total national debt.

In this perspective of intergenerational equity, and abstracting from short–run macroeconomic management considerations, the main criterion governing the access of SNGs (as well as the central government) to borrowing should be their capacity to service the debt over time. By whom and how should the assessment of this capacity be made? Under what conditions can financial markets be relied upon to impose an effective discipline on SNGs' borrowing? When these conditions cannot be fulfilled in practice, is a rules–based approach to SNGs' borrowing preferable to direct controls — when legally feasible — by the central government?

Alternative Approaches to the Control of Subnational Borrowing[3]

Reliance on Market Discipline

Lane (1993) has suggested a number of conditions for financial markets to exert effective discipline on SNG borrowing:

—   markets should be free and open, with no regulations on financial intermediaries (such as reserve or other portfolio composition requirements) that place SNGs in a privileged–borrower position;

—   adequate information on the borrower's outstanding debt and repayment capacity should be available to potential lenders;

—   there should be no perceived chance of bailout of the lenders by the central government in cases of impending default[4]. An assumption by the central government of the debt of a subnational government imposes an externality on taxpayers in the rest of the country; and

—   the borrower should have institutional structures which ensure adequate policy responsiveness to market signals before reaching the point of exclusion from new borrowing.

These are indeed stringent conditions, unlikely to be realised in most countries. Typically, especially in developing countries, available information on SNG finances still suffers from serious weaknesses in coverage, quality and timeliness. Many countries still use various forms of portfolio constraints on financial intermediaries to facilitate placement of government securities (including those of SNGs) at reduced cost. More importantly, in many, especially developing countries, SNGs maintain ownership or controlling stakes in financial institutions which provide a captive market for their bond issues or borrowing. Many countries have seen various forms of intervention by the central government (or the central bank) to prevent SNG defaults. Relatively short electoral cycles tend to make SNG politicians short–sighted and unresponsive to early warnings by the financial markets.

Recognition of these realities may be a major reason why reliance solely on market discipline to control SNG borrowing is not usual. Examples can be found in Canada, at least for provincial governments' borrowing, and earlier (through the late 1980s) in Brazil. They point to the dangers of an unfettered reliance on market discipline. The problems created by the build–up of state debts in Brazil are of course well known and need no repeating here. Yet even in a country like Canada, with well developed and relatively transparent financial markets and no history of bailouts by the federal government, market discipline has not proven fully effective. Despite a clear deterioration in ratings and sizeable increases in risk premiums on provincial bonds — more marked for the more indebted provinces — provincial debt has risen steadily over the last several years (to about 23 per cent of GDP in 1994), and only in the last few years have the provincial governments begun to design and implement fiscal retrenchment programmes. Some of the provinces have also instituted legal or constitutional limits to their own borrowing. Perhaps market discipline is finally starting to work, but only after a "recognition lag" which will necessitate a sharper and more painful retrenchment than would have been necessary if provincial debts, and their service, had been curtailed earlier.

Thus, although appealing in principle, sole reliance on market discipline for SNG borrowing will unlikely become appropriate in most countries under present circumstances. Over the longer term, however — as financial markets become more developed, transparent and free from government intervention; as public banks are privatised; as information on recent and prospective developments in the finances of SNGs improves and has wide dissemination; and as the centre establishes a sustained, no–bailout record — the scope for effective reliance on market discipline can progressively expand.

Rules–based Approaches

A number of countries, both federal and unitary, have relied on approaches to the control of SNGs' borrowing based on standing rules specified in the constitution or in law. Some of these rules set limits on the absolute level of SNG indebtedness; others stipulate that borrowing can occur only for specified purposes (typically investment projects); yet others permit new borrowing only up to a level consistent with predetermined maximum debt–service ratios. Some countries prohibit or severely restrict types of borrowing which involve greater macroeconomic risks (e.g. borrowing from the central bank or from abroad). Many countries use a combination of such rules.

Rules that limit SNGs to borrowing for investment (the so–called golden rules) are quite common in industrial countries — in Germany, Switzerland and most of the state constitutions in the United States. In principle, a good case can be made for golden rules, but they may not be sufficiently restrictive in countries which need to generate government savings to finance at least a part of public investment. Moreover, it may not be desirable to allow government borrowing to finance investments which do not have adequate rates of economic and social return. (Indeed, in many countries, efficient current expenditures on health and education may have higher rates of return than many capital projects.) Finally, it may be difficult in practice to avoid circumvention through the labelling of certain current expenditures as investments.

Countries which allow short–term borrowing for liquidity generally stipulate that it must be repaid by the end of each fiscal year. This applies, for instance, in some of the US states and to regional and local governments in Spain. Enforcement of such rules must watch for creative accounting and build–ups of temporary payments arrears at year end.

Rules that "mimic" market discipline by linking limits on the indebtedness of SNGs to projected debt–service ratios or other indicators of debt–servicing capacity (such as past revenues or the tax base) also occur in several industrial countries such as the United States (Stotsky and Sunley, 1997), Korea (Chu and Norregaard, 1997),

Spain and Japan (Mihaljek, 1997). Their effective use requires, of course, that projections of debt service and revenues used in testing compliance with the ceilings be realistic and preferably conservative.

Rules–based approaches have the obvious advantages of transparency and even–handedness, and avoid protracted bargaining between the centre and the SNGs, a process whose outcome often is determined more by short–term political factors than considerations of sound macroeconomic management. Yet by their very nature rules–based approaches lack flexibility and often foster behaviour and practices aimed at circumventing them. Such practices include, for instance:

— the reclassification of expenditures from current to capital, to escape budget–balance requirements:

— the creation of entities whose operations — albeit governmental — are kept off–budget, and whose debts are not counted against the debt ceilings;

— the use of state or local government–owned enterprises to borrow for purposes which should get funded through the relevant government budget;

— the use of debt instruments — such as sale and leaseback arrangements or the so–called private revenue bonds in the United States (Stotsky and Sunley, 1997), not included in the debt limits; and

— resort to arrears toward suppliers, which are typically difficult to monitor for inclusion in the public debt ceilings.

This non–exhaustive listing suggests that an effective rules–based approach needs support from clear and uniform accounting standards for government entities, strictly limiting and preferably eliminating the scope for off–budget operations; comprehensive definitions of what constitutes debt; modern government financial management information systems capable of providing timely and reliable data on all phases of expenditure[5] as well as on financial operations of the various levels of government; and policies, like privatisation, which minimise the scope for using financial and non–financial enterprises for government purposes.

Direct Central Government Controls Over Subnational Borrowing

A number of countries empower the central government with direct control over SNG borrowing. It may take alternative forms, including annual (or more frequent) limits on the overall debt of individual subnational jurisdictions (or some of its components, e.g. external borrowing); review and authorisation of individual borrowing operations (including approval of terms and conditions), and/or the centralisation of all government borrowing, with authorisation of lending to SNGs for approved purposes (generally investment projects). Control powers generally encompass not only the *ex–ante* authorisation of proposed borrowing, but also the *ex–post* monitoring, on a more or less detailed and timely basis, of the SNGs' financial operations.

Direct central government control over subnational deficits and debt is of course more common in unitary countries than in federations. Examples in different forms exist in the United Kingdom, France, Spain, Japan and a wide range of unitary developing countries. Among federal countries, the Indian Constitution empowers the central government to approve or disallow borrowing by those states (in practice all) which have outstanding indebtedness to the centre (Hemming, Mates and Potter, 1997). In Brazil, the Senate can set limits on state indebtedness, and recently, in their debt–restructuring operations, the states have entered into agreements with the central government which has a degree of control over further state recourse to borrowing (Ter–Minassian, 1997).

Several arguments favour direct central government controls on the external borrowing of SNGs. First, external debt policy links intimately with other macroeconomic policies (monetary and exchange–rate policies, and foreign reserve management) which are the responsibility of the centre (especially the central bank). *Second,* a well co–ordinated approach to foreign markets for sovereign borrowing likely will result in better terms and conditions than a fragmented one. *Third,* a deterioration of foreign ratings for one or more of the subnational borrowers may well have "contagion" effects on ratings for other borrowers, both public and private. Finally, foreign lenders frequently require an explicit central government guarantee for subnational borrowing. Even in the absence of such a guarantee, pressures on central governments to come to the rescue of insolvent SNGs will be more compelling when the external creditworthiness of the whole country risks damage from default by those SNGs. If central governments then bear ultimate *de facto* responsibility for SNGs' external debt, they should have approval power over the SNGs' recourse to it.

The case for direct central government controls over SNGs' *domestic* borrowing is clearly less compelling. As already mentioned, such controls can conflict with the legal and often constitutional status of SNGs in federal countries. Moreover, such controls entail the centre's involvement in micro–level decisions (e.g. about the financing of individual investment projects) best left to the relevant subnational authorities. Finally, administrative approval of individual SNG borrowing operations may well make it more difficult for the centre to refuse financial support in the event of an impending default. Thus, on balance, effectively monitored aggregate limits on the overall debt of individual jurisdictions, set in law and based on market–type criteria, would seem preferable to either centralised government borrowing or the pre–approval by the central government of individual borrowing operations of the SNGs.

Concluding Remarks

This paper has attempted to provide an overview of the complex issues relating to decentralisation and macroeconomic management, and to draw a few lessons from country experiences. Decentralisation, as desirable as it might be on efficiency as well as political grounds, can entail costs in terms of the central government's ability to carry out effectively its traditional macroeconomic management functions. Indeed, one can argue that countries facing acute macroeconomic and fiscal imbalances should "put their house in order" before embarking on substantial further decentralisation of revenue and spending responsibilities.

Ways do exist to minimise the macroeconomic costs of decentralisation. *First,* the greater the degree of revenue and spending devolution, the more important it is for the central government to seek an active dialogue with the SNGs and involve them in macroeconomic management and adjustment efforts. The model of co–operative federalism discussed briefly above is likely to acquire increasing relevance worldwide if the decentralisation trend continues and deepens. *Second,* SNGs need hard budget constraints — comprehensive, transparent, and effectively monitored limits on their indebtedness. These limits preferably should exist in standing rules, enshrined in law and based on sustainability criteria relating to the capacity to service debt with own resources or non–discretionary transfers from the central government. Market discipline, promoted through dissemination of information and removal of government interference, can usefully complement and support the rules.

All these considerations give cause for cautious optimism that the progress made in recent years by most Latin American countries in stabilisation will not be lost, the maintenance of low rates of inflation will go hand in hand with strong and balanced economic growth, and governments will persevere with and expand the scope of reforms of the public finances.

Notes

1.   For a broad survey of country experiences with intergovernmental fiscal relations, focusing in particular on macroeconomic aspects, see Ter–Minassian (1997).

2.   See e.g. Schwartz and Liuksila (1997); Ter–Minassian (1997).

3.   See Ter–Minassian and Craig (1997) for a fuller discussion of these issues and of country experiences.

4.   See Bayoumi, Goldstein and Waglom (1995).

5.   Timely and reliable information on obligations to pay, as well as on actual payments, is essential to prevent the accumulation of arrears.

Bibliography

AHMAD, E. (ed.) (1997), "Financing Decentralised Expenditures: An International Comparison of Grants", Edward Elgar, Cheltenham.

BAYOUMI, T., M. GOLDSTEIN AND G. WAGLOM (1995), "Do Credit Markets Discipline Sovereign Borrowers? Evidence from the United States", *Journal of Money, Credit and Banking*, Vol. 27, No. 4, part 1.

CHI, K.Y. AND J. NORREGAARD (1997), "Korea", in T. TER–MINASSIAN (ed.), *Fiscal Federalism in Theory and Practice*, International Monetary Fund, Washington, D.C.

CRAIG, J. (1997), "Australia", in T. TER–MINASSIAN (ed.), *Fiscal Federalism in Theory and Practice*, International Monetary Fund, Washington, D.C.

HEMMING, R., N. MATES AND B. POTTER (1997), "India" in T. TER–MINASSIAN (ed.), *Fiscal Federalism in Theory and Practice*, International Monetary Fund, Washington, D.C.

LANE, T.D. (1993), "Market Discipline", *Staff Papers*, Vol. 40, International Monetary Fund, Washington, D.C., March.

MCKINNON, R. AND NACHYBA (1997), "Competition in Federal Systems: The Role of Political and Financial Constraints", unpublished, Stanford University, March.

MIHALJEK, D. (1997), "Japan", in T. TER–MINASSIAN (ed.), *Fiscal Federalism in Theory and Practice*, International Monetary Fund, Washington, D.C.

SPAHN, P.B. AND W. FÖTTINGER (1997), "Germany" in T. TER–MINASSIAN (ed.), *Fiscal Federalism in Theory and Practice*, International Monetary Fund, Washington, D.C.

SCHWARTZ, G. AND C. LIUKSILA (1997), "United States", in T. TER–MINASSIAN (ed.), *Fiscal Federalism in Theory and Practice*, International Monetary Fund, Washington, D.C.

STOTSKY J. AND E. SUNLEY (1997), "United States", in T. TER–MINASSIAN (ed.), *Fiscal Federalism in Theory and Practice*, International Monetary Fund, Washington, D.C.

TER–MINASSIAN, T. (1997), "Brazil", in T. TER–MINASSIAN (ed.), *Fiscal Federalism in Theory and Practice*, International Monetary Fund, Washington, D.C.

TER–MINASSIAN, T. AND J. CRAIG (1997), "Control of Subnational Government Borrowing", in T. TER–MINASSIAN (ed.), *Fiscal Federalism in Theory and Practice*, International Monetary Fund, Washington, D.C.

Bibliography

Chapter 4

Fiscal Federalism in OECD Member Countries

Jon Blondal

Introduction

Fiscal federalism — a convenient but perhaps misleading term because it does not apply only to federal systems — presents one of the most complex public management issues facing OECD Member countries. It poses largely the same questions for both unitary and federal countries. This paper offers both an overview of current fiscal federalism arrangements in OECD Member countries and a general discussion of some of the key fiscal federalism issues that they face.

Overview

A quick overview of fiscal federalism arrangements in OECD Member countries reveals the wide range of possibilities available to governments. One finds countries with very strong subnational governments (SNGs), those with very weak ones and everything in between. No single "OECD model" exists. Table 4.1 presents data on the share of SNGs in total government expenditures and revenues. As a first generalisation, federal countries tend to have the larger SNGs — which is what we might expect and has been the case historically. Next in line are the Nordic countries and the Netherlands, all unitary countries and in many ways sharing similar governance traditions. Significantly, SNGs in this group have grown stronger in recent years. One finds the weakest SNGs in unitary countries with Napoleonic or Westminster traditions of governance. Examples include France, Greece, Italy, New Zealand and the United Kingdom.

Table 4.1. **Subnational Government Shares, 1994**

(per cent)

	Share of total government expenditures	Share of total government revenues
Australia	45.4	29.4
Austria	25.2	22.9
Belgium	11.3	7.0
Canada	55.3	50.0
Denmark	51.7	29.1
Finland	28.2	21.9
France	14.2	10.7
Germany	32.0	29.0
Greece	7.9	3.6
Iceland	19.4	19.1
Ireland	26.4	5.4
Italy	23.1	9.9
Japan	36.6	22.9
Netherlands	25.7	7.0
Portugal	8.3	7.1
Spain	20.4	12.6
Sweden	34.5	31.3
Switzerland	43.6	39.5
United Kingdom	25.3	6.0
United States	38.7	34.3

Source: OECD.

Table 4.1 also suggests that the SNGs' share of total expenditure exceeds their share of total revenue. The difference arises mostly from transfers of funds by central governments to SNGs. No obvious groupings emerge from these figures. Some federal countries, notably Australia, have very significant transfers to SNGs, whereas others such as the United States make relatively low transfers. Some unitary Nordic countries, for example Denmark, have very substantial ones but others such as Iceland have relatively few; although other unitary countries do tend to have more substantial transfers from the centre to lower levels.

The figures require caveats. *First,* different accounting regimes for government revenues and expenditures and divergent treatment of social security funds can significantly affect the reported financial flows. *Second,* the figures, by definition, capture only financial flows and do not incorporate mandates from the central government to SNGs. Nonetheless, anecdotal evidence tends to confirm the general conclusions. Also, current fiscal federalism arrangements largely reflect each country's history and entrenched traditions; if Member countries could set up their systems today from a clean slate, they would no doubt look different. The definite trend in Member countries is to strengthen SNGs, giving them more responsibility for revenues and expenditures, but legacies of the past act as a check on the pace of such reforms. Nonetheless, central governments will always dominate. Even in countries with strong SNGs, such as the United States, the federal government still accounts for about two–thirds of all activity.

Issues

OECD Member countries face *five* wide–ranging, often complementary fiscal federalism imperatives, essential for successful outcomes:

i)   Aggregate fiscal discipline;

ii)   Economic stabilisation measures;

iii)   Allocative efficiency;

iv)   Regional equity considerations; and

v)   Operating effectiveness and efficiency.

Aggregate Fiscal Discipline

The overriding goal of any fiscal system is or should be to maintain aggregate fiscal discipline, i.e. to control the totals. Central governments generally fear that some SNGs will behave less than responsibly and accumulate excessive and unsustainable levels of debt. Member countries have adopted three approaches to impose fiscal discipline on SNGs. The first simply imposes no central government restrictions on the borrowing activity of SNGs and leaves it to the market to impose the necessary discipline. The United States and Canada employ this approach.

The second approach, "administrative control", requires SNGs to consult with the central government on their borrowing plans, in aggregate or for individual loans. These consultations commonly cover other aspects of SNG finances as well, i.e. overall levels of revenue and expenditure. They are not quite "consultations"; the central government's view generally prevails if disagreements arise. OECD Member countries most commonly adopt this approach. Prime examples include the Nordic countries, Germany with its Financial Planning Council and Australia with its National Loans Council.

The third approach prescribes at the centre general rules for permitted levels of borrowing by SNGs. Rules–based systems, often combined with administrative control systems, commonly distinguish between capital and operating expenditures and allow borrowing only for the former. The clearest example of a stand–alone, rules–based system, albeit different in nature, is the package of Maastricht criteria for European Monetary Union, with its benchmark budget deficits and government debts of 3 per cent and 60 per cent of GDP, respectively.

Strikingly, only two Member countries — the United States and Canada — rely on the market to impose fiscal discipline on SNGs. OECD Member countries have advanced financial markets and high–quality fiscal reporting, suggesting that market discipline should be effective. It has worked very well in the United States and Canada. SNGs in the United States have relatively low levels of debt; those in Canada accumulated heavy debts in the early 1990s, but downgradings by credit rating agencies and higher interest–rate differentials forced them to adopt strong fiscal consolidation programmes. On this evidence, why do more OECD Member countries not adopt this approach? The reason lies in bailout policies. The United States and Canada offer no comfort that the central government would bail out SNGs if they got into financial trouble. Markets in other Member countries still generally believe that central governments would render assistance. Central governments could try to change this belief over time, primarily by not coming to the rescue of SNGs in financial trouble, but, failing that, a need remains for more direct central government involvement by the in SNG borrowing operations, through either rules–based or administrative control approaches.

Rules–based systems have the advantages of transparency, speed and efficiency, yet they generally have a poor reputation based on their alleged inflexibility; their vulnerability to loss of all credibility if ever the rules are breached; and their openness to all sorts of perverse behavioural incentives when participants try to get around the rules. This critique contains elements of truth, but the Maastricht criteria and their impact on fiscal consolidation efforts in Europe highlight the powerful role that such rules–based approaches can have. OECD Member countries will almost certainly move towards such systems and away from administrative controls which can often be cumbersome and tedious despite their flexibility.

Economic Stabilisation Measures

All OECD Member countries acknowledge that fiscal policy is an important tool for economic stabilisation and that only central governments can run the automatic stabilisers effectively. The Maastricht criteria, however, open a new issue for European Union (EU) member countries, which one can view as emerging SNGs because they are locking themselves into maximum permitted fiscal deficits. The maxima do not differentiate between members that enjoy robust economic growth and those suffering from recessions. Each country operates its own automatic stabilisers with no central EU funds, which can lead to significant adjustment problems. The EU Growth and Stability Pact has recognised this. It offers some debatable flexibility to operate with higher deficits during economic downturns. The US federal government, in contrast, largely controls the automatic stabilisers. Should a severe recession hit California, for example, financial streams to the state from the federal government (unemployment and other welfare benefits) would increase significantly and those in the other direction (less taxation resulting from less economic activity) would decrease greatly. This would ease California's adjustment. This example highlights why the automatic stabilisers should be located at the centre and not in the SNGs. It will be interesting to see whether the EU evolves toward more centralisation.

Allocative Efficiency and Regional Equity Considerations

Allocative efficiency refers to the optimal distribution of resources — spending public money where it is most needed. The key benefit of strengthening SNGs lies in their proximity to the population, which better positions them to reflect the wishes and needs of each community, more innovatively and flexibly. A "one–size–fits–all" standard no longer applies. Almost by definition, therefore, stronger SNGs equal greater allocative efficiency.

At the same time, regional equity considerations — disparities among SNGs either in the financial resources at their disposal or the costs of providing services — need recognition. Should people in more affluent areas enjoy premium services while those in poorer areas struggle for basic services? Should urban areas enjoy better services than less densely populated ones? Such disparities argue for a strong central government to ensure equity.

Fiscal federalism thus becomes a balancing act between two poles: strong SNGs to achieve allocative efficiency versus strong central governments to achieve equity. One school of thought holds that regional inequity is the price to pay for strong SNGs. Another says that regional inequity should preclude strong SNGs. No OECD Member illustrates these extremes. The United States leans towards the former and countries such as the United Kingdom towards the latter. On the middle ground, the centre typically fills the gap between the revenue–raising capacities and the expenditure requirements of SNGs through transfers.

Many types of transfer arrangements exist, along a continuum defined by the degrees of discretion available to SNGs. Some are relatively simple while others involve complex formulas; many incorporate detailed conditions for the use of the transfers. From the central government's point of view, these conditions ensure that the money is spent uniformly throughout the country on improving the services that form the national rationale for having the transfers in the first place. For example, if the central government decides to improve educational standards and supports this policy with transfers to the SNGs that operate the schools, it will want to ensure that the money goes to that purpose. It may go further and insist that the money flows to more specific objectives, such as improving science education, or further still to earmark funds for buying laboratory equipment. Multiply this by the hundreds, or thousands, of individual transfer programmes in operation.

We now see the pendulum swinging in the other direction, towards fundamental reforms in OECD Member countries. The broad outlines of these reforms are very similar, as most countries consolidate multiple transfer programmes and relax substantially the conditions attached to the transfers. Their primary motivation generally is to reduce central government expenditures; cuts in the total amount of transfers usually accompany the reforms. The allocative–efficiency argument provides justification: SNGs can make better use of the money with increased freedom in its use; therefore they will need less. While it is too early to evaluate the impact of these reforms, the OECD record so far suggests a win–win situation. Central governments win because they can reduce expenditures. SNGs win because they can use the transfers in more appropriate ways.

Other reforms in OECD Member countries to promote allocative efficiency include measures to clarify the role of each level of government in specific sectors, to avoid duplication. Other efforts seek to clarify responsibilities for financing expenditure programmes, to avoid situations where the central government is responsible, either fully or on a cost–sharing basis, for financing expenditure programmes operated by SNGs. This should increase the incentive for SNGs to limit expenditures. Canada, for example, has embarked on a major programme of change in the system of federal transfers to provinces. It will consolidate a complex system of separate transfers for social assistance, post–secondary education and health care, now partly on a cost–sharing basis, into a single Canada Health and Social Transfer — a block grant, not an open–ended, cost–sharing transfer. This reform will accompany a decline in total transfers to provinces of one–fifth of GDP over a three–year period.

Operating Effectiveness and Efficiency

This issue has two aspects: whether SNGs have the managerial and technical capacity to carry out the functions assigned to them; and whether they provide "value for money" efficiency by carrying out their functions at least cost. An SNG's managerial and technical capacity generally relates to its size; below a certain size threshold it cannot achieve the necessary economies of scale in operation. Most OECD Member countries have some insufficiently large SNGs and have tended to alleviate the problem in one of two ways — first, by merging SNGs to form larger units, and second, by creating special–purpose organisations operated by several SNGs. Thus a secondary school may be operated jointly by several small jurisdictions. Although the second option has proven easier in political terms, the first should be preferred for operating effectiveness and efficiency, because a plethora of specific–purpose organisations can obscure accountability.

OECD Member countries also want to ensure that SNGs operate public services at least cost. Most leave the problem to the electorate in each jurisdiction, which highlights the importance of clear lines of accountability. The United Kingdom offers a notable exception to this "hands–off" approach. It has formed an Audit Commission for Local Governments, established a Citizen's Charter to set performance standards for public services and instituted a programme of Compulsory Competitive Tendering by local governments. All three initiatives appear to have been highly effective in promoting effectiveness and efficiency in the delivery of service by SNGs.

The Audit Commission audits the finances and performance of each local authority. Its primary influence stems from the respect it enjoys and its provision to the electorate of information by which to hold local authorities accountable. Its "league tables" compare how effectively and efficiently different local governments perform the same service. The Citizen's Charter establishes a framework for "setting, monitoring and publication of explicit standards for the services that individual users can reasonably expect ... (and) ... publication of actual performance against these standards". Citizen's Charters have been established for a variety of local government services, including education and public housing. These charters touch the level of individual users and provide benchmarks for them to judge the performance of public services. The Compulsory Competitive Tendering programme requires local governments to "market–test" specific activities. Market–testing is essentially contracting out, but in–house personnel can compete against outside contractors in the bidding process, with no presumption that activities will necessarily go to private suppliers. This exposes in–house personnel to the discipline of the market and fosters efficiency. The programme began with blue–collar activities such as trash removal and janitorial services, but is now being expanded to include white–collar activities such as legal and financial services.

Conclusion

No single "OECD model" can describe fiscal federalism arrangements in OECD Member countries. They are too diverse. The major fiscal federalism issues in the OECD area highlight the vast array of considerations that apply to designing successful fiscal federalism programmes. Institutional arrangements, very important of course, do not by themselves guarantee success or failure. In the end, political will determines the outcome.

Chapter 5

Strengthening Municipal Financing:
Difficulties and New Challenges for Latin America

Gabriel Aghón and Carlos Casas

Introduction

The fulfilment of their new responsibilities by local governments in Latin America under the fiscal decentralisation process that started in the 1980s has confronted a lack of financial resources to meet citizens' needs. Local governments need an appropriate system of revenue mobilisation. By law, several countries in the region have delegated functions such as education and health to local governments within a legal framework of autonomy and accountability; but an appropriate fiscal system requires an adequate division of fiscal revenues. Taxes assigned to each level of government must equal, on average, its expected expenditures. This criterion is not fulfilled in practice, an issue central to the autonomy and decentralisation debate in the region.

The distribution of fiscal revenues and expenditures for a group of Latin American countries (Argentina, Brazil, Colombia and Chile) reveals a limited participation of subnational governments (SNGs). Other countries, such as Peru, Bolivia, Paraguay, Ecuador and those of Central America, tend to exhibit a higher concentration of revenues and expenditures at the centre. Latin American countries generally show more expenditure concentration in the central government than industrialised countries; they have a long way to go to reach high levels of fiscal decentralisation.

A common pattern describes functions and expenditures assigned to local governments in the region. As Table 5.1 shows, they focus on items such as local public services, sewage and local infrastructure. Their financing comes mainly from user charges and contributions, which promotes efficiency. Urban planning, security and general administration are local public goods and hence local taxes most appropriately finance their provision. Medium and large cities in some countries partially fund urban infrastructure by borrowing, but central governments have extensive

Categories	Local responsibilities	Responsibilities shared with the central government	Financing
Public Services			User charges are the main
Sewage	x		source of financing. In some
Electricity	x		cases municipalities have
Telephone	x		access to the financial system.
Urban and Transport Infrastructure			The financing of these activities
Road construction	x		are shared with central
Highways	x	x	government. Other forms are
Bridges	x		participation of private sector
Street lighting		x	(concessions) and contributions.
Public transportation			
General Urban Services			These activities are financed by
Solid waste	x		local taxes and user charges.
Recreation	x		
Street cleaning	x		
Administration	x		
Social Services			Principal financing source are
Primary education		x	subsidies from central
Basic health		x	governments and in many cases
Welfare		x	transfers from the same source.
Housing		x	
Local Development Promotion (agriculture, manufacturing and mining, tourism, environment and telecommunications		x	National taxes, debt and private participation

control over local–government indebtedness. In small cities or rural villages, local authorities have no access to capital markets and central governments co–finance the provision of local infrastructure.

A second group of fiscal responsibilities concerns social services (education, health, sports, social assistance). Here municipalities only manage service delivery and sometimes cofinance expenditures. The centre usually finances and establishes the general policies. Middle–tier governments also play a part in providing social services by acting as technical advisors to local governments. In federal countries, provincial or state governments participate in the design and financing of social programmes in the municipalities under their jurisdictions. In recent years, local governments have received greater roles in social programmes such as health and education, boosting their need for technical assistance from intermediate levels.

A third group of responsibilities, not explicitly local, relates to economic development — promoting private–sector development and access to the domestic financial sector. This activity is co–ordinated by the central government and, in large cities, local governments design and implement specific policies.

Four main principles define the role of local governments. *First,* the benefit principle states that local taxes and user charges must finance the provision of local public goods. Accordingly, every household is charged in exact proportion to the satisfaction derived from such goods, to reach an efficient allocation of resources in the local economy. The *second* principle is efficiency in tax collection; local governments must prefer taxes levied on goods and services with little inter–jurisdictional mobility, to avoid tax competition between them. These taxes must also be neutral with respect to income distribution. The *third* principle is equity: every citizen must pay according to his/her income level. The *fourth* principle relates to autonomy and accountability: taxes must be set transparently.

Main Instruments of Municipal Finances

An adequate description of fiscal decentralisation in Latin America requires a review of the main revenue sources in the region. Local governments have greater autonomy for local taxes or user charges than with respect to transferred funds or debt management, which are particularly important in local budgeting. Table 5.2 shows the variant structures of local revenues in several Latin American countries, with their great dependency on intergovernmental transfers and limited self–generated resources. In comparison with the industrialised world (Aghón and Letelier, 1996; Bird 1993; Musgrave, 1983; Shah, 1994), Latin American local governments have limited ability to mobilise resources locally.

Table 5.2. **Municipal Revenue Structure in Selected Countries in Latin America**
(Percentage of total revenues)

	Brazil	Bolivia	Colombia	Chile	Peru
Transfers	62.7	54.7	47.8	42.7	58.1
Taxes					
Property tax	8.3	7.4	12.4	12.6	9.1
Commercial permission		18.1	9.2	2.6
Vehicle tax	22.3	7.3	3.2	7.4	1.3
Other taxes		22.8	5.2	3.7	13.0
Total Taxes			38.8	32.9	
User Charges	14.1	4.6	10.4	12.4	13.3
Other Revenues	15.0	17.9	3.0	12.0	15.6
Total	100.0	100.0	100.0	100.0	100.0

Source: Case studies, Regional Project ECLAC/GTZ Fiscal Decentralisation in Latin America.

In recent years, local taxes have gained larger shares in the total revenue of Latin American local governments. In almost every country, national legislation sets bases and tax rates and local governments act mainly as tax collectors without discretion or autonomy. The main local taxes are property and vehicle registration taxes. Commercial and professional permits follow. The chief problem of tax–base assignment is to find taxes that perform efficiently and do not breach basic principles of tax administration.

An important property–tax issue concerns the undervaluation of its base. In some countries, the declared base is one–third of its commercial value, despite efforts of local tax administrators to modernise tax collection systems. Two complementary measures form a basis for strengthening this revenue source: improvement of the property register through modern valuation techniques, computerised geographic information and up–to–date property values; and improved collection through better guidelines to taxpayers and adequate sanctions for tax evasion.

Bogota (Colombia) and La Paz (Bolivia)

To compare recent progress in property tax reform, Bogota (Colombia) and La Paz (Bolivia) represent good case studies[1]. Property taxes, the main source of local revenue in Colombia in the last decade, represented only about 25 per cent of tax revenues for Bogota in 1990–94, but this now is true only for districts of small industrial and commercial activity. In La Paz, property taxes represented 55 per cent of total revenues in 1990–95.

Recent increases in revenue coincide with reforms in both cities. In Bogota, the reform allowed for self–valuation to assess the tax base, a move justified by the small proportion of registered properties (of a total of 1.25 million estates, only 30 per cent were formally registered) and the negative impact of the delay that commercial valuations would have caused. Despite initial difficulties, tax revenue increased considerably (Table 5.3). The rise came from growth in the number of registered estates that began to pay taxes rather than a heavier per capita tax burden; this led to a better distribution of the tax charge and a considerable reduction in evasion. The experience enabled assessment of the benefits of self–evaluation mechanisms, and other cities such as Cali and Barranquilla now use the system.

In La Paz, the Law of Popular Participation (*Ley de Participación Popular*), which devolved property taxes to municipal jurisdictions, produced a significant increase in tax collection (Table 5.4). Cities that demonstrate adequate administrative capacity now may levy this tax. Higher revenues also came partly through local efforts to modernise the tax collection system through an integrated, computerised system for the register of taxpayers. As in Bogota, La Paz also has undervalued tax registers (in many cases less than half of the real value of the property). Several monitoring activities in recent years have worked to mitigate this problem. The participation of the private sector offers an interesting alternative in the development of an adequate register system. It is also important to consider incentives and control mechanisms to avoid tax evasion.

Table 5.3. **Bogota, Unified Property Tax, 1993-96**
(million pesos)

	1993	1994	1995	1996
Base	8 921 098	17 724 125	22 155 156	30 305 924
Total revenue	45 662	104 000	128 000	157 635
Number of declarants	550 00	950 000	997 500	1 047 375
Effective rate (percentage)	0.51	0.59	0.58	0.52

Source: Piza (1996).

Table 5.4. **Property Tax in Relation with Total Local Taxes and Total Revenue, La Paz, 1991-96**
($ million)

Year	Property tax (a)	Local taxes (b)	Total local revenue (c)	Percentage ratio (a/b)	Percentage ratio (a/c)
1991	3.7	6.5	35.1	56	56
1992	4.8	8.1	41.0	58	58
1993	4.6	9.3	40.7	50	50
1994	8.2	13.4	37.4	61	61
1995	10.3	19.9	41.9	52	52
1996	9.3	19.4	45.9	48	48

Source: Cuevas (1996).

Recent decades have seen greater use of user charges[2]. Evaluating them requires consideration of the benefits and costs of the services provided[3]. In contrast with local taxes, such charges increase autonomy over the determination of tariffs, tax administration and tax collection. User charges constitute the clearest example of Latin American legislation enabling local governments to play an active role in generating resources and self–financing[4]. Nevertheless, they still have a relatively small share in the revenue structure of Latin American local governments, because of legal impediments limiting their use, several exceptions in their collection, the low quality of services and, in general, political resistance.

Some recent experience with private sector involvement in municipal infrastructure financing deserves mention[5]. Concessions represent a possibility worth exploration by local governments, as in countries such as Chile and, more recently, Colombia and Peru, where municipalities are considering private–sector participation in the development of infrastructure projects[6]. In environmental management, mobilisation of private sector resources represents a major task for coming years. Tax mechanisms to control pollution are becoming urgent in the major Latin American cities.

Intergovernmental transfers often provide a considerable portion of the total revenue of local governments, especially in medium and small municipalities. The criteria used in determining them concern different variables such as population, poverty indicators, fiscal effort and administrative efficiency[7]. The last two have become more important in recent years. Discretionary or conditional transfers mainly finance basic health and educational services; the central government defines the main features of

the programme and the municipalities simply manage the funds without any cofinancing ,
requirement or active participation in quality control. Other transfers seek redistributive
and efficiency goals or compensation for severe externalities.

Although transfers have an equity justification, their use as the basis of decentralised
finance creates several problems. Local attitudes towards transfers versus local taxes
matter, because a lack of local fiscal effort leads to a decrease in local autonomy[8].
Another problem concerns the lack of transparency and efficiency in administration;
in countries such as Argentina and Brazil, the criteria for the distribution of transfers
often are based more on regions than on people, so that in many cases the poor in rich
regions subsidise the rich in poor ones[9]. Also, rigidity in using the resources transferred
can lead to overfinancing some services which probably causes losses in quality. This
doesn't mean that transfers are unnecessary and that they do not promote the desired
goals, but it emphasises the need for an adequate balance between the different types
of financing and the level of local autonomy.

Finally, the different financial mechanisms that enable municipal leverage for
priority projects can easily be combined with traditional local revenue mobilisation.
With some exceptions (e.g. Brazil, Colombia and Ecuador), the financial system
commonly encourages low use of local leverage capacity. This prevents adequate
evaluation of some important projects' profitability. Evaluations also should estimate
the resources that the present generation can mobilise in order to finance top–priority
projects for future generations (intergenerational equity). If the population's ability
to pay is low relative to the extent of leverage, so is the amount of local investment
financed via leverage. This can also occur if the legal framework for credit is inadequate
or if financial evaluation of payment capacities is inefficient. In countries such as
Argentina, Venezuela and Chile, municipalities cannot conduct public credit operations
because they must be approved by the National Congress.

This type of financing offers little evidence of any negative macroeconomic
consequences. In these countries, inadequate economic management by central
governments, not local government finance, has caused macroeconomic disequilibria.
Nevertheless, financial discipline requires clear regulation concerning municipal
borrowing[10]. Recent efforts of countries such as Brazil, and particularly the legal
initiative of Colombia, include some interesting suggestions for evaluation of the
paying capacity of local governments.

New Challenges in Municipal Finances

If citizens do not pay at least part of the costs of projects from which they obtain
some benefit, financial deficits will inevitably appear. The experiences of many Latin
American countries reveal the main challenges that municipalities will have to face.
Despite the benefits and limitations of different financial instruments, the principal
issues concern the financial self–sufficiency of local governments to ensure minimum
levels of investment and the lack of adequate administrative and technical capacities

to carry out decentralisation programmes. Policies to promote municipalities' fiscal responsibilities must aim not only at financial self–sufficiency but also at increasing expenditure quality. One of the goals of decentralisation is the creation of a political and administrative environment that encourages financial responsibility. This requires the devolution of more authority to local governments to generate revenues and manage larger funds.

Increasing fiscal autonomy at the local level constitutes a major part of fiscal reform. Several options exist. *First,* some relate to the actual structure of tax revenues and charges, which requires taking municipal diversity into account to promote financial creativity. Local tax bases must grow and the use of existing taxation mechanisms be rationalised, giving local governments more autonomy to determine and monitor tax revenues. It is important to strengthen the tax instruments which local governments can use more efficiently, such as bases with low inter–regional mobility and instruments encouraging the use of local facilities and the development of municipal activities with localised externalities. *Second,* new sources of revenue at the local level must also be found, such as user charges, special contributions for specific purposes and the mobilisation of private capital through concessions. These instruments would not only raise local revenue but also reduce dependency on transfers from the central government and enable local governments to cover local costs of service delivery.

According to the theory of fiscal federalism, local governments must charge, when possible, for the services they offer so that they cover at least their current delivery costs. In general, a certain degree of flexibility in the tax system would allow them to set their own tax rates[11] and user charges. This flexibility must also extend to expenditure management to allow local governments to play an active role in the design and control of priority projects. The lack of autonomy, political responsibility and accountability encourages evasive behaviour in local governments, which usually blame the central government for the fragility of their finances.

This paper suggests a clearer division of expenditure functions among the different levels of government. A greater balance between revenue and expenditures requires the assignment of functions according to the principles of fiscal subsidiarity and political responsibility. With respect to intergovernmental transfers, and because of their importance in local finances, the accomplishment of redistributive (equity and fiscal compensation) and efficiency goals depends on transparency and simplicity in the design of institutions (Wiesner, 1995). On leverage, one of the most controversial themes for central government, lessons exist in those countries where local governments may issue debt (always under clear and strict control by the monetary authorities). Municipal governments should understand their administrative and paying capacities to ensure a solid financial structure and adequate assessment of investment projects based on a clear perception of their benefits or financial returns.

Despite the great diversity of financial mechanisms in operation, attention should focus on co–ordination across different levels of government. The risks of inefficient resource use increase in decentralised administrations, particularly when the process of decentralisation leads to the atomisation of resources, a lack of adequate investment projects and poor co–ordination. Local governments must improve their administrative and technical capacities, which requires more local autonomy and accountability. The greatest challenges they face involve increasing the efficiency of resource allocation and the promotion of self–financed activities.

The experiences of Latin America reveal interesting institutional schemes and instruments that have shown efficiency in solving some of the problems. They include some successful innovations in the decentralisation of service delivery. Different financial instruments have been introduced in the local tax system, along with new sources of locally mobilised revenues and interesting schemes of community participation which promote greater political responsibility. Diffusion of these innovations can be promoted among local governments domestically and through international co–operation.

Notes

1. These cases are treated with greater detail in Piza (1996) and Cuevas (1996).

2. For analytical purposes, it is important to make a distinction between local taxes and non–tributary revenues as charges and contributions (Edling, 1996).

3. Charges provide certain information about the costs and the demand for a specific service, promoting a more efficient allocation between the public and private sectors (Edling, 1996). The crowding–out effect is mitigated by this instrument.

4. The recovery of costs through this instrument not only promotes a higher degree of autonomy but also generates incentives for more efficient production.

5. As noted by the World Bank (1994, 1995), the possibilities for private participation in municipal infrastructure usually refer to: *i)* private property and exploitation, *ii)* public property and private exploitation (concessions), *iii)* privatisations, and *iv)* services charged to the community.

6. The Peruvian experience demonstrates how recent legislation on the participation of the private sector through concessions for public infrastructure and services has promoted the interest of local governments (the district of Miraflores). Also, one of the themes concerning the Decentralisation Commission in the Peruvian Congress refers to the modification of local taxing and the explicit incorporation of concessions.

7. For a better description, see the national case studies from the CEPAL/GTZ project of Fiscal Decentralisation. For a comparative analysis, see CEPAL (1996).

8. In countries like Colombia, investigations have attempted to verify the hypothesis that an increase in transfers has led to fiscal sluggishness. They have tried to determine causal relationships between the tax incomes of local governments and the total amount of central transfers, using uni–equational elasticity models and cross–sectional and panel estimations. The econometric results do not validate the hypothesis, due probably to the lack of a good measure for fiscal effort and of local statistical information.

9. A recent investigation conducted by A. Porto and P. Sanguinetti for the CEPAL/GTZ project for Fiscal Decentralisation on the intergovernmental transfers and the regional and personal distribution of income shows that fears concerning the regressive nature of regional distribution are unfounded. Evidence for a selected group of countries shows that regional redistribution in fact favours a positive effect on personal redistribution.

10. This theme has promoted a very important discussion in Latin America with the participation of specialists R. López Murphy, A. Porto and P. Sanguinetti in Argentina; J. Roberto Rodrigues Afonso, and Rui A. Britto in Brazil; L. C. Valenzuela y Ferreira in Colombia; J.A. Ocampo, G. Perry and E. Weisner in Venezuela. Also, international specialists from the IMF, for example, Teresa Ter–Minassian, have discussed this theme suggesting some interesting criteria that must be considered.

11. In Brazil and Colombia, municipalities have relative autonomy to establish their own tax rates, but in Bolivia, Chile, Mexico and Peru, tax rates remain the responsibility of the centre.

Bibliography

AGHON, G., AND L. LETELIER (1996), "Local Urban Governments Financing: A Comparison between Countries", *Estudios de Economía*, 23.Department of Economics, University of Chile.

BIRD, R. (1993), "Threading the Fiscal Labyrinth: Some Issues in Fiscal Decentralisation", *National Tax Journal*, 46.

CEPAL (1996), "Descentralización Fiscal en América Latina: Balance y Principales Desafíos", *Informe del Proyecto Regional CEPAL/GTZ de Descentralización Fiscal*, Santiago de Chile.

CUEVAS, J. (1996), "El impuesto a la Propiedad Inmueble: El caso de la ciudad de la Paz, Bolivia", paper presented to the third seminar of the joint CEPAL/GTZ project on fiscal decentralisation in Latin America.

EDLING, H. (1996), "Los Ingresos no Tributarios: Una Perspectiva Internacional", Working paper for the joint CEPAL/GTZ project on fiscal decentralisation in Latin America.

MUSGRAVE, R. (1983), "Who Should Tax, Where and What?", *Tax Assignment in Federal Countries*, Camberra, Australian National University, Center of Research on Federal Financial Relations.

PIZA, J.R. (1996), "El Autoavaluo, Una Alternativa para Incrementar la Base Gravable del Impuesto Predial: La Experiencia de Santafé de Bogota", paper presented to the third seminar of the joint CEPAL/GTZ project on fiscal decentralisation in Latin America.

SHAH, A. (1994), "The Reform of Inter–Governmental Fiscal Relations in Developing and Emerging Market Economies", World Bank, Washington, D.C.

WIESNER, E. (1995), "La Descentralización, el Gasto Social y la Gobernabilidad en Colombia" National Planning Department and the National Association of Financial Institutions, Bogota, Colombia.

WORLD BANK (1994), *Informe sobre el Desarrollo Mundial: Infraestructura y Desarrollo*, Washington, D.C.

WORLD BANK (1995), *Better Urban Services: Finding the Right Incentives*, Washington, D.C.

Bibliography

A Comment

by Rakesh Mohan

Introduction

Visiting Latin America after more than 10 years, some 17 years after I did any substantive work in this continent, I find that many of the issues connected with urban development have remained the same, except that, relative to the 1960s and 1970s, the rate of urban growth has fallen significantly. Indeed, I believe the debt crisis of the 1980s was a consequence of very rapid urbanisation during the previous quarter century. After a lost decade, the continent has again begun to find a self–sustaining growth path.

The paper by Carlos Casas and Gabriel Aghón describes very well the arrangements for urban infrastructure development in Latin America. It focuses on the need to strengthen municipal financing and addresses some of its new challenges. Some of the changes now taking place in governance at the subnational level in different countries also provide new opportunities for innovative and self–sustaining arrangements for municipal finance. My general remarks focus on how some of the changes taking place in the world impact on municipal financing.

Urbanisation: A Historic View

Generally, it takes an extremely long time for a country or an economy to reach urbanisation of 25 per cent to 30 per cent, during which the population remains dispersed in small settlements and urban infrastructure needs stay limited. As agricultural productivity increases, with fewer people required for food production, urbanisation accelerates. Once a country reaches urbanisation of about 25 per cent or more, its pace of development is highly likely to accelerate along with that of urbanisation, which then rises to levels in the region of 60 per cent to 70 per cent within a very short historical span of 25 to 30 years. The Latin American region went through such a great urban expansion in the third quarter of this century, roughly between 1950 and

1975. Much innovation took place in different Latin American cities to cope with the pressures generated by such fast urbanisation. Many new institutions, usually structured as parastatals of central, state or city governments, arose to deliver urban services. At the same time, a good deal of innovation at the community level gave rise to a whole host of self–help activities that added considerably to the stock of urban infrastructure.

Debt generally financed parastatals, sometimes from higher governmental levels but more usually from banks, development banks and multilateral institutions. National or state borrowing often was passed on to local entities. This had two broad consequences. *First,* most countries in Latin America exhibited large fiscal deficits which usually resulted in long periods of high inflation. *Second,* excessive exposure developed in foreign debt to both multilateral institutions and private commercial banks. All these activities resulted in reasonably successful investment in urban infrastructure and the cities' absorption of large migrant populations over a short period, but they also bruised fiscal systems and contributed to the well known debt crisis of the 1980s.

Some parts of Asia, e.g. Korea and Chinese Taipei, also went through similar fast urbanisation in the quarter century after 1960, but this was not Asia's general experience. Now, China, India and Indonesia have entered the fast–urbanisation phase which will last at least until about 2025. The world now sees 2.2 billion or more people going through fast urbanisation at the same time. This will put intolerable pressures on fiscal and financial systems and enhance demand for international capital to fund the huge infrastructure needs arising from it. The competition for international capital will intensify. It thus becomes very important for Latin American cities to strengthen their systems of municipal administration, municipal financing and urban management, so that they can compete for scarce international capital.

The late 1990s differ greatly from the 1960s and 1970s. World capital markets are much more integrated and global capital flows much more rapid. Much more development has taken place within capital markets in developing countries, including in Latin America. Municipal entities now can feasibly take recourse to impersonal financing options such as municipal bonds. In the past, transactions between banks or multilateral institutions, the only source of financing, and the recipients of funds were often not fully transparent and sometimes irresponsible — because sovereign guarantees often protected lenders from exposure to the risk inherent in such lending. Similarly, the ultimate recipients, local authorities or parastatals, faced no real risks because they also operated under the umbrella of government guarantees. Both lenders and borrowers encountered rampant moral hazard. In an impersonal financing system, a borrower has difficulty in raising finance without intrinsic financial strength. Finally, the worldwide wave of increasing interest in democratic decentralisation has resulted in much greater attention to municipal administration and its strengthening.

Urban Financing

Two key categorisations affect the methods of financing of urban infrastructure. First is the distinction between public and private goods. In principle, public goods should be financed through taxes and private goods through user charges. In practice, some urban infrastructure services fall somewhere between these two ideal types and therefore their financing needs appropriate blending between taxes and user charges. The second distinguishes between capital and current expenditures. Equity or debt can finance capital expenditure, but current tax revenues or user charges generally must finance current outlays — as well as, of course, equity or debt servicing.

Financing of capital expenditures for infrastructure services provided by enterprises can come either through borrowing or from equity. The equity in state–owned corporate entities would have to come from the government. Before the changes taking place today began, parastatals usually depended almost fully on their parent governments for both equity and borrowing, either directly or indirectly; now, with the development and integration of capital markets, they can borrow independently if their financial strength is adequate. The credit rating process itself contributes to better financial management and financial health.

Government borrowing and taxes must finance public goods. Some Latin American countries, however, have used other innovative methods such as valorisation (particularly in Colombia) and variations on land readjustment schemes. In the absence of well functioning capital markets, funds were channelled through governments or through their agencies, with effective credit rationing and limited independence for recipient municipal governments or entities generally highly dependent on higher government levels. The new possibilities now emerging, which municipal financial management must exploit, include raising resources directly from the capital market — an ultimately more self–sustaining process because the market will not lend without adequate financial disclosure to enable credit ratings. When financing comes from high–level governments, it is quite possible for local governments or their entities to receive funds on a political basis without financial prudence in their own management. Direct recourse to the capital market prevents this.

Current expenditure must be fully financed either by current revenues for public goods or user charges for private goods. Different countries have had different fiscal systems for sharing taxes from higher to lower levels of government. Different cities have had different systems to raise local taxes and have found it generally difficult both to levy and to collect local taxes efficiently, essentially because local vested interests are often difficult to counter because of their proximity to decision makers. During fast urban growth, when urban land values rise rapidly, property tax becomes an important source of revenue which most cities have found difficult in practice both to levy and to collect adequately.

The reasons for this difficulty relate both to the power of vested interests and to technical problems in property assessment and the continuous re–assessment of property tax values. Some Latin American cities have made considerable progress in instituting modern methods of property assessment and the computerisation of property records. The technical issues related to property assessment are simplified tremendously if the urban land market is allowed to operate efficiently. Observation of property values becomes easier and changes in them can be regularly captured. Addressing some of these technical issues would very significantly enhance the promotion of increased power in the hands of local governments for financing urban development. Improved information technology and better operation of land markets provide new opportunities for local governments to improve their property tax systems. This requires intensified training programmes.

Fiscal subsidy systems differ quite significantly among countries and thus resist general comment. Once again, however, transparency and stability in these systems enhance significantly the ability of local governments to maintain public–good urban infrastructure services. In many cases the predictability of revenue–sharing arrangements is not very high.

In Latin America, parastatals quite commonly have delivered most of the services on which user charges can be levied. Despite the aura of seeming disorganisation in many cities, these organisations have done quite well, in the presence of very rapid urbanisation, in delivering basic urban services such as water supply, electricity and transportation. The change needed in the future involves promoting increased financial independence for these entities so that they can raise resources independently and service them through user charges.

Raising Urban Finance

Most countries provide some degree of governmental assistance in raising finances for urban infrastructure. In the United States, the federal government provides a significant subsidy by making municipal bonds, the main method for raising resources, tax free. This recognises the public–good element in many urban infrastructure services. The subsidy makes it possible for municipal authorities to pay lower interest rates to their bondholders and thereby to levy lower user charges or taxes than would otherwise be the case. This system represents a well designed, performance–related subsidy. Arguments in most countries support subsidies for urban services, because they are seen as public goods, or a good section of their consumers is seen as too poor to pay economic charges. Usually the subsidy is given *ex ante* and has a limited relationship to how well it is delivered. The American tax–free municipal bond system is a performance–related subsidy because the ability of municipal authorities to access it depends on their credit ratings. A good rating can be obtained only if the local authority keeps its accounts in order and observes tight fiscal discipline. The more efficient the municipal authority, the higher its credit rating and therefore the higher the federal subsidy available. This system has a lot to offer in terms of conceptual neatness.

In Germany, designated mortgage banks issue mortgage bonds called Pfandbriefs. In principle, the banks act as bond banks on behalf of the municipal or state authorities. The government contributes to this system through guarantees by state or local governments. The mortgage banks essentially raise the resources on behalf of state and municipal authorities and then pass on the proceeds for infrastructure investment. This system also maintains great pressure on the state and local authorities to maintain healthy financial conditions so that mortgage banks can accept their guarantees in full faith. Tradition now regards Pfandbriefs as among the safest financial instruments available in the market after sovereign bond offerings. They have never defaulted throughout this century, despite the severe disruption caused by the two world wars.

Japan provides a third example, where a good deal of urban infrastructure financing occurs essentially through resources raised by a very efficient national postal savings system which competes well with other savings instruments available to the public. The resources it raises are passed on through the Ministry of Finance to development banking institutions which in turn lend to local authorities. The development banks evaluate the fiscal health of the local authorities, making the system less impersonal than the American one, where credit rating agencies do the evaluation.

These examples demonstrate that urban infrastructure financing has received attention in all countries in favour of some interference by government in the market. The systems observed around the world differ quite significantly, making it difficult to point to a particular one as using a preferred methodology. The differences tend to reflect the relative development of capital markets. The United States, with the most developed capital market, can finance local authorities directly in the market without the need for intermediaries. By contrast, the Japanese system, in the least developed capital market among developed countries, channels resources through development banks.

With the considerable economic reforms and capital market development taking place in different Latin American countries, they should tend increasingly towards direct financing of municipalities by the capital market without necessarily going through intermediaries. Each country must use a procedure consistent with the sophistication of its capital markets.

Conclusions

The key point in my comments is that systems of urban finance must change with changes taking place worldwide, particularly widespread capital market development. Pro–active measures need to create credit rating agencies where they do not exist. Subsequently, municipal bodies need help to improve their credit quality so that they can receive credit ratings adequate to raise resources of the required volume. Each country will have to use institutional methods consistent with its own level of development and that of its market. Changes like Chile's pension reform should be watched. The future opens wide possibilities for institution building and capital market development. Municipal governments must improve the quality of their officials; a great need exists for training of municipal staff across the continent.

The provision of private goods by parastatals is in principle very amenable to privatisation. Wherever possible, it may be desirable in the interest of greater efficiency and service quality — provided that appropriate regulation of potential monopolies accompanies it.

A Comment

by Kathryn Gordon

The OECD experience broadly confirms many of the principal lessons drawn in Anwar Shah's paper: *i)* intergovernmental transfer systems need careful design to balance diverse and sometimes competing aims — enhancing competition for the supply of public goods, fiscal harmonisation, regional accountability and regional equity; *ii)* the integrity and independence of the financial sector contribute to fiscal prudence in the public sector; *iii)* monetary policy is best entrusted to an independent central bank with a mandate for price stability.

Nearly all OECD governments have engaged in fiscal consolidation, although some of it has involved creative accounting and cash management induced by the high stakes created by the Maastricht deficit criteria. The average OECD deficit peaked at 6.2 per cent of GDP in 1993, but has since declined to an estimated 2.5 per cent in 1997. All OECD countries now participate in this effort, which has brought about a marked convergence in their fiscal positions The convergence process has brought down the OECD average deficit to roughly its 1980 level, but has left the OECD with a much tighter distribution of deficits (i.e. with fewer of the exceedingly high deficits observed in the 1970s and 1980s). Both debt and tax burdens have also converged, but on higher levels. The convergence reflects the influence of a number of factors operating on all OECD Member countries. For example, financial market liberalisation and capital mobility have enhanced the scope for financial market monitoring of fiscal policies and created an economic environment less tolerant of fiscal "outliers". Likewise, the successful reform of monetary policies and institutions has meant that fiscal policy, rather than relying on inflation–related transfers to governments, now has to do its job the hard way — by reducing expenditure or raising taxes.

Deficit levels are dropping in unitary and decentralised states alike. Successful fiscal control does not seem strongly correlated one way or another with unitary versus federal arrangements. In terms of cyclically adjusted budget balances, the most concerted consolidators have been Canada, Belgium, Greece, Norway, and Sweden. Only Belgium and Canada are federal states. The others are unitary. The impetus behind consolidation appears to have been fear of impending crisis; none of these countries had a debt–GDP ratio below 75 per cent when they started consolidating and in all cases the debt ratios were climbing rapidly. While several countries have moved or will move toward various forms of devolution (Belgium, Canada, Italy, Spain and the United States), domination by complex political agendas often makes it hazardous to assess them only with respect to fiscal impacts.

Another impetus for consolidation has arisen because OECD governments — especially those with very high tax burdens — now face an increasingly unmanageable dilemma in taxation. With globalisation and financial market liberalisation, capital tax bases become ever more mobile and difficult to tax. The growing tax burden in OECD countries has tended to fall disproportionately on labour. In countries with restrictive labour market practices and regulations, this has aggravated unemployment problems. Thus, countries, especially high–tax countries, have come to realise that their ability to raise taxes without causing large economic distortions is very limited indeed. This dilemma may get worse as other tax bases become more mobile. For example, there is some indication that technological progress has made certain types of consumption more mobile and difficult to tax.

Difficult choices will have to be made in many spending policies between the numerous competing demands for scarce government resources. This competition has a regional dimension (the focus of Anwar Shah's paper), but also a very important programmatic one. The challenge is not just to cut, but to establish priorities and restructure programmes and services without compromise of fundamental public objectives. So far, OECD governments have had relatively little success in these deeper reforms. The most intractable have been social spending and especially pensions and health care (and in some countries unemployment benefits and related programmes). These programmes lie at the heart of social protection that most OECD countries have spent the better part of the twentieth century developing and refining. It is not surprising that such reform is difficult. So far, the principal failings have been political; policy makers have not convinced the public of the need to reform and they have not communicated how service outcomes will change as a result of the reforms (in some cases, the actual change in service quality may be low, as waste is eliminated).

Main Dimensions of Reform

The OECD fiscal picture is striking in the degree to which a diverse set of countries has encountered similar problems — run–ups of debt levels and tax burdens are almost universal, and not only have these problems centred on social spending, but the particular problem areas (health, pensions, etc.) are also the same among countries. This suggests that the difficulties arise from shared problems in governance and financial control that may indeed be common to all governments. OECD Members nevertheless have worked to improve their performance and their ability to make financially disciplined decisions. The thrust of their experiences so far suggests the following as the main axes for future efforts:

— Learn to manage incentives: Government tax and spending programmes have often created perverse systems of incentives which have plagued almost every sphere of government endeavour — tax policy, labour markets and social programmes, intergovernmental relations, health care, pensions etc. Governments are now trying to refine their management of incentives in these and other areas.

— Get intergovernmental relations right. Although this is no panacea and the actual implementation of reforms tends to be a trial–and–error process, OECD experience has shown that inappropriate specification of these relations can be very costly.

— Improve the information systems that support public financial decision making. Promote the effectiveness of fiscal monitoring by markets and the political institutions by improving the information systems used for external reporting of fiscal positions. Here the thrust of OECD efforts will focus on harmonisation of reporting standards, more stringent disclosure and reporting requirements, accrual accounting and improving accounting practices at lower levels of governments.

— Reform budgeting processes. OECD governments have experimented with budget rules and associated penalties.

Learn to provide "core government services" better and more efficiently. OECD governments are attempting to withdraw from non–essential activities (e.g. state–owned banks) and to put appropriate programmes in place where government involvement is deemed essential (social services, infrastructure, defence, etc.). This applies especially to "big ticket" spending items. Many of these reforms involve re-structuring intergovernmental relations, with the exact form of such redesign depending on the types of service and the countries in question.

A Comment

by José Roberto Afonso

Teresa Ter-Minassian's paper should be required reading for anyone who is interested in the decentralisation of public finance. Ms Ter-Minassian sensibly and impartially analyses the links between budgetary federalism and unbalanced public finances, without failing to mention the problems that greater autonomy of local authorities *vis–à–vis* the central/federal government could pose in terms of macroeconomic stability. For all that, she does not conclude that decentralising decision making with regard to budget revenues and expenditures is undesirable. She merely states that it is neither a cure–all for unbalanced budgets nor the cause of macroeconomic instability.

This point is of particular interest for Brazil. Decentralisation has picked up speed since the promulgation of the 1988 Constitution, which gave the lower levels of government greater autonomy with regard to tax collection and spending. It had been thought that this type of fiscal structure would be ill–suited to checking hyperinflation. However, the introduction of the real in mid–1994 was the most positive component in the process of economic stabilisation, even though no structural changes occurred in the way the Brazilian federation works either prior to and after this move. The usual order of recommended reforms was reversed: public services were decentralised first, and the economy was stabilised afterwards. There is nothing unusual in the fact that the "federative issue" has not been fully resolved. Moreover, this international conference shows Brazilians who are concerned by such issues, but have little or no interest in the experience of other countries, that "federative crises" are not confined to developing countries, and even less so to Latin America. The budget deficits faced by some wealthy nations are even more serious than the situation in less developed countries, which have greater flexibility to restructure and fine–tune their fiscal and tax–collection systems.

Although decentralisation and budget discipline encompass issues that range from tax collection to spending commitments, Ms Ter–Minassian restricted her paper to the issue of public debt. This issue, of particular interest to the conference organisers, is the *key point* of tax relations between the various levels of government in the context of efforts to achieve macroeconomic stability in highly decentralised countries. This does not mean, however, that there are no other subjects of dispute among the

97

various levels of government. For example, Brazil decided to eliminate the "state VAT" (ICMS) on exports and investment to open the economy outward and promote capital accumulation. This decision resulted in lower revenue for authorities below national level and higher transfer payments by the federal government to compensate for this. There are also conflicts in the area of *public service tariffs*, where the goal of stable prices has to be reconciled with the need to adjust electricity, telecommunications and water rates in order to put public enterprises on a sound financial footing and/or to privatise them.

Returning to the issue of public debt, a central government must have access to instruments that will enable it to manage macroeconomic aggregates efficiently when it has little control over the taxation, transfer payments and budgets of lower levels of government. Ms Ter–Minassian draws on experiments in a number of countries to describe mechanisms used to control public debt incurred by lower levels of government and assess their effectiveness. In conclusion, it should be remembered that central governments are advised to establish closer dialogue with lower levels of government and implement institutional standards that reconcile budget restraint with effective control of regional and local debt. This means adopting realistic rules and fairly evaluating the borrowing and debt management capacity of the various levels of government. The speaker attributes only a minor role to market discipline.

The IMF economist's two conclusions are pleasantly surprising. *First,* because she broached the somewhat unusual concept of "co–operative federalism". This assumes a change in attitude on the part of the central government, which should no longer simply impose its policy, but discuss it with lower levels of government in order to ensure their support and responsible behaviour. (This is an innovative track in relations among the various levels of government in Brazil, where the role of the central government has shifted to allow room for ongoing negotiation with lower levels in order to support and promote privatisation of public services in the various states, thereby improving the competitiveness of Brazilian enterprises.) *Second,* even more surprisingly, Ms Ter–Minassian attaches little importance to the role of market discipline in managing local debt; she also emphasises the fact that the most heavily indebted states are those where the central government exercises little control. (Brazil is not short of rules and regulations, including constitutional ones, aimed at controlling state and local debt. In those cases where debt is uncontrolled, I believe there should be more faith in market sanctions, with the offenders being told that this is the last time that the federal government will bail them out, that the risk will subsequently be assumed solely by the creditors of states or municipalities.)

The only suggestion to be made with regard to Ms Ter–Minassian's informative paper concerns credit policy. In less developed countries whose financial systems are still shaky, the bulk of long–term loans, especially to the public sector, is provided either directly or indirectly by sources controlled by the central government (federal banks, external debt, Treasury loans, etc.) — not to mention measures taken by the central bank and the budget authorities in the context of a traditional credit policy, such as a cap on bank loans granted to regional and local governments.

PART TWO

CASE STUDIES: LATIN AMERICAN PERSPECTIVES

Experiences of Decentralisation and Intergovernmental Fiscal Relations in Latin America

Ernesto Rezk

Review of Some Theoretical Issues

Although fiscal decentralisation now attracts interest from economists and policy makers, one could hardly think of any unique focus, not to mention the lack of consensus on whether all decentralised spending and taxing functions are in reality beneficial. Theoretical and policy–oriented interest arose during the 1980s as countries all over the world faced unprecedented situations. According to Bird (1993), the revival of decentralising processes was motivated in Eastern Europe by a need to recreate systems of intergovernmental finance and in developing countries by an endeavour to escape from ineffective and inefficient governance, macroeconomic instability and insufficient economic growth.

Tanzi (1995) argued that the creation of a central entity, transcending European Union member states in some economic functions, opened a debate on fiscal federalism and decentralisation. He thus acknowledged the growing disenchantment with powerful central governments (especially in industrialised countries), whose policies fell short of stabilising the economy or improving income distribution and created a presumption towards the convenience of trusting more the market and subnational and local governments. Although it has become generally accepted that decentralising has grown in importance and that decentralised decision making permits governments to perform their assigned tax and spending duties in accord with efficiency and equity objectives, the overall notion is far from a single concept as the different ideas of deconcentration, delegation and devolution (each involving a different degree of independent decision making at the subnational and local levels) illustrate.

Bird (1993) suggested two different, somehow "synthesising", approaches to the general notion. The first refers to decentralisation from the top down, when the central government seeks to transfer deficits downwards, delegate authority to subnational governments (SNGs) to better achieve allocative goals or enhance national welfare. The second works from the bottom up, to uphold political values apart from allocative efficiency, such as improved governance arising from local responsiveness and political participation[1]. While the two variants refer to whose preferences (those of central or subnational governments) prevail, Bird suggests further that the whole subject could be better dealt with in a combined approach that includes both federal finance and fiscal federalism. Federal finance depicts a situation in which both jurisdictional boundaries and tax and spending functions are constitutionally set, intergovernmental transfers tend to be unconditional (and generally equalising) and relations between central and subnational governments occur in a bargaining situation between principals with no presumption of central dominance. Fiscal federalism applies when the central government alters or decides on boundaries, assignments, transfers, and other elements involved in intergovernmental fiscal arrangements[2].

According to Tanzi (1995), the concepts of administrative and fiscal decentralisation imply similar notions. The former covers situations in which the central government levies most taxes and transfers funds to SNGs, which carry out their spending activities under guidelines and controls imposed at the centre; the latter describes most federations, where SNGs have constitutional or legal powers to raise taxes and perform spending functions with complete local autonomy. In the theoretical approach underlying collective decision making and its degree of independence at different government levels, the idea of fiscal federalism (as defined above) entails a principal–agent framework whereby the central government (the principal) transfers funds to lower levels (through either categorical or categorical matching grants), expecting them to provide public goods or services according to "obligations" and goals. SNGs (the agents) accept this delegation, expecting to maximise their own economic and equity goals[3]. Because SNGs must meet presumed central government priorities and policy objectives, the notion of fiscal responsibility means that lower governments are accountable to their principal (the central government) and not to local taxpayers or residents (Wiesner, 1994).

The federal–finance variant introduces a new way of regarding fiscal decentralisation and gives room to alternative theoretical approaches upon which to base collective decision making as, for instance, the well known public–choice theory. This approach, as developed by Black, Buchanan and Arrow and preceded by Wicksell's work in the past century, favours the idea that different government levels finance most of their spending functions out of their own taxes and revenue (the principle of financial autonomy), with enhanced accountability of SNGs to their taxpayers and not to the centre. The link between taxing and spending ensures in turn what Bird (1995) referred to as "... the maintenance of a legitimate system of governance in terms of public support of government". Wiesner (1994) stresses how public choice models pose another proposition, that SNGs' spending autonomy must be subject to a budget constraint to induce efficient resource allocation. Dillinger (1995) takes a similar stance, that decentralisation ensures accountability and eliminates the "soft budget constraint". Estache (1995) argued that a clear division of functional expenditure responsibilities between government levels based on the benefit jurisdiction model will be conducive to SNGs' higher accountability, as the distorting separation between the level bearing nominal responsibility and the one actually and ultimately responsible for providing specific goods and services disappears.

The different variants suggest that some measure of fiscal decentralisation (depending on institutional mechanisms) should gather widespread acceptance. In reality, the notion and its conditions for success have not passed unchallenged. Prud'homme (1990) pointed to "basic contradictions" to suggest that a case against decentralisation could be built upon an alleged dual relationship; decentralisation does boost allocative and productive efficiency[4], but it also leads to likely negative results for both equity goals and macroeconomic management. Contending that tax decentralisation aggravates jurisdictional inequities because tax bases are unevenly distributed among jurisdictions, Prud'homme concludes that decentralisation failures make it more difficult to carry out redistribution policies.

His rather gloomy assessment, however, runs counter to empirical evidence from the extended Barro and Sala–i–Martín model (1992), to which Oates and Sang Loh Kim added measures of fiscal decentralisation and financial structure to explain per capita GDP growth in 40 countries. According to Oates (1995), apart from enhanced allocative efficiency when decentralisation can offer a menu of local outputs that reflects local preferences and conditions, the initial results clearly suggest that countries which allowed greater revenue self–reliance by local governments experienced higher economic growth rates, with a significant and robust positive correlation between fiscal decentralisation and per capita growth.

A slightly different view put forward by Hommes (1995), contends that decentralisation's positive economic impact depends on overcoming institutional conflicts and political dilemmas. He presented a paradox: decentralisation first demands more economic and political skills at the centre, central governments that learn "... when to impinge on local autonomy for the sake of stability and when to refrain from intervention to avoid inhibiting good government at the local level"[5]. Hommes suggested local government capacity to raise own revenues (financial sufficiency and autonomy) as the second key requirement for successful decentralisation, the third being a properly functioning local democracy to ensure that local collective decision making works.

Overview of the Latin American Experience

Intergovernmental Fiscal Relations in Argentina[6]

Argentina is a three–tiered federation composed of the central government, 23 provinces, the autonomous city of Buenos Aires and over 1 000 municipalities; its federal character is constitutionally guaranteed; apart from political powers, subnational and local governments have ample independent fiscal and spending functions.

Except for defence (an exclusive responsibility of the central government) and law and order (the country has one federal and 23 provincial judiciary systems and police forces), the constitution reserves practically no spending function to any single level; all three levels have concurrent jurisdictions in most types of expenditure, even when one level dominates in practice. (The central government largely manages social security while education is mostly a provincial responsibility, for example.) The constitutional tax assignment also stresses a highly federalist fiscal setting; only export and import duties fall exclusively to the central government. Both the central and subnational levels can raise indirect taxes, but the former can levy direct taxes[7] only for limited periods and on the grounds of defence, common security and general welfare. Municipal fiscal powers normally apply to user charges for services rendered to residents, although municipalities also collect property, business, energy consumption and "special benefits" taxes. The assignment of revenue sources to various governments levels is broadly consistent with the widely accepted Musgravian principles. Overlapping tax systems[8] have led since 1935 to revenue sharing as the main intergovernmental fiscal arrangement and the preferred tax co–ordination method.

Table 6.1 shows that primary distribution (allotment of shared revenues between the central government and the provinces) also involves national and provincial social security systems and diverse funds accruing to provinces as principal–agent transfers. Revenue–sharing systems also exist at the subnational level, whereby provinces and their municipalities divide the main provincial tax revenues and national shared taxes[9]; similarly to the national case, primary distribution entails diverse funds for specific purposes.

Table 6.2 indicates the evolution of secondary distribution (the division of the distributable tax pool among provinces) since it started in 1935, from a pattern of almost exclusive use of devolution criteria to that in 1973–84 when equalising criteria, mostly based upon spending needs, predominated. Objective devolution or equalising parameters ceased to exist in 1985 and revenue assignment among provinces took place thereafter on the basis of fixed coefficients (last column in Table 6.2), agreed upon in political negotiations (Law 23548). Almost all provincial–municipal revenue–sharing schemes, however, have explicit distribution criteria based on factors such as population, area, own revenues and efficiency in tax collection. Equalising principles generally consist of an equal allotment of funds among local governments, or distribution to municipalities' social spending, expenditure budgets or estimated salary needs for basic public services. Some provinces use population and fiscal capacity inversely as equalising measures to favour low–density and poorer municipalities.

Table 6.1. Tax Assignment in Argentina: Responsibilities for Administration, Collection and Disposition of Revenues

(percentages of participation in tax revenues)

Taxes Levied by the Central (National) Government	Nation	Provinces and Buenos Aires	National social security system	Provincial social security systems	Various provincial funds
Personal and Corporate Income Tax	22.82	35.04	29.60		12.54
Value added tax	31.74	43.16	22.15	2.20	0.75
Excise taxes (internal taxes) and others	35.66	48.49	15.00		0.85
Tax on assets	17.83	24.25	7.50		50.42
Tax on personal goods			90.00	10.00	
Tax on fuel sales	29.00				71.00
Energy tax					100.00
Tax on salaries			100.00		
Stamp duty	100.00				
Import duties	100.00				
Export duties	100.00				
Statistics tax	100.00				

Taxes levied by the Provinces	Provinces	Municipalities	Provincial social security systems	Various municipal funds
Turnover Tax	80.00	16.10		3.90
Urban and rural property tax	80.00	16.10		3.90
National tax–shared revenues	80.00	16.10		3.90
Tax on provincial and municipal payrolls			100.00	
Stamp duty	100.00			
Tax on motor vehicles		100.00		
Social infrastructure tax	100.00			
Tax on gambling	100.00			
Tax on turf activities	100.00			
Fees and user charges	100.00			

Municipalities' Fiscal Revenues*: Property Tax, Contribution on Improvements, Business Tax, Advertisement and Publicity Tax, Tax on Raffles and Other Games of Chance, Tax on Energy Sale, Tax on Cemetery Occupancy, Various Fees and User Charges.

Notes: Existing provincial funds mainly include conditional transfers to provinces for their use in the following fields: energy, infrastructure, roads, public works, housing and education. There exists also a subsidiary fund for regional compensation and another one for unconditioned treasury grants to provinces. Notwithstanding marked similarities, Argentina has 23 provincial tax–sharing systems. Revenue disposition has been illustrated here with the prevailing scheme in the province of Cordoba, which fairly represents the rest.

This is the fiscal revenue pattern belongs of the city of Cordoba municipal government but, again, most local governments in Argentina share the same revenue structure. Municipalities normally collect fees for streets, pavements and public space occupancy and for all public applications or requests to the local government for administrative actions. User charges normally cover sanitary protection and inspections in public places, as well as approval, supervision and inspection of gas networks and the construction of houses and buildings within the Municipal Boundaries.

The constitutional reform of 1994 created new conditions for revenue sharing, granting it constitutional status for the first time and dictating a new system for implementation on 1 January 1997[10]. The system entails objective distribution criteria and built–in fund transfers to provinces and the city of Buenos Aires; it relates primary and secondary distribution to subnational jurisdictions' services, functions and competences; it not only includes but strengthens equalising criteria; and its constitutional mandate literally states that the system "... will be fair, solidarity–framed and give priority to the achievement of similar degrees of development, quality of life and equal opportunities throughout the country". In a clear reassurance of the country's federal character, the Constituent Assembly introduced a clause which favours better future decisions on delegation or devolution from the centre to the provinces, stating that no transfer of competences, functions or services may occur without a previous revenue reassignment through a Congressional law reaffirmed by the legislature of the province concerned.

Table 6.2. **Argentina: Tax Sharing Systems (1935–84):**
Criteria for Secondary Distribution
(percentages)

Periods and legal regimes	Spending needs				Tax capacity	Total for eq. criteria
	Devolution criterion	Current spending	Minimum spending	Supply cost		
Period (1935–53) 1. Law 12139 (1935)						
Internal taxes on consumption	91		9			9
Internal taxes on production	100					0
2. Law 12143 (1935)	40	30	30			60
3. Law 12147 (1935)	40	30	30			60
4. Decree 14342 (1946)	40	30	30			60
5. Law 12956 (1947)	36	27	27	10		64
6. Law 14060 (1951)	100					0
Period (1954–72)						
7. Law 14390 (1954)	16		82		2	84
8. Law 14788 (1959)	25	25	25	25		75
Period (1973–84)						
9. Law 20221 (1973)	0		65	10	25	100

Source: Own estimates based on legal regimes cited.

Decentralisation in A "Formal" versus A "True" Federation

Many studies have reported that although Argentina has long had a formally federal constitution, its political and fiscal institutions have normally operated in a centralised fashion[11]. Rezk (1996), in particular, sees intense use of the principal–agent model in inter–jurisdictional fiscal arrangements other than revenue–sharing schemes. The overview of actual government tax collection in Table 6.3 stresses revenue concentration; the central government gleans more than 77 per cent of the tax yield while provinces and municipalities account for about 19 per cent and 4 per cent respectively. This concentration results from taxes raised exclusively by the central government (import and export duties and taxes on income). Some important taxes collected by the central government (such as VAT, income tax, excises and liquid fuels tax) get partly transferred to provinces through revenue sharing and grants that reassert preferences for delegation rather than devolution[12]. Table 6.3 also highlights the primary role of indirect taxes (overwhelmingly the turnover tax) in provincial revenues; property taxes (collected mainly by SNGs) come second. The municipalities' modest share indicates that, unlike in other federations, they play a minor role in consolidated tax revenue; their main sources—property and business taxes, user charges and fees—finance on average less than half of their spending needs.

Table 6.3. **Argentina: Distribution of Total Tax Revenue by Source and Level of Government, 1995**
(percentages)

Levels–Items	Income tax	Social security contributions	Property tax	Indirect taxes		Other taxes	Total
				Domestic	International		
Central government	100.00	89.30	11.70	73.80	100.00	53.00	77.30
Provinces	0.0	10.70	67.90	21.30	0.0	41.50	18.90
Municipalities	0.0	0.00	20.40	4.90	0.0	5.50	3.80
Percentage of total	11.30	24.00	6.80	42.30	9.00	6.60	100.00

Source: Own estimates based on figures from Argentina, Secretary For Economic Programming (1996).

The figures for expenditure assignments in Table 6.4 indicate some overlapping, attributable to constitutionally granted, concurrent competences in almost all spending fields. The data suggest that expenditure decentralisation does not match revenue centralisation. The table also shows that spending decentralisation has not yet reached the municipal level (only 7.75 per cent of total public spending), whose fiscal role remains confined to general administrative control functions, inspection and supervision, and traditional community services including primary education, preventive health care and social welfare; municipal spending in Argentina lags well behind that of local governments in other federations in the world.

Table 6.5 shows that unconditional grants to provincial governments dwindled in 1983–96 from 80 per cent to 70 per cent of total transfers, while conditional grants rose from 20 per cent to 30 per cent. The important 9 per cent to 10 per cent share of conditional grants for transferred services (mainly primary and secondary education) suggests that agency problems undermine decentralisation to the detriment of SNGs' financial autonomy and fiscal responsibility. Local decision making does have support in unconditional grants, however, because they are almost exclusively automatic transfers (mainly shared revenues). Vertical imbalances persist in intergovernmental transfers (Table 6.6), due to the mismatch in the decentralisation of expenditures and revenue sources. The fiscal gap is reflected as well; after accounting for intergovernmental transfers, revenues reached 96 per cent of central government spending in 1995, but resources from all sources amounted to only 90 per cent of total subnational expenditures.

Table 6.4. **Argentina: Percentage of Total Government Spending
by Government Level and Function, 1993**

	All government levels	National level of government	Provinces	Municipalities
Total Expenditure	100.00	57.13	35.12	7.75
I. Administration, Law and Order	100.00	51.72	32.40	15.88
I.1 General Services	100.00	39.15	29.36	31.49
I.2 Justice	100.00	54.55	45.45	0.00
I.3 Defence	100.00	100.00	0.00	0.00
I.4 Public Order and Safety	100.00	45.13	54.87	0.00
II. Social Expenditure and Spending in Human Resources	100.00	55.60	37.69	6.71
II.1 Education, Science and Technology	100.00	25.21	72.49	2.29
II.2 Health	100.00	48.03	45.79	6.18
II.3 Housing	100.00	12.50	87.50	0.00
II.4 Welfare	100.00	5.81	79.07	15.12
II.5 Social Security	100.00	80.65	19.35	0.00
II.6 Labour	100.00	100.00	0.00	0.00
II.7 Other Expenditure	100.00	0.00	0.00	100.00
III. Infrastructure for Economic Affairs and Services	100.00	54.62	40.16	5.22
III.1 Primary Sectors	100.00	26.47	73.53	0.00
III.2 Fuel and Energy	100.00	78.13	20.83	1.04
III.3 Manufacturing	100.00	66.67	8.33	25.00
III.4 Services	100.00	53.01	39.76	7.23
III.5 Other Expenditure	100.00	0.00	87.50	12.50
IV. Public Debt	100.00	92.77	7.23	0.00

Source: Based on data provided by the Secretary for Economic Programming.

Table 6.5. Argentina: Unconditional and Conditional Transfers to Provinces and Buenos Aires, 1983–96

(percentages)

| | Unconditional transfers | | | | | Conditional transfers | | | | | | | | | |
| | Automatic | | | Non-automatic | | Automatic | | | | | | Non-automatic | | | |
	1	2	3	4	5	6	7	8	9	10	11	12	13	14	15
1983–84	27.0	0.0	8.1	45.8	0.0	4.3	0.0	0.0	0.0	0.0	0.0	3.4	0.3	9.7	1.3
1985	28.9	0.0	8.8	40.4	0.0	4.4	0.0	0.0	0.0	0.0	0.0	2.3	0.4	13.8	1.0
1986	65.3	0.0	10.9	1.7	0.0	6.4	0.0	0.0	0.0	0.0	0.0	3.7	0.8	9.7	1.5
1987	60.9	0.0	11.6	4.6	0.0	5.6	0.0	0.0	0.0	0.0	0.0	3.8	0.9	10.7	2.0
1988	55.5	1.9	8.9	5.7	0.0	4.6	0.0	0.0	0.0	0.0	0.0	6.2	0.7	15.2	1.3
1989	57.9	7.5	11.8	1.0	0.0	5.8	0.0	1.8	0.0	0.0	0.0	1.5	0.6	11.2	0.9
1990	60.3	8.8	7.6	1.7	9.4	2.1	0.0	1.2	0.0	0.0	0.0	1.3	0.0	7.4	0.3
1991	65.6	2.0	8.1	0.9	3.8	1.7	0.0	2.1	0.0	0.0	0.0	2.5	0.1	11.5	1.7
1992	73.8	2.2	4.9	1.2	1.7	0.7	0.0	0.6	2.2	2.9	0.3	1.9	0.2	8.6	1.1
1993	66.3	1.5	4.1	1.7	0.0	1.7	8.9	0.9	4.2	2.1	0.9	3.4	0.6	5.6	0.2
1994	62.7	3.8	3.8	2.5	0.0	1.9	9.0	1.4	5.4	1.1	1.0	1.6	0.7	5.8	0.6
1995	61.7	3.6	3.4	3.5	0.0	1.9	8.7	1.2	6.1	0.8	1.0	1.8	0.5	6.2	0.2
1996	63.5	3.8	3.8	2.0	0.3	2.0	9.2	0.8	6.8	0.4	0.8	1.2	0.6	5.2	0.4
	63.6	3.7	–	2.0	–	2.4	9.0	1.3	6.8	0.2	1.2	1.5	0.7	6.7	0.9

Notes and Source: Own estimates based on figures from the Secretary for the Assistance to the Provincial Economic Reform. 1. Tax Sharing System. 2. Disequilibria Fund. 3. Royalties. 4. National Treasury Grants (Atn). 5. Anticipated Taxes. 6. Road Construction. 7. Decentralised Services. 8. Social Security. 9. Income Tax (Infrastructure). 10. Educational Fund. 11. Infrastructure Transfer. 12. Others 13. Energy Fund (Fedei). 14. National Housing Fund (Fonavi). 15. Regional Disequilibria Fund.

Table 6.6. **Vertical Imbalances in Argentina, 1995**
(percentages of total revenue and expenditure)

| | Before transfers | | | | After transfers | |
	Central gov.	Prov. gov.	Central gov.	Prov. gov.	Central gov.	Prov. gov.[a]
Revenue share[b]	81.80	18.20	58.06	41.94	54.26[c]	39.20[c]
Expenditure share	64.30	35.70	56.39	43.61	56.39	43.61
Surplus/deficit	17.50	(17.50)	1.67	(1.67)	2.13	(4.41)

a.   Figures include transfers due to any existing inter–jurisdictional fiscal arrangement between the central government and
      the provinces.
b.   Includes revenues of all kinds (except borrowing).
c.   After accounting for the overall central and subnational fiscal deficit.
Notes and Source: Own estimates based on figures from Argentina, Secretary for Economic Programming, (1996) and on
                     data from the Secretary for Assistance to the Provincial Economic Reform.

Fiscal Federalism and Decentralisation in Brazil

Brazil also is a three–tiered federation including the federal government (the Union), 26 states, the Federal District (where Brasilia is located), and 5 225 municipalities. Unlike Argentina, Brazil exhibits one of the most decentralised federal patterns, compared even to other federations among developing nations (Shah, 1991). Rezende (1995) stresses some important features of fiscal federalism in Brazil. First, the country has huge regional disparities and the Union uses fiscal instruments and the tax system to check them; this engenders conflict between the demands of more developed states for higher tax autonomy and the pressures of less developed ones for larger compensatory grants. Second, the country's marked "municipalist" tradition strengthens local governments' tax powers and their access to federal compensatory transfers; Rezende emphasises that the relative independence of local governments *vis–à–vis* the states worsens vertical and horizontal disequilibria in national revenue distribution, and makes negotiations for a new federative equilibrium more difficult[13]. Third, a disequilibrium in congressional representation represents the political element in fiscal federalism; the predominance of representatives from poorer regions produces imbalances in the sharing of fiscal revenues.

Table 6.7 depicts a situation completely different from Argentina's. Fiscal concentration is much less evident. SNGs' own revenues in 1992 stood at more than a third of total tax revenue. After accounting for intergovernmental transfers, states and municipalities controlled almost half of disposable revenue. Local governments' total receipts (including transfers) reached three times their own revenue — clear evidence of the municipalist element.

Table 6.7. **Brazil: Tax Yield And Disposable Tax Revenue
by Government Level**
(percentages)

Year	Tax collection			Disposable revenues			Tax yield
	Union	States	Local gov.	Union	States	Local gov.	% of GDP*
1960	63.9	31.3	4.7	59.4	34.0	6.5	17.4
1980	72.8	24.0	3.2	66.2	24.3	9.5	22.4
1989	65.4	31.7	2.9	57.3	19.8	12.9	20.6
1992	62.2	32.3	5.5	52.2	31.0	16.9	23.7

a.   Inclusive of Social Security Contributions.
Source: J.R. Afonso (1996).

Table 6.8 looks at vertical fiscal imbalances. No fiscal gaps appear at the state and municipal levels because recent constitutional amendments improved the SNGs' share of total revenue. Major benefits accrued to municipalities when they doubled transfers received relative to GDP between 1970 and 1991. Rezende (1995), despite his critical view of the decentralisation process, points out that demands for more state and municipal spending on social programmes and civil servants' wages matched the increased transfers, which explains the expenditure percentages in Table 6.8 (9.1 per cent and 4.3 per cent of GDP in 1991, against 7.9 per cent and 1.6 per cent in 1970, for states and municipalities respectively).

Table 6.8. **Brazil: Some Revenue and Expenditure Items
per Government Level**
(percentage of GDP)

Items	Union		States		Local government	
	1970	1991	1970	1991	1970	1991
Current revenue	17.3	18.6	11.3	11.2	1.8	5.5
Own current revenue			10.1	9.3	1.1	2.0
Transfers			1.2	1.9	1.7	3.5
Current expenditure	15.0	16.4	7.9	9.1	1.6	4.3
Consumption	5.0	5.0	4.9	5.6	1.4	4.0
Wages	3.5	2.7	3.9	4.2	0.8	2.3
Investment	1.6	0.7	1.9	0.9	1.0	1.3

Source: J.R. Afonso (1993).

Table 6.9 shows how tax assignments take place. The absence of revenue concentration at the centre makes Brazil an exception to other countries in the region. The constitution dictates the exclusive responsibility of the Union for taxes on income, foreign trade and rural property. Taxing powers over production, consumption and services overlap across different government levels. The states tax automobile registrations, inheritances and donations, while municipalities, apart from the services tax, derive the rest of their own revenue from urban property and property transfer taxes. The VAT on goods and services (ICMS) is not only the states' main own revenue but also the single most important tax in the country—almost 30 per cent of total tax revenue.

Table 6.9. **Tax Assignment in Brazil**

Revenue source	Percentage	Revenue disposition (%)		
		Union	States	Municipalities
Union	66.1			
Social security contributions	21.6	33.3	66.7	–
Income tax (IR)	16.6	53.0	24.5	22.5
Industrial products tax (IPI)	9.8	43.0	32.0	25.0
Finsocial	4.9			
Pis/Pasep	4.2			
Import and export duties (IM IE)	2.0	100.0	–	–
Tax on credit operations (IOF)	1.9	100.0	–	–
Social contribution on benefits	1.6			
Rural property tax (ITR)	0.2	50.0	–	50.0
Other revenues	3.3			
States	30.1			
General value added tax (ICMS)	29.5	–	75.0	25.0
Motor vehicles tax (IPVA)	0.5	–	50.0	50.0
Inheritance and gift taxes (ITCD)	0.05	–	100.0	–
Income tax additional[a]	0.05	–	100.0	–
Municipalities	3.8			
Service tax (ISS)	2.1			100.0
Urban property tax (IPTU)	1.2			100.0
Property transfers tax (ITBI)	0.3			100.0
Tax on retail sales of fuels (IVVC)[a]	0.2			100.0

a.   Suspended since 1 January 1996.
Sources: Shah (1991); Lagemann and Bordin (1993).

Brazilian revenue–sharing systems also play a heavy role[14], as the primary distribution of resources described in Table 6.9 shows. The municipal orientation emerges again; local governments participate (as in Germany) in the distribution of some federal and state taxes. Revenue decentralisation (specially in favour of municipalities) followed spending decentralisation in Brazil; the federal, state and municipal spending shares are, 51 per cent, 32 per cent and 17 per cent of total expenditure respectively, Affonso (1997).

Decentralisation in Venezuela[15]

The concept of gradualness, an institutional arrangement whereby regional governments can decide when to ask for transfer of administrative competences to them, distinguishes Venezuela from other countries in the region. It too is a federal country, with a central government and SNGs including 22 states. The centre levies the most important taxes (on income, fuel, consumption and sales, including VAT, excises, and import duties) whose yield represented 17 per cent of GDP, in 1995. Intermediate governments' fiscal powers are restricted to stamp duties, taxes on non-metallic minerals, and user charges on roads, ports and airports. SNGs have in practice no opportunity to change the quality and volume of decentralised services. Municipalities have more fiscal alternatives; they can levy taxes on business, urban property and automobiles, user charges, and service and licence fees.

Venezuela has a fairly standard assignment of spending functions, with some expenditures restricted to specific government levels and some overlapping. The centre has the sole responsibility for defence, justice, policing and mining, but shares with the states public health, housing, infrastructure and environmental protection. States in turn have responsibility for education, labour services, ports, and airports. Local governments cover mainly water and electricity, urban development, public transport, local environmental policy and public works.

Against this background, gradualness is not without problems: additional spending burdens on the central government, higher transaction costs during the transition to shared service provision, more room for lobbying groups opposed to decentralisation and risks of losing transparency and neutrality during negotiations. An imbalance between spending and revenue assignments explains the need for transfers, carried out under two principles: the constitutional *situado*[16], and the intergovernmental fund for decentralisation. The former amounts to an unconditioned grant that assigns 20 per cent of current national revenues to the states (in a twofold process whereby states share 30 per cent in equal parts and 70 per cent in proportion to population); the latter is a revenue–sharing mechanism (resembling a categorical matching grant) through which states and municipalities receive up to 30 per cent of the VAT yield (net of the constitutional *situado*) to finance their projects and services. State revenues clearly suffer from vertical imbalances. On average, their own taxes reached only 1.2 per cent of the total in 1996, while transfers provided 98.8 per cent (*situado* at 78.7 per cent and special grants at 20.1 per cent). Thus decentralisation prevails only in expenditures (partly on the basis of principal–agent mechanisms). Estimates show potentially transferable functions at around 30 per cent of the national budget.

Fiscal Decentralisation in Colombia

Bird and Fiszbein (1996) point out that the outcome of conflicts between centralists and federalists in the latter part of the 19th century explained Colombia's highly centralised federal structure—until very recently, when decentralisation has stemmed from strains on central government finances caused by the expansion of local public services, increasing urbanisation, and economic and fiscal regionalism. Although not formally a federal country, Colombia has a central government, 33 intermediate governments (including departments, the capital city and national territories), and over 1 000 municipalities, the chief beneficiaries of recent decentralisation.

The available figures on tax assignment indicate a marked concentration of revenue at the centre, at 82 per cent of the total *vis–à–vis* 11 per cent and 7 per cent for intermediate governments and municipalities, respectively. After transfers, the three figures are 68 per cent, 17 per cent and 15 per cent. Table 6.10 shows that intergovernmental transfers and borrowing (0.54 per cent of GDP) check vertical imbalances for departmental and municipal governments. Excessively relaxed norms for borrowing[17] make it relatively easy for municipal governments to borrow (Aghón and Letelier, 1996).The fiscal gap reflects the departments' more inelastic revenue compared to local governments' lucrative instruments (property and business taxes, mainly). Aside from that, decentralisation has facilitated increased municipal and departmental spending.

Table 6.10. **Colombia: Revenue and Spending by Level of Government, 1994**
(percentage of GDP)

Departments		Municipalities	
Expenditures	3.12	Expenditures	3.98
Financing	2.91	Financing	4.08
Own source fiscal		Own source fiscal	
revenues		revenues	
Liquor tax	0.36	Property tax	0.48
Tobacco tax	0.11	Industry & commerce	0.64
Beer tax	0.39		
Stamp tax	0.16	Other current revenue	0.93
Other taxes	0.77	Transfers	
		National	1.43
Other current revenues		Other	0.06
(including transfers)[a]	0.82		
Net domestic credit	0.30	Debt	0.54
Surplus/Deficit	−0.21		0.10

a.   Transfers are Exclusive of Fiscal *Situado*.
Source: World Bank Report No. 15298–Co (Volume II – 1996).

Colombia has three types of intergovernmental grants: the fiscal *situado* (SF), the municipal participation (PM), and the national cofinancing system (SNC). The fiscal *situado* consists of 24.5 per cent of national revenue and accrues to departments and districts according to population. The municipal participation takes an increasing portion of national current revenue (up to a maximum of 22 per cent in 2002) and goes to municipalities on the basis of parameters aimed at favouring smaller and poorer ones (Bird and Fiszbein (1996). The national cofinancing system transfers around 0.8 per cent of GDP, on a matching basis and for specific subnational projects.

The central government uses earmarked transfers extensively to ensure the proper attainment of policy objectives, especially the provision of minimum service levels and infrastructure, and increase the SNGs' fiscal capacity. This has been widely criticised on the grounds that local fiscal autonomy did not increase and transfers impeded the promotion of more effective and efficient SNGs through decentralisation. SNGs could always count on national government funds and thus had few incentives for local fiscal effort. A critical assessment of decentralisation in Colombia (World Bank, 1996*b*) suggests the revision of the *situado* and participation systems and the inclusion of some general purpose grants, more flexible use of resources at the subnational level and the elimination of earmarking not responding to clearly established needs.

Decentralisation in Peru

Although not a federation, Peru has a central government; intermediate governments (12 regional entities[18], 25 departments, 189 provinces and 1 799 districts); 189 provincial municipalities (all provincial capital cities, according to the constitution); and 1 799 district municipalities. Despite recent developments, the country's incipient decentralisation (Casas, 1997), is conditioned by a rigid unitary political and institutional structure reflected in tax assignments. SNGs have no constitutional power to create taxes. The centre levies the main taxes (income, assets, sales and consumption taxes, and customs duties), while local governments may only, as determined by the centre, collect (but not create or modify) urban and rural property tax, automobile registration tax, estate transfer tax, and excises (Table 6.11). Property taxes (5.64 per cent of current revenue in 1994) are the most important revenue of local governments. Regional entities have no taxing powers. Municipalities have access to user charges, service fees and special benefit contributions which represent around 4 per cent of their total revenues.

Intergovernmental fiscal arrangements in Peru do not clearly distinguish revenue sharing from categorical or non–categorical transfers. On one hand, taxes and participations from the central level to municipalities include 20 per cent of the municipal promotion tax (a 2 per cent surtax on the general sales tax), petrol sales tax and municipal betting taxes[19], oil royalties and customs duties share (2 per cent of total yield). On the other, the municipal compensation fund (FCM) includes 80 per cent of the municipal promotion tax, the petrol sales tax and municipal betting taxes. unlike in Argentina and Brazil, it is not easy to speak here of a revenue–sharing scheme (despite the existing mechanisms for primary and secondary distribution), because local governments can neither change the system's structure (taxes, bases or rates) nor (at least in the case of FCM) freely use the funds[20].

Table 6.11. **Peru: Revenue By Level of Government, 1994**

(Percentage of total at each level)

Items	Central government	Provincial municipalities	District municipalities
Tax resources	82.9	31.00	23.04
Tax on income	15.4	0.01	–
Tax on assets	2.8	10.35	5.64
Import duties	10.9	–	–
Taxes on production, consumption and sales	51.1	3.12	12.91[a]
Other taxes	3.7		
Negative taxes	–1.0		
Service fees		16.55	4.36
Contributions		0.97	0.13
Non–tax current Resources	13.8	27.91	26.27
Capital revenues	3.3	41.09	50.69
Capital good sales		0.60	0.81
Borrowing		3.55	4.00
Municipal compensation Fund		36.47	44.34
Others		0.47	1.54

a. Includes transfers of municipal promotion tax.
Sources: Banco Central de Reserva del Perú and Dirección General de Presupuesto Público, MEF.

Tax assignments and spending functions produce strong vertical imbalances; the central government collects more than 95 per cent of total tax revenues, leaving the rest (less than 5 per cent) to local governments (Table 6.12). Even the modest scale of expenditure decentralisation occurs only through massive transfers. As a consequence of the fiscal assignment pattern and the nature of transfers, analysts agree that local accountability must be strengthened by enhancing municipal fiscal autonomy, and that transfers need correction to address externalities, minimum service standards, and similar fiscal capacity criteria.

Table 6.12. **Peru: Vertical Fiscal Imbalances, 1993**
(percentages)

Items	Before transfers			After transfers		
	Central level	Regional level	Local level	Central level	Regional level	Local level
Revenue share	95.45		4.55	77.24	11.38	11.38
Expenditure share	79.04	11.38	9.58	79.04	11.38	9.58
Surplus/deficit	16.41	−11.38	−5.03	−1.80		1.80

Source: Own estimates based on Casas (1997).

Notes

1.   According to Bird, while in the top–down approach the main criterion for judging fiscal decentralisation should be how well it serves presumed national policy objectives, the main feature of the bottom–up variant is that it improves local welfare most by freeing SNGs from central dictates.

2.   As Bird (1993) pointed out, central government's policy preferences are clearly dominant in this case.

3.   In assuming a straight application of the principal–agent relationship, with implied symmetric information and agents' fair behaviour, the problems of adverse selection and moral hazard are here ruled out.

4.   Although in another article Prud'homme (1995) also challenges merits of decentralisation, as regards allocative efficiency, on grounds that it assumes hypotheses not easily defensible in developing countries and for privileging the concept of demand efficiency instead of supply efficiency.

5.   In Hommes's thinking, the equivalent idea was that central governments — mainly in developing countries — should be capable of directing reforms and steering institutional changes towards more democratic and efficient societies.

6.   This section draws heavily on Rezk (1996).

7.   Since 1935, Personal and Corporate Income Tax in Argentina has levied by the central government and shared with the provinces through revenue–sharing schemes.

8. Tax source separation was the prevailing situation until 1935, when the first revenue–sharing scheme came into being.

9. A marked difference with other federations (e.g. Brazil or Germany) is that municipalities in Argentina do not participate directly in revenue–sharing schemes including taxes managed by the central government.

10. This date has recently been changed.

11. See for instance Rezk (1995, 1996) and World Bank (1996a).

12. Although the degree of fiscal centralisation is decreased by intergovernmental transfers of all kinds, almost 60 per cent of total tax revenues is still retained by the central government (see Table 6.4).

13. Along the same line of analysis, Afonso (1996) pointed out that, especially after the reform brought about by the 1988 Constitution, the general trend of decentralisation through redistribution of public resources entails that (in vertical terms) local governments internalise almost all relative gains, while (in horizontal terms) most additional resources go to poorer states and municipalities.

14. Revenue sharing flows through different funds as for instance the state and municipal participation funds (FPE and FPM), the special state fund for less developed regions (FE), the fund for financing productive sectors in northern regions (FFR) or the state fund for export compensation (FPEx).

15. This section heavily relies on Barrios (1997).

16. There is also a municipal *situado*, whereby local governments receive an unconditional transfer distributed among them half in equal parts and half in relation to population.

17. It is easy to see that excessive access to credit by municipal governments can create an accountability problem when the financial burden is ultimately transferred to the central government; in such a case, there will be no chance for the community to control spending.

18. As of 1992, regions were replaced by the so called Transitory Councils for Regional Administration (CTAR), which in practice are the central level's decentralised entities in charge of sectoral current and investment spending of Treasury funds.

19. In this case, only 25 per cent of the total yield goes to the Municipal Compensation Fund.

20. Central government demands that municipalities use FCM for investment spending.

Bibliography

AFONSO, J.R. (1996), "Descentralização Fiscal, Efeitos Macroeconômicos e Função de Estabilização: O caso (peculiar) do Brasil", VIII Seminario Regional de Política Fiscal, ECLAC, Santiago de Chile.

AFFONSO, R.B. (1997), "Os Estados e a Decentralização no Brasil", *Serie Politica Fiscal 93*, ECLAC, Santiago de Chile.

AGHON, G., AND L. LETELIER (1996), "Local Urban Government Financing: A Comparison between Countries", ECLAC, Project CEPAL/GTZ on Fiscal Decentralisation in Latin America.

ARGENTINA, Secretary for Economic Programming (1996), *Informe Económico 1995*, April.

BARRIOS, A. (1997), "Decentralizacion Fiscal y Establidad Macroeconomica en Venezuela", *Serie Politica Fiscal 94*, CEPAL, Santiago de Chile.

BARRO, R.J. AND X. SALA–I MARTIN (1992), "Convergence", *Journal of Political Economy*, 100.

BIRD, R.M. (1993), "Threading the Fiscal Labyrinth: Some Issues in Fiscal Decentralisation", *National Tax Journal*, XLVI.

BIRD, R.M. (1995), "Fiscal Federalism and Federal Finance", *Anales de las 28 Jornadas de Finanzas Públicas*, Cordoba, Argentina.

BIRD, R.M. AND A. FISZBEIN (1996), "Fiscal Decentralisation in Colombia: The Central Role of the Central Government", Conference on Fiscal Decentralisation in Developing Countries, Montreal University, Canada.

CASAS, C. (1997), "Descentralización Fiscal: El Caso de Perú", *Serie Política Fiscal 92*, Proyecto Regional de Descentralización Fiscal, CEPAL/GTZ.

DILLINGER, B. (1995), "Decentralisation, Politics and Public Service" in A. ESTACHE (ed.), *Decentralising Infrastructure, Advantages and Limitations*, World Bank Discussion Papers 290, World Bank, Washington, D.C.

ESTACHE, A. (ed.) (1995), *Decentralizing Infrastructure, Advantages and Limitations*, World Bank Discussion Papers 290, World Bank, Washington, D.C.

HOMMES, R. (1995), "Conflicts and Dilemmas of Decentralisation" in M. BRUNO AND B. PLESKOVIC (eds.), Annual World Bank Conference on Development Economics, World Bank, Washington, D.C.

LAGEMANN, E. AND L.C. VITALI BORDIN (1993), "Decentralização Fiscal no Brasil: A Percepção do Estado do Rio Grande do Sul", Secretaria da Fazenda, Governo do Estado do Rio Grande do Sul.

OATES, W. (1995), "Comment on 'Conflicts and Dilemmas of Decentralisation'" by R. HOMMES, in M. BRUNO AND B. PLESKOVIC (eds.) Annual World Bank Conference on Development Economics, World Bank, Washington, D.C.

PRUD'HOMME, R. (1990), "Decentralisation of Expenditure or Taxes" in R. BENNETT (ed.) *Decentralisation, Local Governments and Markets*, Clarendon Press, Oxford.

PRUD'HOMME, R. (1995), "On the Dangers of Decentralisation", Policy Research Working Paper No. 1252, World Bank, Washington, D.C.

REZENDE, F. (1995), "Federalismo Fiscal no Brasil", *Revista de Economia Politica*, 15, 3(59).

REZK, E. (1995), "Federal Finance in the Argentine, Germany and Brazil", *Annals of the Arnoldshain Seminar I*, J.W. Goethe University, Frankfurt.

REZK, E. (1996), "The Performances of Fiscal Federalism and Decentralisation: Lessons for Argentina", *Anales de las 29 Jornadas de Finanzas Públicas*, Cordoba, Argentina.

SHAH, A. (1991), "The New Fiscal Federalism in Brazil", World Bank Discussion Papers No. 124, World Bank, Washington, D.C.

TANZI, V. (1995), "Fiscal Federalism and Decentralisation: A Review of Some Efficiency and Macroeconomic Aspects" in M. BRUNO AND B. PLESKOVIC (eds.) Annual World Bank Conference on Development Economics, World Bank, Washington, D.C.

WIESNER, E. (1994), "Fiscal Decentralisation of the Public Sector", in *Economic and Social Progress in Latin America, 1994 Report, Special Report: Fiscal Decentralisation*, Ch. 1, Inter–American Development Bank, Washington, D.C.

WORLD BANK (1996a), Report No. 15487–AR "Argentina: Provincial Finances Study", *Selected Issues in Fiscal Federalism*, Vol. I, Washington, D.C.

WORLD BANK (1996b), Report No. 15298–CO "Colombia, Reforming the Decentralisation Law: Incentives for an Effective Delivery of Services", *Selected Issues in Fiscal Federalism*, Vol. I, Washington, D.C.

Chapter 7

Decentralisation, Intergovernmental Fiscal Relations and Macroeconomic Governance: the Case of Argentina

Ricardo Lopez Murphy and Cynthia Moskovits

Introduction

Argentina is a federal state organised on three levels, national or central, provincial and municipal. The national constitution directly regulates only the first two. The country's history points to a progressive centralisation of power in the hands of the national government over public spending as well as tax collection, which has given rise to increasingly prevalent "vindication politics" among provincial governments and towards the national government. The results have been weak autonomy for the lower levels of government; inequity among provinces; increased, competing demands by different jurisdictions; and a lack of autocorrection mechanisms, which depend on central government action due to the marked vertical imbalance.

Distribution of Functions

Article 1 of the constitution lays out the federal system. It distributes fiscal responsibilities geographically according to criteria explicit for the national government and implicit for provincial governments. The provinces have exclusive powers (those not explicitly delegated to the federal government), concurrent powers (those exercised simultaneously with the national government), and superseding powers (which must abide by federal regulations). The general rule gives the provinces jurisdiction over functions not delegated to the national government, whose powers cover international and interprovincial relations and regulations.

The constitution limits itself to assigning responsibility for organising and guaranteeing municipal systems to the provinces. The first ruling of the Supreme Court considered the municipalities as autarchic entities organised along territorial lines, which should apply the norms set out by higher levels of government. In recent years, however, some provinces have modified their constitutions to recognise municipal autonomy (power to determine their own governing norms, especially for management). Recent Supreme Court rulings guarantee municipal autonomy on the following grounds: *a)* a municipal regime has a constitutional origin in contrast to the merely judicial basis of autarchic entities, and consequently cannot disappear or be suppressed; *b)* municipal ordinances are by nature local legislation; *c)* the municipality is a legal public entity whose existence is guaranteed by the constitution; *d)* the scope of its decisions includes all the inhabitants of the municipal territory; and *e)* municipalities can create autarchic entities. In sum, the present definition of municipal powers is somewhat confusing. This constitutes a serious obstacle to setting municipal regulatory powers, because if they are autonomous units their powers to regulate matters hitherto not within their jurisdiction must be recognised.

The national constitution allocates taxing powers to both the centre and the provinces. In principle, the law supports their separation, but in reality they have been concentrated in the hands of the national government, which legislates and collects the lion's share of taxes (VAT, income taxes, specific consumption taxes, and fuel taxes). The federal government has exclusive powers over import and export duties and direct taxes "for a limited time". The nation and provinces have concurrent powers over indirect taxes. The provinces "maintain all powers which are not delegated" to the federal government and could thus impose permanent direct taxes — a power restricted in practice because direct taxes imposed by the nation have taken on a permanent character through constant renewal by law.

The constitutional reforms of 1994 prospectively give the revenue–sharing regime constitutional weight for the first time and establish a general framework; it thus will acquire higher status than it currently enjoys. This guarantees that, for example, funds will go automatically to the provinces and their primary and secondary distribution "will be directly correlated with the jurisdiction, services and functions of each province and will reflect objective sharing criteria", which will show "equity [and] solidarity, and will give priority to achieving an equivalent level of development, quality of life, and equality of opportunities in the whole of the national territory".

Other constitutional reforms also are relevant to the federal tax–sharing system. They include Buenos Aires as an independent jurisdiction in it[1]. The revenue–sharing law will originate in the Senate, where all provinces are equally represented, so that smaller jurisdictions will enjoy relatively greater influence in negotiations. Transfers of services and responsibilities between nation and province will be restricted unless accompanied by the corresponding funds and consented to by legal representatives of both levels of government. A federal fiscal entity will be created to control fiscal relationships between the nation and the provinces; it will include representatives of each province and Buenos Aires, although the presence of a national representative is not mentioned. The federal government's powers to modify taxes subject to revenue sharing through specific allocations (pre–co–participation) are increased, although these measures will require absolute majorities in both houses. For municipalities, the debate on autonomy versus autarchy will directly influence whether they have taxing powers. As autarchic entities, they could charge fees for services but not collect taxes[2]. If current judiciary trends continue, nothing in the constitution disallows taxation at the municipal level; these powers will depend on provincial legislation[3].

Fiscal Federalism and Argentina's Experience

During the first period of institutional organisation (1853–1890), the criteria governing tax–raising powers were the predominant issue: the nation retained the revenues from foreign trade and the indirect taxes which it collected in the federal capital and national territories. Provincial financing depended on their capacity to collect their own taxes. Between 1890 and 1935, increased public–sector functions — in areas such as education, justice, health and defence — created a necessity for new resources. The crisis of the 1930s forced adoption of a set of emergency measures, including the introduction of income tax, sales taxes and taxes to be shared between the national government and the provinces; this introduced an incipient regime of federal tax co–participation. The system of revenue sharing consolidated as time passed, acquiring greater weight in financing provincial spending as well as a greater share of total tax receipts.

Until 1960, the co–participation regime corrected some of the asymmetries in spending capacities which differences in tax bases had caused. In 1973 the Federal Co–participation Law was passed to reduce the financial dependency of provincial governments, specify distribution criteria for provinces to give added weight to redistribution and surmount the complex and fragmented character of the system. The law's criteria, however, deepened the separation of spending and financing decision making, gave added spending incentives to the provinces and created a very rigid system for increased receipts. Decentralisation continued apace with the transfer of responsibilities for social spending (pre–primary and primary education, health) to the provincial level. Provincial spending increased enormously. By 1980, the provinces' per capita spending had doubled from 1960 as a share of GDP.

Between 1977 and 1980, some large permanent expenditures (primary and adult education, health, water, and local distribution networks) were transferred to the provinces — unaccompanied by the funds necessary to pay for them. This not only substantially altered secondary resource distribution but also encouraged provincial fiscal irresponsibility and higher spending, irrespective of the criteria of efficiency, equity or necessity[4]. The revenue–sharing regime expired at the end of 1984, to be replaced only in 1988. The ensuing legislative vacuum led to the substitution of co–participation for Treasury contributions. As a result, spending grew to incredible levels during 1986, due especially to out–of–control provincial employment, which reached 60 per cent of total public employment. Provincial spending now represented 85 per cent of total spending on pre–primary education, 91 per cent of that on primary and 36.7 per cent for secondary education, 65 per cent of law and order outlays and 70 per cent of spending on justice.

The new Law of Federal Co–participation came into effect at the start of 1988, accompanied by a series of special laws creating national taxes whose revenues would be distributed to the provinces to promote transparency and predictability and eliminate discretion in determining the amount and distribution of collected tax. This law conceded the greatest share of primary distribution to the provinces in Argentina's history, from a wider tax base[5]. Attempts to justify it pointed to the spending responsibilities shunted to the provinces in the late 1970s without corresponding taxing powers[6]. The law also implied greater redistribution of funds among the provinces as secondary co–participation — essentially the continuation of the *ad hoc* participation of 1985–87, the consequence of no definition of objective criteria and powerful incentives to spend when another level of government bears the political cost of taxation. The new redistribution scheme deepened disparities in per capita spending. Provinces with low population densities could spend 3.58 times more than the developed provinces and the underdeveloped ones almost twice.

Public Spending, Revenues and Transfers

Public Spending

Since the early 1980s, Argentine public spending[7] at all levels has moved erratically. During the 1990s, a strong upward trend became clear, especially for primary expenses, with a small decrease in interest payments on the public debt noticeable in recent years. The trend becomes even stronger when state–owned enterprises (SOEs) are excluded from primary spending (SOEs were an important part of total spending before rapid privatisation began in the early 1990s).

Municipal and provincial outlays had already reached 36 per cent of total expenditure in 1990, up from an average of 31.5 per cent during the 1980s. A combination of factors caused the shift: first, the decentralisation of public expenditure itself; second, growth in the nation's resources (as a consequence of economic growth, improved tax controls and improvements in the tax system) and transfers to the provinces through the federal co–participation regime; third, the privatisation of SOEs, which were in essence national, allowed reductions in central government spending; and finally, restructuring of the maturity of national debt.

A more accurate evaluation of the effects of decentralisation emerges from looking at primary expenses only, with the SOE sector netted out. This reveals that during the 1980s, provincial and municipal spending together accounted for 41.4 per cent of total public spending. The provinces' share then increased progressively from 1989, reaching 49.9 per cent in 1993 and then stabilising at around 49 per cent, with the average for the 1990s at almost 48 per cent. It is improbable that any decentralisation took place at lower levels, because the municipalities' fraction of the combined municipal/provincial share has decreased somewhat in recent years.

Artana *et al.* (1994) have pointed out that direct federal government expenditure decreased between 1983 and 1992 in both relative and absolute terms. The nation's share of primary expenses, excluding SOEs, health insurance and private education (whose funds come wholly or in part from different levels of the public administration but with final execution by the private sector) was 52.3 per cent in 1983. It dropped to 42.8 per cent in 1992. The nation financed 68.1 per cent of primary expenses excluding SOEs in 1983 but only 57.8 per cent in 1992. Provincial expenditures grew from 30.1 per cent in 1983 to 36.6 per cent in 1992. Provincial financing of these expenditures, through own resources, non–conditional transfers or debt[8] also increased, from 26.5 per cent in 1983 to 34 per cent in 1992. The municipalities' share remained virtually unchanged between 1983 and 1992, although their provision of financing decreased. The private sector's share also remained stable.

The provinces' share of total public–sector social spending increased considerably from an average of 16.5 per cent during the 1980s to 24.3 per cent in the first years of the 1990s and 26.3 per cent in 1995. Spending on education had three phases: in the first part of the 1980s through 1983, the central government carried out around 47 per cent of spending on culture and education; from 1984 through 1991, its share dropped to 38 per cent; and during 1992–95 it dropped by another 16 per cent. The provinces clearly absorbed the slack, as the municipalities showed only minor variations throughout. Provincial expenditures on medical services also increased due to the transfer of social services. The three levels of government share general administration expenses, while almost all urban services are offered by the municipalities.

Tax Resources

The discussion so far has emphasised the provinces' loss of tax powers in practice. The provinces legislate, manage and collect[9] four main taxes and other minor ones. The first group consists of a turnover tax (sales tax), stamps[10], automobile registration and real estate taxes. The latest fiscal agreement between the central government and the provinces established a retail sales tax or a VAT to replace the turnover tax. If this occurs, the structure of provincial taxation would come into line with economic theory[11]. Two of the more important taxes (automobile registration and real estate) have relatively fixed tax bases, which impedes tax exportation and greatly restricts the possibility of "tax wars" and of "voting with one's feet".

The provinces have not put their tax systems to good use. They now collect only around 17 per cent of the total for the central government and provincial jurisdictions put together (this figure averaged 16 per cent during the 1980s, and increased slightly to 16.6 per cent during the first six years of the 1990s)[12]. Funds collected from provincial taxes amounted only to around 29 per cent of provincial expenditures (30.9 per cent in 1995). The turnover tax, which distorts economic activity and is highly procyclical, historically has generated the most revenue for the provinces (56 per cent of total tax collections in recent years, with automobile and real estate taxes at only ten per cent and 20 per cent, respectively).

Clearly, the provinces have had no incentives to collect taxes, due largely to the structure of the revenue–sharing scheme, their opportunities to acquire debt (in the past through national banks, suppliers and rediscounts) and the near certainty of national bailouts in the event of default. The harmful consequence, a very low correlation between expenditure and tax collection, becomes even less with expenditure decentralisation. A related and continuing problem involves the provinces' loss of tax–raising powers to the central government. This constraint would be lifted if, for example, the central government transferred fuel and excises (on alcohol and cigarettes) to the provinces. The national government also could stop imposing some direct taxes, leaving them to the provinces (e.g. some personal income taxes, although the levies should not be progressive). This would lead to an increase in fiscal accountability, better correlation between taxes and spending and, of course, a more efficient allocation of resources that would reduce the importance of the federal tax co–participation regime.

Municipalities should charge fees for services. Such fees are in practice more akin to transaction taxes, because they exceed the cost of the services rendered. Some limits placed on the municipalities' ability to acquire debt have allowed for higher correlation between collected funds and expenditure than that seen at the provincial level. An important share of municipal revenues also originates in provincial co–participation. This system functions along the same lines as the federal co–participation system, although primary distributions from province to municipality are much smaller in relative and absolute terms.

Transfers

The federal revenue–sharing regime, the most important mechanism for transfers to the provinces, has accounted for almost 71 per cent of total explicit transfers (automatic and non–automatic, conditional and non–conditional) in the 1990s. Although the system's criteria were initially based on devolution (funds transferred according to their origin), other criteria such as population were subsequently adopted. Transfers to provinces (including National Treasury Contributions) accounted for 52 per cent of central government expenditure in 1995. A considerable spread exists in the provinces' shares of expenditure funded by transfers. Developed provinces such as Buenos Aires, Cordoba and Santa Fe depend on them (so in far this decade, Buenos Aires financed 43.8 per cent of its expenditures with transfers, Cordoba 47.9 per cent and Santa Fe 53 per cent). Less developed provinces such as Catamarca, Santiago del Estero and La Rioja fund more than 80 per cent of their expenditures with transfers. San Luis, one of the "middle income" provinces, was the most dependent, at 83 per cent of its expenditure.

Transfers from the nation to the municipalities practically do not exist. The provinces, to a certain degree, copy the mechanism of federal co–participation relative to their municipalities, using federal co–participation funds. This generally includes shares of taxes collected within their jurisdiction such as turnover taxes, automobile registration (often almost all that is collected) and real estate taxes. In contrast to the federal system, primary distribution allows much smaller shares to the municipalities. Finally, transfers from municipalities to provinces are minimal.

The mechanism of federal revenue sharing does not include incentives for the efficient provision of services or for increasing their coverage. Correcting this would involve fixing levels of expenditure as well as objectives for the growth of coverage. Even with such measures, fulfilment could be uncertain and control costly, leading to moral hazard for local officials. A similar problem occurs when funds transferred for specific programmes (e.g. conditional transfers such as FONAVI or other health or education programmes) get diverted to general funds and then are spent in other, politically profitable ways (e.g. temporary jobs for potential supporters or simply deficit reduction). The central government cannot immediately detect if this has an effect on the local government's housing, health or education budget, nor can it legally prevent it unless legally or constitutionally authorised[13].

Improving fiscal accountability requires systematic knowledge of the government's activities as well as an institutional framework that allows the community to participate. The best way to promote community participation for programmes financed by the central government is through local–government cofinancing. Linking performance to tax payments creates a powerful incentive for community involvement. A complementary solution would sanction laws which impose a strict code of conduct on local administrators, making them personally responsible and legally liable when they do not serve the best interest of the community. These laws could serve as a powerful disincentive against corruption if civil institutions could bring class–action suits against local politicians.

Macroeconomic Policy and Fiscal Decentralisation

Counter–cyclical Policies and Debt

A decentralised government will always allocate resources more efficiently than a centralised one, adjusting expenditure decisions and financial alternatives to citizens' preferences. Nevertheless, a nation should have a unique, central government macroeconomic policy; but certain prerequisites must be satisfied. For example, the design of the tax system must make predominant at the national level those taxes which fluctuate with the cycle and can raise considerable revenues (i.e. VAT, corporate profits), while local governments should levy taxes with more stable and fixed bases.

The design of transfer regimes is another important element of macroeconomic policy. When fiscal correlation (revenue to expenditure) in lower levels of government is low, the cost of financing public deficits is borne by higher levels of government and citizens perceive only the benefits of public services without immediately incurring the costs. Even without significant imbalances, horizontal equity requires transfer mechanisms. The *first* requirement of a transfer regime is that it not be cyclically sensitive; local governments should make long–term expenditure plans with the financing available, abstracting from current economic circumstances.

The debt policy of local governments, perhaps the most important factor in macroeconomic policy making, affects the sustainability of the debt/GDP ratio and control of the debt/net internal investment ratio[14]. Fundamentally, the central government must not bail out local governments faced with default, although this restriction will often get bypassed for reasons of public order or when health or education spending are affected. If politicians, bureaucrats, banks or other lending institutions believe that the central government will not allow lower levels of government to default, problems of moral hazard arise and contribute to the creation of structural deficits. Jurisdictions' expectations that the centre will come to their rescue will allow them to act as if they had only minor budget restrictions, which does not force them to reduce spending (or boost revenues)[15] to keep their budgets in equilibrium in the short term and even less on a continuous basis. Financial institutions will have added incentives to lend if they anticipate bailouts.

If a provincial or local government is too important or too big to be allowed to fail, central government intervention could involve restrictions on levels of allowed indebtedness or other regulations — or reduce the size of local governments. Separation of the big urban economic centres from the main governmental centres (functional decentralisation) or fragmentation of large SNGs into multiple jurisdictions (spatial decentralisation) could help to strengthen controls over lower–level budgets.

The debt of subnational governments (SNGs) should not be left to their own management. Local government debt accumulation can be limited in various ways: *i)* reliance on market discipline; *ii)* co–operation between different levels of government in the design and implementation of debt controls; *iii)* controls based on rules; or *iv)* administrative controls. For reliance on market discipline, financial intermediaries must not face rules that privilege the government in acquisition of loans; lenders must have adequate information on borrowers' outstanding debt obligations and their ability to pay; and bailouts should be limited effectively to prohibit using federal transfers as collateral. The role of credit rating agencies is essential. Giving free reign to market forces and assimilating local governments into the private sector probably are not viable; nevertheless, policies could allow the floating of medium–term bonds, prohibit the use of federal transfers as collateral, and oblige debts to be qualified.

The *second* option would establish local government debt limits through a process of negotiation with the central government, thus defining global debt targets and estimates for the growth of the principal categories of revenues and expenditures. The *third* fixes limits on the absolute levels of SNG debt and/or on the purposes for which it may be used (e.g. investment). Another restriction could link debt to the ability to service it (e.g. ratios of debt servicing to total debt, past revenues or the tax base) Some types of financing (e.g. central bank loans) could be prohibited. This policy approach implies the existence of clear and uniform accounting norms for government entities that strictly limit or eliminate extra–budgetary operations. Clear definitions of debt must be set (not forgetting contingent assets from SNG pension systems, for example) and modern information systems for government financial management established. The *fourth* possibility implies annual or more frequent limits on SNGs' global debt (or of some of its components, such as foreign debt); the approval of debt operations; or the centralisation of all government loans combined with their conditional reissue to SNGs.

The problem with debt goes beyond its level to the increased risk caused by its growth and the difficulties this implies for the private sector. In Argentina the regime of fiscal relationships is strongly procyclical (even with the effects of pre–co–participation on the most important taxes) and the provincial and municipal governments depend heavily on these funds[16]. Both the provinces and the municipalities have the capacity to issue debt. Only the provinces can borrow abroad and they require the approval of Congress to do so, especially if they use transfers from the central government as collateral. For municipalities, authorisation to acquire debt usually requires a qualified majority in the Deliberating Council (*Concejo Deliberante*); other cases require approval by the provincial legislature. In general, limitations on debt issuance mainly involve not allowing debt servicing payments to exceed a percentage (often 25 per cent) of a municipality's revenue[17].

Characteristics of Distribution

The centre's redistributive policy should aim at eliminating horizontal inequity by equalising the initial opportunities of individuals with different incomes through a minimum supply of public goods, i.e. compensating for the weakness of the tax base. A high level of personal and capital mobility limits the ability of SNGs to implement redistribution programmes financed by their own resources. Therefore, income redistribution should constitute one of the basic objectives of an intergovernmental transfer regime. Personal or family income redistribution programmes need engineering at the national level, although administration can be decentralised.

Musgrave and Musgrave (1980) have proposed that federal subsidies redress differences in the tax bases of different jurisdictions, to finance a standard level of spending according to the characteristics of the population[18]. Assuming a uniform system of taxation applies to all jurisdictions with similar levels of compliance, such transfers will allow the financing of a jurisdiction's weak tax base, or greater expenditures in response to the composition of the population (e.g. a greater demand for old–age subsidies).

There is no reason why the region rather than the individual should be the objective of the distributive scheme; policies should prevent subsidies by the poor of a rich jurisdiction to the rich of a poor one. The Argentine revenue–sharing system has had a strong redistributive content, with the larger proportion of transfers organised along regional, not personal lines. Those that are aimed at individuals or families include the FONAVI and the school meals programme at the national level, and some provincial health services (especially in the province of Buenos Aires).

The organisation of transfers on a regional basis does not necessarily mean that they cannot improve personal income distribution, although this appears true for Argentina. The practice of correlating each province's per capita transfers to the proportion in the total population of households with basic needs unsatisfied does not necessarily provide information on the effectiveness of the transfers in improving personal income. Moreover, an analysis of social expenditures in households with unsatisfied basic needs reveals that the objective of levelling per capita social expenditure has not been attained. The transfers tend not to compensate for the weakness of provincial tax bases (for example, provinces with equal relative tax–base weaknesses, such as La Rioja, Corrientes, Misiones, San Juan and Santa Cruz, received very different federal co–participation transfers).

Argentina illustrates an increase in transfers not commensurate with consolidation of an "equivalent expenditure" level, along with skyrocketing spending in jurisdictions receiving the greater part of the transfers. In 1934, the federal co–participation system did not exist and the provinces were practically auto–financed. This allowed the relatively more developed jurisdictions to make per capita expenditures almost triple those of the least–developed provinces. The introduction of the federal co–participation regime in 1935 allowed the balancing of per capita public expenditure in each group of jurisdictions. By 1959 developed, middle income and less developed provinces all had similar per capita outlays, while the provinces with low population densities (Patagonia area) spent 15 per cent more per capita than the national average. A substantial imbalance surfaced in 1992 when the low–density provinces had per capita expenditure triple that of the more developed provinces, while the least developed almost doubled it, with significant differences among similar provinces.

Although the general rule holds that richer jurisdictions should subsidise poorer ones, the policy based on regional redistribution, which presumably attempted to achieve greater settlement of the country's interior, was not based on rational assumptions. The significant territorial redistribution provoked a profound inequality in the per capita distribution among different provinces: residents of the more developed provinces receive through co–participation 64 per cent less than the less developed provinces, 60 per cent less than the provinces with low population densities and 55 per cent less than the middle income provinces. Residents of Buenos Aires receive a per capita co–participation 48 per cent of the national average. Moreover, if households with unsatisfied basic needs are used as a proxy for personal income distribution, the more developed provinces receive co–participation for each of these households 17 per cent less than the less developed provinces and 51 per cent less than the provinces with low population densities. A disadvantaged household in Santa Cruz receives six times as much as a similar household in Buenos Aires, while one in La Rioja receives four times as much.

From a historic point of view, regional redistribution policies — in addition to showing poor results relative their objectives — have probably resulted in net losses for society. The loss of fiscal correlation in provincial management of public funds has led to skyrocketing public expenditure and a weakening of provincial tax collection. The provinces receiving smaller per capita transfers (i.e. the more advanced ones) have smaller per capita expenditures and exploit their theoretical bases relatively more. Exactly the opposite is true of the less advanced provinces.

Conclusions

Numerous difficulties can be highlighted in the organisation of Argentina's tax system. The system's initially good design began to deteriorate as the activities of the public sector became more complex. The central government gained powers which had previously belonged to the provinces, particularly in taxation but also in social spending (e.g. primary education during the first steps of national organisation). The lack of clarity regarding municipal powers permitted provinces to take them over while the central government was taking over theirs[19]. As a result, a state with a federal government structure, in which the provinces had existed before the nation, became more centralised; with this came the reduction of benefits inherent to resource allocation in a decentralised regime.

The transfer of expenditure functions from nation to province deepened an already considerable imbalance because the central government did not relinquish any of its taxing powers *pari passu* with the decentralisation of functions. The system of fund transfers favours a set of perverse behaviours. For example, neither the national nor a subnational government has an incentive to collect taxes, for two main reasons. *First,* the transfers can pay for expenditure or be used as debt mechanisms during periods of imbalance. *Second,* a large part of the effort to collect taxes goes only to finance provincial and municipal expenditure, thus increasing the necessity to finance the whole of the public sector. The central government's efforts to reduce expenditures does not produce an exemplary effect on lower levels of government in the absence of mechanisms forcing them to adopt similar strategies.

The Argentine tax–sharing system also engenders for macroeconomic policy the loss of central control over stabilisation policies. The regime's design favours the acquisition of debt by lower levels of government. Argentine provinces face no restriction on acquiring debt because they can use future funds transferred to them through this regime as collateral. The basic objective of a transfer mechanism, to serve income distribution policies of the central government, is frustrated as well. The regime has not succeeded in improving the personal distribution of income, whether through financing a minimum level of per capita public expenditure or trying to equalise the tax bases. It serves only to benefit certain provinces at the expense of others; poor citizens in rich provinces subsidise rich ones in poor provinces.

Notes

1. In 1981, Law 22451 eliminated the Municipality of Buenos Aires from the federal tax co–participation regime.

2. At the moment, the municipalities collect taxes disguised as fees for services.

3. The present Federal Co–participation Law obliges the provinces to set limits on the revenue–raising powers of municipalities. They may not impose "local taxes analogous to those distributed by the national government". The situation of the Municipality of Buenos Aires has peculiar characteristics. The central government imposed certain taxes on it (i.e. stamps) while recognising its powers to collect real estate taxes and the gross revenues tax.

4. As an example of provincial fiscal decontrol, provincial government employees reached 750 000 in 1983, clearly outnumbering the national central administration.

5. In addition, it was established that the amount to be distributed to the provinces would not be less than 34 per cent of the central administration's tax revenues, part of the co–participation system or not. The funds are transferred automatically and their use is not subject to conditions or predetermined objectives.

6. The transfers of spending obligations to the provinces are restricted to education and public health. Distribution of drinking water and electricity should not require additional transfers since these services can be financed by fees.

7. The whole of public spending analysed here includes health insurance and subsidies to private education. Expenditures financed by compulsory payments made by workers (health insurance) and the public sector's financing aimed at education (even if carried out by private entities) are included .

8. Financing with conditional transfers is not considered. These are funds whose destination is pre–established by a higher level of government, such as the FONAVI.

9. Some provinces have delegated power to collect some taxes. In Chubut, Santa Cruz, Chaco and Corrientes urban and suburban real estate and automobile taxes are collected by the municipalities.

10. Since the different provincial jurisdictions approved the second fiscal pact, stamp duties on financial activities had to be eliminated; most provinces did so.

11. In this case, some doubts emerge relative the possible effects of mechanisms imposing taxes on the importation of goods and not on exports (border adjustments).

12. If only tax revenues are counted (not including revenues from taxes on salaries) the figures are: 19.8 per cent and 22.1 per cent, respectively.

13. The same problem could arise if an administrator who is a representative of the central government pursues his personal political interests with government funds. This activity implies even higher costs, as well as risks, since local voters will have no incentives to replace him because they cannot choose his successor. This in turn increases the central government's costs of detecting him.

14. When measuring debt, contingent liabilities should be noted (e.g. implicit debt in the state pension system).

15. This same opportunistic *modus operandi* would occur if transfers were strongly procyclical and if they finance an important part of local expenses — which is the case in Argentina.

16. Because of this successive stabilisation programmes have opted for the reduction of the co–participation percentages, the transfer of services or changing the destination of resources.

17. In some cases, the provinces are also subject to this type of restriction.

18. It should be noted that the criteria of compensating the differences in tax bases does not necessarily lead to an equalisation of per capita public spending, because the redistribution criteria compensate for the existing differences in order to provide a minimal public expenditure and not the whole of expenditure.

19. For example, in 1948, the provinces had delegated the power of collecting the gross revenues tax to their municipalities. The amplification of national government taxing power led them to reassume this function. To compensate, the provinces allowed municipalities to charge an "Inspection Fee for Commercial Security and Hygiene".

Bibliography

ARTANA, D., O. LIBONATTI, C. MOSKOVITS AND M. SALINARDI (1994), "La descentralización fiscal en América Latina: problemas y perspectivas. El caso de Argentina", *IDB Work Series No. 184*, Inter–Americain Development Bank, Washington, D.C.

MUSGRAVE, R. AND P. MUSGRAVE (1980), *Public Finance in Theory and Practice,* McGraw–Hill, New York.

Chapter 8

Fiscal Federalism and Macroeconomic Stability in Brazil: Background and Perspectives

Luiz R. de Mello Jr

Introduction

Fiscal federalism concerns the decentralisation of public–sector fiscal activities and the partition of revenue sources and expenditure functions across different levels of government. It requires a great deal of intergovernmental fiscal co–ordination which often exceeds the fiscal efforts of separate units of government in a multilevel structure. The organisation of multilevel government has a direct bearing on the allocation of public finance; the division of revenue and expenditure responsibilities across different levels of government is often complex and conflicting, and goes beyond institutional arrangements. Under subsidiarity, expenditure functions are assigned with the objective of making "regionally grouped diversities" (Livingstone, 1956; Dikshit, 1976) compatible with a unitary state. Taking into account local differences in culture, environment, natural resources, and economic and social factors can then make the performance of public functions more efficient.

To analyse the scope, limitations, and prospects of fiscal federalism in Brazil, one must understand the organisation of the Brazilian public sector. Its units encompass the central government (referred to here as the Union); intermediate governments (27 states[1]); local governments (over 5 000 municipalities); state–owned enterprises (SOEs, federal, state and municipal); the social security system; and state–owned financial/ banking institutions, included here to take account of the impact of quasi–fiscal[2] imbalances on overall macroeconomic performance. Brazilian fiscal federalism, complex in both institutional arrangements and current governance practices, is characterised by great autonomy of subnational governments (SNGs)[3].

From an historical perspective, a consensus exists in Brazil that the long period of economic deceleration between the mid–1980s and early 1990s reflected to a great extent a crisis in the regime of fiscal federalism adopted since the late 1960s. Growth based on import substitution, which prevailed until the 1980s, relied heavily on public investment, particularly in infrastructure. The 1970s and 1980s saw little scope for legislative scrutiny of the federal budget, with administrative centralism exercised to the extent that the Union collected a significant share of total tax revenue and then distributed it to SNGs. More importantly, the monetary authorities had a quasi–fiscal role to facilitate preferential lending, opening special credit lines to the private sector in accordance with the government's industrial and development policies, and to finance public spending in general. The lack of transparency in the management of fiscal and monetary policies persisted until the late 1980s, when most credit facilities within the Union were progressively transferred from the central bank to the Treasury. Nevertheless, not until 1988 did the expenditures and revenue of the Union become consolidated, with management of the public debt by the Treasury. More recently, the devolution of tax revenue to SNGs has not been matched by sensible efforts towards decentralising expenditures and rationalising revenue sharing.

This paper focuses on two important aspects of Brazilian fiscal federalism. One relates closely to the microeconomic and institutional aspects of fiscal federalism in a country characterised by sizeable regional disparities in economic and social indicators and great complexity in fiscal arrangements across different levels of government. This setting not only explains specific institutional features of the Brazilian fiscal federalism regime, but also provides valuable lessons to other large federations. The second aspect concerns the impact of macroeconomic instability and chronic inflation on fiscal policy making. Specific factors in Brazilian intergovernmental fiscal arrangements explain, among other things, the difficulties in the management of economic policy in Brazil in pursuit of economic stability in recent years.

Macroeconomic Stability and Fiscal Federalism

Macroeconomic Background

Three important phenomena characterise the Brazilian inflationary process and macroeconomic instability. *First,* the combination of persistent high inflation in the 1980s and early 1990s, and formal and/or informal, backward–looking indexation of prices and wages led to the progressive demonetisation of the Brazilian economy, with a steady fall in the stock of M1 as a share of GDP over the years (Table 8.1). The converse is true for the ratio of M2 to GDP (except for 1990 and 1991, due to the financial asset confiscation of the Collor administration[4]). As a result, the rise in inflation coincided with the replacement of monetary wealth by financial assets, in a process that reflected more the hypertrophy of the financial/banking sector than financial deepening. Financial innovation contributed to an increase in the liquidity of otherwise illiquid interest–bearing assets, which allowed for a steady process of domestic (rather than foreign) currency substitution in response to chronic inflation.

Table 8.1. **Macroeconomic Indicators, 1980–96**

Year	M1*	M2*	Private consumption (percentage of GDP)	Government consumption (percentage of GDP)	Consumer price inflation (per cent)	Parallel exchange premium (per cent)	Current account balance (percentage of GDP)
1980	11.94	18.14	69.34	9.15	82.9	11.75	−5.45
1981	11.43	22.01	68.32	9.70	105.6	15.28	−4.46
1982	9.35	21.22	70.77	10.18	98.0	47.46	−5.79
1983	8.05	18.75	73.28	9.94	141.9	55.39	−3.36
1984	7.50	24.19	73.59	8.67	196.7	13.24	0.02
1985	8.07	29.12	65.54	9.81	226.9	26.18	−0.12
1986	12.39	23.84	67.51	10.63	145.0	54.81	−1.98
1987	8.95	32.21	62.06	12.12	229.8	30.94	−0.49
1988	8.02	43.94	59.47	12.55	682.8	44.42	1.26
1989	9.37	76.22	50.00	16.49	1 286.9	101.20	0.23
1990	8.37	17.91	58.72	16.87	2 938.0	40.96	−0.79
1991	6.89	23.90	63.22	15.06	369.0	13.09	−0.35
1992	6.13	38.27	60.41	16.48	1 345.0	7.18	1.50
1993	6.04	48.50	60.89	16.49	2 146.0	0.64	−0.13
1994	6.39	20.40	62.67	15.35	2 669.0	0.99	−0.35
1995	4.51	16.96	65.10	15.20	23.2	0.47	−2.81
1996	3.68	21.26	65.00	15.00	9.12	3.27	−3.16

Sources: *International Financial Statistics*, IMF, and Central Bank of Brazil.

Second, the response of private consumption/saving behaviour to fiscal disequilibria, and the composition and sources of finance of public deficits, determine to a large extent the macroeconomic effects of fiscal imbalances. With private and government consumption figures disaggregated, Table 8.1 evidence gives of a dramatic rise in the latter, particularly after 1988, which suggests significant payroll and administrative costs imposed by the new fiscal arrangements enshrined in the 1988 Constitution[5]. The higher the dissaving of the public sector (the sum of the primary balances[6] of the central government, the subnational governments and the SOEs), the higher the savings of the private sector (Figure 8.1). Nevertheless, very little empirical evidence of debt neutrality[7] in developing countries exists (Easterly *et al.*, 1994), whereby an increase in public sector borrowing requirement (PSBR) figures would lead to a one–to–one rise in private saving in anticipation of future tax increases.

The *third* important phenomenon is that conventional, non–financial public deficits were moderate by international standards in the early 1990s (Table 8.2), as was also the total outstanding net debt of the public sector (Table 8.3) which, despite the recent increase in 1996, lies significantly lower than the OECD average (over 42 per cent of GDP, in 1995), and stands at roughly half of the EU average (over 57 per cent of GDP, in 1995). Although it is widely accepted that conventional inflationary processes are deeply rooted in fiscal imbalances, non–financial PSBR and net domestic debt figures in the early 1990s cannot explain *per se* the very high inflation rates, a paradox.

To complicate matters further, the fall in inflation after the implementation of the latest stabilisation programme in July 1994 coincided with an increase in the PSBR, leading to operational deficits in 1995 and 1996 after two consecutive surpluses. In fact, Tables 8.2 and 8.3 indicate that the deterioration of the fiscal balance in the last two years, believed to be the main threat to the consolidation of macroeconomic stability and disinflation, seems to have been caused by the stabilisation effort since 1994.

Figure 8.1. **Savings Patterns and Fiscal Stance**

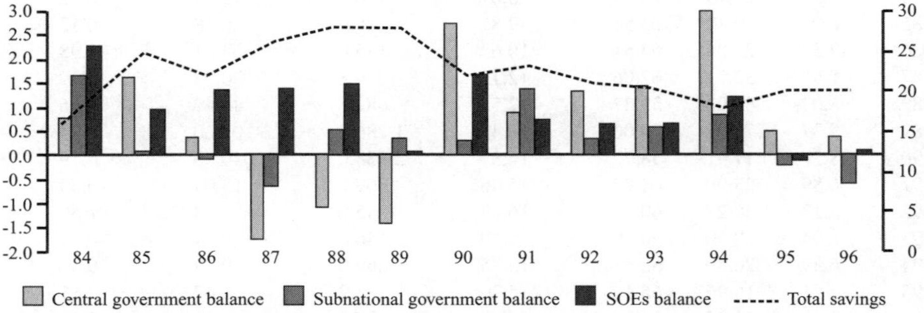

Note: The government balance figures are measured on the left hand side scale and refer to the primary result (negative figures denote a deficit). Subnational government figures aggregate states and municipalities.

Thus a lack of fiscal discipline alone, as implied by non–financial PSBR figures, cannot explain the persistence of high inflation in Brazil in the late 1980s and early 1990s. Rather than denying the fiscal nature of most inflationary processes, the solution to this paradox calls for examination of the composition of non–financial fiscal imbalances across different levels of government instead of their aggregate magnitudes, on the one hand, and consideration of quasi–fiscal or financial disequilibria on the other. The former addresses explicitly the problems facing the fiscal federalism regime in Brazil, whereas the latter deals with the financial components of fiscal imbalances at the heart of chronic macroeconomic disequilibria. In the former, aggregate figures may understate the fiscal effort of the federal government and overstate that of subnational governments, or vice–versa, because apparent aggregate fiscal discipline may hide both considerable fiscal imbalances across the different levels of government and significant differences in fiscal austerity efforts in SNGs (Table 8.2).

Table 8.2. **Public Sector Borrowing Requirement (PSBR), 1988–96**
(percentage of GDP)

	1988	1989	1990	1991	1992	1993	1994	1995[a]	1996[a]
Primary Result	−0.94	1.00	−4.68	−2.99	−2.32	−2.64	−5.03	−0.3	0.1
Real Int. Payments	5.74	5.90	3.38	1.57	4.53	2.39	3.76	5.2	3.8
Domestic	2.83	2.71	0.10	−0.38	3.09	0.84	3.07	–	–
Union	0.86	0.70	−1.53	−0.67	1.22	0.28	1.00	2.2	2.1
States/Municipalities	0.72	0.73	0.52	0.12	1.09	0.27	1.37	2.2	1.3
SOEs	1.25	1.28	1.11	0.17	0.78	0.29	0.70	0.8	0.4
Foreign	2.91	3.19	3.28	1.95	1.44	1.55	0.69	–	–
Union	1.55	1.84	1.96	1.24	0.89	1.15	0.47	–	–
States/Municipalities	0.17	0.18	0.16	0.09	0.07	0.05	0.04	–	–
SOEs	1.19	1.17	1.16	0.62	0.48	0.35	0.18	–	–
Operational Result	4.80	6.90	−1.30	−1.42	2.21	−0.25	−1.27	4.9	3.9
Domestic	3.80	1.60	−6.50	−3.66	3.29	−0.22	−2.52	–	–
Union	–	–	–	−2.59	2.03	0.02	−2.90	1.7	1.7
States/Municipalities	–	–	–	−1.10	0.74	−0.27	0.49	2.3	1.9
SOEs	–	–	–	0.03	0.52	0.03	−0.11	0.9	0.3
Foreign	−2.60	0.30	0.40	−0.05	−3.82	−2.42	−2.85	–	–
Union	–	–	–	0.01	−3.98	−2.41	−2.72	–	–
States/Municipalities	–	–	–	0.09	0.06	0.04	0.07	–	–
SOEs	–	–	–	−0.05	0.10	−0.05	−0.20	–	–

a.   Figures for interest payments and the operational result include the foreign balance.
Notes: (+) Deficit, (–) Surplus.
Source: Central Bank of Brazil.

Table 8.3. **Net Debt of the Public Sector, 1991–96**
(percentage of GDP)

	1991	1992	1993	1994	1995	1996
Total debt	43.5	42.7	38.4	29.7	29.9	34.5
Union and central bank	14.6	14.0	11.2	12.8	13.0	16.4
States/Municipalities	8.2	10.6	10.8	9.9	10.4	12.0
SOEs	20.7	18.1	16.3	7.0	6.5	6.1
Domestic debt	15.9	21.2	21.6	21.0	24.5	30.4
Union and central bank	−2.5	0.9	2.1	6.5	9.6	14.8
Securitised debt outside the central bank	3.5	10.3	10.8	11.7	15.3	22.2
Social security system	0.0	−0.3	−0.3	−0.4	−0.2	0.0
FAT	−1.1	−1.5	−1.7	−2.0	−2.5	−2.6
States/Municipalities	7.0	9.4	9.6	9.5	10.1	11.6
Securitised debt outside the central bank	2.1	3.8	4.3	2.1	2.0	2.4
SOEs	11.4	10.9	9.8	5.1	4.8	4.1
Foreign debt	27.6	21.5	16.8	8.6	5.5	4.0
Union and central bank	17.0	13.0	9.1	6.3	3.4	1.6
States/Municipalities	1.3	1.2	1.2	0.3	0.3	0.4
SOEs	9.2	7.2	6.5	2.0	1.7	2.0

Note: FAT denotes the Unemployment Benefit Fund, administered by the National Savings Bank (CEF).
Source: Central Bank of Brazil.

Fiscal and Quasi–Fiscal Imbalances

Federalism and Fiscal Imbalances

In the composition of public deficits across different levels of government, Table 8.2 shows that although primary aggregate surpluses, which do not incorporate interest payments, obtained throughout the post–1989 period, SNGs had an operational deficit of almost 0.5 per cent of GDP in 1994, while the Union and the SOEs taken together had an operational surplus of over 3 per cent of GDP. The SOEs displayed a significant fiscal effort from 1988 to 1996 by reducing both interest payments and their outstanding net debt, domestically and internationally (Tables 8.2 and 8.3). They achieved it to a great extent at the expense of public investment, however, rather than by streamlining and rationalising their activities, which reflects the use of such firms for quasi–fiscal purposes. Moreover, the fall in the outstanding foreign debt of the public sector as a whole since 1990 has come partly from appreciation of the domestic currency, which reduces the value of the external debt expressed in domestic currency.

Table 8.3 also shows a dramatic increase in the securitised debt of the Union outside the central bank. For the states and municipalities taken together, this debt nevertheless remained stable as a share of GDP in 1991–96. Yet the fiscal effort of states and municipalities cannot be overestimated because, in aggregate terms, the fall in the outstanding net debt of the public sector in the period came mainly from effort of the Union (particularly the SOEs) and debt rescheduling with the central bank, including extensive debt–swap operations. Although debt swaps may underestimate the indebtedness of SNGs at the expense of the Treasury and the central bank, such operations likely strengthen the control of the Union over subnational finances, so that the federal government can impose fiscal retrenchment as a precondition for debt alleviation. The overall debt of the states and municipalities taken together rose considerably between 1991 and 1996[8].

Table 8.4 provides an additional overview of the fiscal stance of SNGs. With regard to fiscal autonomy, measured as the ratio of tax revenue to total revenue, it is clear that poorer regions/states have limited ability to collect taxes. In general, tax revenue varies from over 25 per cent of total revenue in poorer regions to over 50 per cent in richer regions. The limited taxing capacity implies high dependency ratios, measured as the share of transfers in total revenue, which vary from over 10 per cent in richer regions to over 65 per cent in poorer regions. Table 8.4 also reveals a high level of indebtedness, measured as the ratio of net debt to net revenue, particularly in richer regions which have easier and less costly access to financial markets. The increase in indebtedness was widespread in the 1990s, particularly in the Southeast. In addition, there seems to be an inverse relationship between investment capacity and indebtedness.

Table 8.4. **Basic Fiscal Indicators**
(state level)

Region/state	Ratio of investment expenditure to net revenue		Ratio of net debt to net revenue		Ratio of tax revenue to total revenue		Ratio of transfers to net revenue	
	Average 1985–90	Average 1991–94	Average 1985–90	Average 1991–94	Average 1985–90	Average 1991–94	Average 1985–90	Average 1991–94
North	**0.27**	**0.20**	**0.64**	**1.05**	**0.23**	**0.27**	**0.66**	**0.57**
Rondônia	0.21	0.14	0.42	0.39	0.16	0.30	0.78	0.58
Acre	0.07	0.07	0.71	1.89	0.06	0.07	0.93	0.88
Amazonas	0.28	0.15	1.29	2.04	0.37	0.43	0.37	0.32
Roraima	0.42	0.37	0.23	0.43	0.01	0.06	0.98	0.76
Pará	0.22	0.13	0.58	0.96	0.33	0.31	0.51	0.45
Amapá	0.36	0.32	0.00	0.37	0.03	0.07	0.97	0.90
Tocantins	1.29	0.49	0.71	0.34	0.17	0.17	0.73	0.70
Northeast	**0.17**	**0.10**	**1.97**	**2.33**	**0.31**	**0.33**	**0.44**	**0.46**
Maranhão	0.56	0.18	2.86	3.98	0.16	0.22	0.65	0.66
Piauí	0.24	0.11	2.62	2.66	0.22	0.24	0.70	0.66
Ceará	0.06	0.15	2.91	2.76	0.34	0.33	0.40	0.41
Rio Gr. do Norte	0.15	0.01	1.43	1.88	0.25	0.26	0.66	0.60
Paraíba	0.30	0.08	4.14	4.00	0.26	0.27	0.54	0.59
Pernambuco	0.12	0.08	1.16	1.73	0.42	0.42	0.37	0.41
Alagoas	0.03	0.03	1.77	2.15	0.34	0.29	0.48	0.59
Sergipe	0.28	0.15	0.60	1.12	0.20	0.24	0.51	0.61
Bahia	0.07	0.07	2.07	2.17	0.40	0.39	0.31	0.32
Southeast	**0.08**	**0.08**	**1.19**	**2.12**	**0.53**	**0.48**	**0.14**	**0.12**
Minas Gerais	0.14	0.05	2.49	3.54	0.41	0.39	0.20	0.22
Espírito Santo	0.11	0.06	1.12	1.28	0.44	0.48	0.24	0.26
Rio de Janeiro	0.07	0.04	2.54	3.00	0.54	0.47	0.20	0.15
São Paulo	0.07	0.10	0.46	1.48	0.57	0.51	0.10	0.08
South	**0.05**	**0.05**	**2.55**	**2.61**	**0.52**	**0.50**	**0.15**	**0.17**
Paraná	0.05	0.07	2.11	1.70	0.58	0.65	0.15	0.18
Santa Catarina	0.04	0.04	3.33	3.73	0.54	0.49	0.17	0.20
Rio Gr. do Sul	0.06	0.04	2.50	2.83	0.48	0.43	0.14	0.15
Centre–West	**0.07**	**0.14**	**2.19**	**2.29**	**0.37**	**0.39**	**0.44**	**0.38**
Mato Grosso	0.05	0.15	5.24	4.94	0.35	0.50	0.26	0.25
Mato Gr. do Sul	0.11	0.08	4.13	3.93	0.47	0.55	0.32	0.22
Goiás	0.13	0.16	3.08	3.77	0.51	0.52	0.23	0.18
Federal District	0.03	0.14	0.11	0.39	0.27	0.24	0.66	0.55

Notes: Net revenue figures consist of total tax and non–tax revenue minus transfers (current and capital) and credit operations. Net debt figures comprise domestic and foreign balances. Total revenue figures consist of total tax and non–tax revenue net of transfers (current and capital).

Source: *Atlas das Desigualdades* – IPEA.

An additional important linkage between fiscal federalism arrangements and macroeconomic governance concerns the political economy aspects of voting procedures in the legislature and institutional design. Both factors affect fiscal discipline by highlighting the political determinants of budget imbalances. In general, a move promoted in the 1980s from more hierarchical to more collegial institutions in the fiscal decentralisation process tended to aggravate the lack of fiscal discipline and delay fiscal adjustment. Tax–sharing arrangements and unbalanced, statutory intergovernmental transfers that create a bias in favour of SNGs represent a "tragedy of the commons" situation, in which SNGs favour spending in their jurisdictions, financed by a common pool of tax revenue[9].

Institutional changes detrimental to macroeconomic stability and fiscal governance in part offset efforts towards more transparency in budgetary procedures and accounting practices. In fact, international evidence suggests that fiscal decentralisation most successfully preserves macroeconomic stability when fiscal devolution does not preclude local revenue mobilisation and local governments can handle additional transfers and expenditure assignments. Minimising spillovers and tax overlap across jurisdictional boundaries is also a prerequisite for successful decentralisation. Otherwise, free riding may become rampant and SNGs excessively reliant on tax exporting and funding from transfers.

Quasi–Fiscal Imbalances

Quasi–fiscal disequilibria generally arise from lack of transparency in the relationship between fiscal and monetary authorities (the Treasury, the central bank, and public financial institutions). As a result, public financial institutions become agents (or instruments) of fiscal policy and quasi–fiscal deficits constitute an important source of macroeconomic disequilibria in most developing countries. The consideration of quasi–fiscal deficits makes an implicit source of public deficit finance explicit; that is to say, with significant quasi–fiscal imbalances, conventional non–financial PSBR figures underestimate the actual magnitude of fiscal imbalances and hide important sources of macroeconomic disequilibria. The most important quasi–fiscal activities of the public sector relate to the management of exchange and interest rates, regulation of the commercial banking system, sterilisation of foreign capital inflows, and the costs of bailing out financial institutions in distress.

With regard to deficit–finance alternatives, the correlation between inflation and fiscal imbalances is strong to the extent that money creation finances fiscal deficits. Yet persistent high inflation in Brazil does not stem exclusively or primarily from monetary expansion (Table 8.5). Due to the progressive demonetisation of the economy (low M1/GDP ratios, Table 8.1, and monetary base/GDP ratios, Table 8.5), which reflects the high opportunity cost of holding non–indexed, non–interest–bearing currency, financing even very small public deficits through seignorage requires very high inflation rates. In other words, high inflation increases the seignorage–maximising inflation rate[10]. The average seignorage in the 1980–88 period was 2.5 per cent of

GDP, with average inflation at over 212 per cent and the average monetary base at 2.7 per cent of GDP. In 1989–94, the average monetary base increased to 3.5 per cent of GDP and average seignorage rose to over 3 per cent of GDP (Table 8.5). At the same time, average inflation skyrocketed to an annualised rate of almost 1 800 per cent (Table 8.1). More recently, a combination of low inflation and monetary austerity has led to negative seignorage in 1995 and 1996. The loss in seignorage revenue is associated with the deterioration of the central bank balance since 1994.

Table 8.5. **Monetary Base and Seignorage, 1988–96**
(percentage of GDP)

	1988	1989	1990	1991	1992	1993	1994	1995	1996
Monetary Base	3.60	5.00	4.80	2.29	2.75	2.40	4.10	3.10	2.50
Seignorage	3.94	6.04	4.44	–0.71	3.02	1.94	5.65	–0.42	–0.39
Money Creation	0.80	1.40	–0.20	–2.51	0.46	–0.35	1.70	–1.00	–0.60
Inflation Tax	3.14	4.64	4.64	1.80	2.56	2.29	3.95	0.58	0.21

Note: Seignorage is calculated as the sum of two components: money creation and the inflation tax. The former is calculated as $M_t - M_{t-1}$, where M_t is the monetary base at time t. The latter is calculated as $\pi_t\,(1 + \pi_t)^{-1} M_t$, where π_t is the inflation rate at time t.

Given the deterioration of the PSBR position in the last two years, high real interest rates reflect excessive reliance on tight monetary policy to keep the exchange rate stable after the introduction of the new currency in July 1994, and to reduce inflationary pressures due to increased demand in the phase of macroeconomic consolidation. High real interest rates also reflect the credibility problem of the central bank in light of its frequent use in the recent past of non–orthodox policy instruments to curb inflation, such as successive price and wage freezes between 1986 and 1989 and the financial asset confiscation following the inauguration of the Collor administration in March 1990. High real interest rates have also engendered additional costs associated with the sterilisation of foreign capital inflows, attracted by the differential between domestic and international rates of return. Given that residents may not hold assets denominated in foreign currency, sterilisation incurs an additional financial cost to the central bank, the difference between the rates paid on central bank assets (foreign currency) and liabilities (mainly BBCs, central bank bonuses, in sterilisation operations)[11].

More recently, the effort of the monetary authorities to safeguard liquidity and solvency in banking institutions in financial distress[12] illustrates another important source of quasi–fiscal imbalance — and a reason for concern in the post–1994 period of low inflation, with the financial system under pressure from the fall in inflation–related revenue and profitability. In state–owned financial institutions, high inflation and lack of monetary discipline permitted the accumulation of sizeable portfolios of non–performing loans, due to factors ranging from weak management and careless lending to inadequate collateralisation, loan recovery difficulties, and poor credit worthiness assessment. The use of such institutions as agents of fiscal policy, with preferential credit lines with the central bank and pernicious political interference with lending criteria, enhanced the lack of financial prudence. Resources used to recapitalise troubled financial institutions are transfer payments to their creditors and depositors. In subsidised lending, the central bank incurs a cost associated with the lending–rate differential. Bailout operations have an additional quasi–fiscal cost because they often are off–budget disbursements of the central bank.

An additional important source of quasi–fiscal revenue in Brazil in the early 1990s, before the implementation of the stabilisation programme in 1994, was the adoption of a multiple exchange–rate regime with significant spreads of the parallel rate over the official or commercial rate (Table 8.1)[13]. Given that the Brazilian government is a net buyer of foreign currency and faced severe international liquidity constraints in the 1980s, the central bank could buy foreign exchange at a lower rate than that used in current account transactions (mainly imports and exports). When exporters must surrender foreign–exchange earnings at a high rate, the tax revenue accruing to the government inflates the net income of the central bank, generating a quasi–fiscal revenue. This corresponds to an implicit tax on exports. A unification of multiple rates imposes a fiscal cost on the government, despite the overall welfare gain from the elimination of relative price distortions and their detrimental impact on the allocation of resources.

An important additional source of quasi–fiscal revenue to the central bank concerns reserve requirements[14]. High, non–remunerated reserve ratios allow it to channel resources from the private banking system to finance low–cost lending to the public sector. This equates to a quasi–fiscal tax that artificially reduces the cost of government borrowing. An additional important difficulty of excessive fiscal laxity in a reforming economy is the management of current–account imbalances, given the association between fiscal, quasi–fiscal and balance–of–payments disequilibria. Such association may lead to an unsustainable current account position if the exchange–rate regime is to be preserved. Tables 8.1 and 8.3 show a deterioration of both the current account balance and the fiscal stance of the government after 1994.

Overall, the deterioration of the fiscal stance of the government after 1994 is associated with the fall in quasi–fiscal revenue, which allows the financing of fiscal imbalances at lower cost, and with the increased costs of financing the national debt and sterilising capital inflows, given the increase in real interest rates. Before 1994, fiscal imbalances could be financed at low or even negative real interest rates and from various quasi–fiscal sources of finance, with no sanctions for the use of monetary instruments to finance fiscal imbalances or institutional rewards for fiscal discipline. The inability of the public sector to promote a far–reaching fiscal reform, by which the saving/investment structure of the economy could change in favour of the private sector, contributed to the aggravation of the fiscal imbalances towards the end of the 1980s. With limited access to international capital markets, given the severe international liquidity constraints of the 1980s, the fiscal disequilibrium of the public sector crowded out private investment and led to the stagnation of growth after 1985. More importantly, the rapid increase in the financial burden of domestic debt and the transfer of liabilities from the private sector and SNGs to the Union coincided with the institutional reforms in tax–sharing arrangements that favoured SNGs at the expense of the Union.

Federalism in Brazil: Tax Sharing and Expenditure Assignments

Broad Overview

The 1988 Constitution brought constitutional arrangements in Brazil generally into line with broad expenditure assignment principles in economic theory (Oates, 1977; Bennett, 1980) — but cross–level co–ordination and service delivery practices pose additional problems. For instance, Brazil has no clear division of responsibilities across the levels of government on health and social security, education and social welfare, agriculture, food distribution, sanitation, housing, policing, public transport, natural resources and the environment; this leads to clear duplication of spending assignments. Potential tax overlapping can therefore counteract the scope for revenue separation.

Duplication is particularly evident in the following cases. Ambiguity exists in spending assignments for primary, secondary and higher education. Efficiency objectives imply a hierarchical apportionment of public goods according to their degree of externality and spatial range; hence local governments should have responsibility for primary education, with the Union's role essentially normative (setting minimum standards, providing technical advice, etc.). Nevertheless, given the regional social and economic disparities in the country, the Union remains responsible for spending across subnational jurisdictions in different regions of the country. In urban infrastructure (water services, sanitation, housing, road building, etc.), controversy rages over spending assignments for investment in infrastructure, maintenance, and conservation. In public transport, local needs are best met in a decentralised urban–transport system where the state or federal governments provide technical assistance and subsequent quality screening.

Although it leaves grey areas in education and urban infrastructure, the 1988 Constitution makes significant progress over post–1967 arrangements in clarity of expenditure and revenue assignments to different government levels. Tax sharing remains problematic, however; efforts to transfer taxation revenue, but not necessarily spending assignments, from the Union to SNGs excessively favour lower levels of government at the expense of the Union. The Union faces a severe fiscal squeeze with a detrimental impact on overall macroeconomic performance and stability, while the SNGs face a disincentive to fiscal effort. Union control over SNG spending has also been reduced significantly.

International trade. Foreign trade taxes in Brazil comprise the import tax (II) and the export tax (IE). Because the Brazilian economy remained relatively closed until the early 1990s, they had only a minor share in total tax revenue. Progressive opening of the economy since the early 1990s has led to a fall in average II rates.

Consumption Taxes. Brazil has three consumption taxes: the ICMS, of broad incidence, is a credit–method VAT levied by the states[15], the IPI, of narrower incidence, is levied by the Union on manufacturers' sales, and municipalities levy the ISS on selected goods and services exempted from the ICMS. The management of consumption taxes raises a number of problems. *First,* their collection under different jurisdictions does not preclude partial tax overlapping. *Second,* emphasis is placed on essentially cumulative, selective, multiphase taxes that have a deleterious impact on industrial competitiveness, particularly for exports. *Third,* consumption taxes in Brazil are also used as a regional development instrument by allowing for rate differentiation in interstate trade, opening great scope for interstate fiscal competition. Differentials in tax–deferral regimes also are used in interstate competition for investment.

Financial Transactions Tax. The only such tax in Brazil (IOF) is levied on a broad variety of financial transactions, ranging from capital gains to banking activities and insurance. A particular type of IOF taxes transactions in gold (IOF–Gold) and has an important role in intergovernmental transfers. Currently, a supplementary tax (IPMF) taps certain financial transactions to create an additional source of Union revenue and is due to be earmarked for health spending from 1997.

Income Tax. Although the income tax (IR) is under federal jurisdiction, as in most federations, almost half of its revenue is transferred to lower levels of government. Brazil has three income taxes: the corporate tax (IRPJ), the personal income tax (IRPF), and the personal income tax deducted automatically from workers' salaries (IRF). State governments can levy a further 5 per cent on the corporate income tax. Progressiveness of the income taxes is low; proportional taxation occurs mainly in the IRF and various exemptions narrow the IR tax base.

Property Taxes. As with consumption taxes, property tax revenues have a rather peculiar distribution. The Union levies a tax on rural properties (ITR) and the municipalities tax urban properties (IPTU). In a further complication, the states tax inheritances (ITBCM) and the municipalities tax donations (ITBIV); in principle, both donation and inheritance taxes should be governed by the same provisions and levied at the same level of government. The IPTU tends to be progressive. The ITR tends to be very regressive, given distortions in it to reduce the scope for speculation on rural property prices and to reform land ownership, primarily by providing incentives for the rational use of land and preventing large rural properties from remaining fallow. Both distortions failed to achieve their objectives.

Vehicle Registration Tax. The IPVA tax is levied by the states, which retain half of the revenue and transfer the other half to the municipalities where the vehicles are registered.

Others. Two additional taxes fall under federal jurisdiction, one on the sale of mineral products, including oil prospection and fuels, and a hydroelectricity tax.

Social Security Contributions. Brazil has a broadly defined social security system incorporating both health and social welfare provisions. Contributions divide into two basic types. The first comprises contributions paid into government–managed funds and the second those to private funds related to specific industrial sectors and administered by non–governmental institutions. Private contributions mainly finance vocational education and retraining programmes, and provide technical support and management assistance to small private enterprises. The employers' social security contributions are levied on firms' gross revenue (COFINS and PIS/PASEP[16]), payroll (FGTS) and net profits. The employee's contribution (INSS) is levied on gross earnings.

Contributions levied on firms' gross revenues and payrolls constitute a significant share of total contributions (Table 8.6). Formal education spending is financed by a combination of tax–sharing and social security contributions, including an additional contribution earmarked for education (*Salário–Educação*). Although social security spending concentrates in the Southeast, the region also is the system's main contributor. A redistributive effect towards funding social security spending in poorer regions nevertheless occurs, given their low revenue–raising capacity and fiscal autonomy (Table 8.4). A current overhang of unfunded social security liabilities arises from a combination of demographic factors (very rapidly falling population growth coupled with rising life expectancy) and institutional design (a publicly funded pay–as–you–go system with generous early retirement provisions, particularly for civil servants and SOE employees).

Intergovernmental Transfers. A number of statutory and discretionary or negotiated transfers from the Union to SNGs govern revenue–sharing and equalisation–payment arrangements. General–purpose transfer agreements enshrined in the 1988 Constitution form a number of State and Municipal Funds (FPE, FPEX for exporting states and FPM). The FPM provides selective, non–matching project grants to support regional development, agriculture, education, health, housing and sanitation.

Before 1980, intergovernmental transfers were centralised and mainly determined by annual investment plans and the government's income and development policies. After 1980, two simultaneous processes guided federal transfers. On the one hand, the Union relied increasingly on tax revenues not statutorily transferable to lower levels of government[17]. On the other, lower levels of government consolidated their fiscal stance by imposing progressive increases in statutory transfers from the Union to the participation funds (FPE, FPM, and FPEX[18]), at the expense of the Union's fiscal position during its political weakness after 1985 (Barrera and Roarelli, 1995; Afonso and Ramundo, 1996). Both processes tended to aggravate public sector fiscal and financial imbalances which became evident in the late 1980s.

Table 8.6. **Social Security Contributions, 1980–96**

(percentage of GNP)

Contributions	1980	1990	1991	1992	1993	1994	1995	1996
Public	7.01	10.02	9.02	8.82	9.73	10.60	11.01	–
COFINS	–	1.49	1.53	0.97	1.34	2.51	2.46	2.40
Net Profits	–	0.53	0.27	0.70	0.77	0.95	0.95	0.89
PIS/PASEP	1.02	1.11	1.02	1.04	1.14	1.05	0.99	1.00
FGTS	1.32	1.43	1.30	1.26	1.26	1.34	1.48	–
INSS	4.67	5.01	4.39	4.36	5.22	4.75	5.13	–
Salário–Educação	–	0.32	0.33	0.36	–	–	–	–
Others	–	0.13	0.18	0.13	–	–	–	–
Private	–	0.20	0.17	0.19	–	–	–	–
Total	7.01	10.22	9.19	9.01	9.73	10.60	11.01	–

Note: Constructed from de Almeida and Cavalcanti (1995), Afonso (1996), and Central Bank of Brazil. For quick reference, the employer's social security contributions are: COFINS and PIS/PASEP, levied on firm's gross revenue, and FGTS, levied on payroll. The employee's social security contribution is INSS, levied on gross earnings.

In principle, funds get distributed to SNGs on the following criteria, in order of importance: fiscal needs (proxied by population), fiscal capacity (proxied by the inverse of per capita income), fiscal effort (proxied by the ratio of own revenues to expenditure), and spillover factors such as interstate trade orientation. In general, the highest statutory and negotiated transfers go to the less prosperous regions (North, Northeast, and Centre–West), which are required to receive 85 per cent of total resources against 15 per cent for the South and Southeast. Average transfers exceeded 3 per cent of GDP (over 10 per cent of total tax revenue) in 1989–91, and statutory transfers increased from half the total to over 75 per cent in 1990 — which suggests that promulgation of the 1988 Constitution increased the institutional rigidity of the system. The share of negotiated transfers shows drastic variations over time, perhaps suggestive of their use politically rather than to complement social policy.

Macroeconomic Performance and Tax Collection Over Time

It might be useful to see the Brazilian tax structure from an international perspective. For the OECD countries, the tax burden increased from 30 per cent of GDP in 1970 to over 40 per cent in 1996 (almost 50 per cent for the EU countries and slightly over 39 per cent for the federal states within the OECD). In contrast, the Brazilian tax burden is lower (Table 8.7). In 1994, OECD countries' tax revenues accrued mainly from income, profit, and property sources (over 42 per cent of the total, against over 16 per cent in Brazil and almost 38 per cent in the EU countries), followed by general taxes on goods and services (roughly 30 per cent of total revenue against almost 37 per cent in Brazil and over 31 per cent in the EU countries). In addition to Brazil's imbalance in favour of indirect taxation, particularly in contrast with the OECD's federations, Tables 8.6 and 8.7 show social security contributions in Brazil in the neighbourhood of a third of total revenue, higher than the OECD figures (almost 26 per cent in the OECD and almost 30 per cent in the EU countries).

Table 8.7. **Tax Revenue, 1980–96**

(percentage of GDP)

Government Levels	1980	1990	1993	1994	1995	1996
Federal Government	18.50	20.88	16.20	18.94	20.00	–
IPI	2.20	2.54	2.12	2.15	2.06	2.13
Income Tax	2.95	4.95	3.78	3.51	4.00	4.14
Fin. Operat. Tax	0.94	1.38	0.63	0.68	0.49	0.39
States	5.41	8.74	6.58	8.18	8.60	–
ICMS	4.89	7.68	6.64	8.17	7.17	7.75
Municipalities	0.71	0.91	0.51	1.38	1.70	–
Total	24.63	30.53	23.29	28.50	30.30	–

Source: Central Bank of Brazil.

Several factors explain the pattern of total tax revenue as a share of GDP in Brazil in the 1980s. Inflation tended to erode part of the revenue from non–indexed taxes, generating a Tanzi effect which depressed total tax revenue. Yet gross tax revenue did not collapse despite dramatic inflation in 1985–93, due to the increased complexity of the tax collection system with widespread, albeit imperfect, indexation and the reduction in average collection time from a progressive move towards a pay–as–you–earn system[19]. The Tanzi effect was therefore much milder than in other high–inflation countries, in particular Mexico and Argentina[20]. On the other hand, tax evasion did increase due to distortions brought about by successive price and wage freezes in the non–orthodox policy era of 1986–89 coupled with the increased complexity of the tax system. Non–orthodox interventionism in the late 1980s and widespread indexation mechanisms not only distorted relative prices in the economy but also affected the efficiency of tax collection by making the tax system less equitable and tax rates more distorted.

Macroeconomic instability had several impacts on income taxation. *First,* emphasis was placed on vertical progressiveness by increasing the number of income brackets and differentiating the corresponding marginal tax rates. Horizontal progressiveness to create a broader tax base and ensure more fiscal equity was never pursued seriously. *Second,* the collapse of tax revenue with the acceleration of inflation was avoided by a shift towards capital gains in the composition of income tax revenue. With the increase in the share of financial assets in national income during the rise in inflation after 1983, the taxation of capital gains became increasingly complex and changed dramatically. *Third,* the most important changes related to the maturity of financial investments; income taxation was used as a policy instrument to discourage short–term financial investment, particularly overnight applications, which have an important impact on the financial burden of the public debt. To encourage investment in equity, an important exemption in taxation of capital gains is spot market applications. To limit the inflation–related erosion of tax revenue, the collection system changed towards a pay–as–you–earn one under which payments (with indexation) could be made at any time instead of only at the end of the fiscal year.

A key distortion in the tax system was the increase in the selectivity of general consumption taxes, in sharp contrast with international trends. The disproportionate increase in financial revenue and capital gains, with persistent high inflation and the ensuing hypertrophy of the financial/banking sector, encouraged the government to focus on taxing firms' revenue, payroll, and financial transactions. The share in GDP of the IOF has varied a great deal over 1980–96, depending primarily on the rate of inflation (Table 8.7). Excessive taxation through social security contributions levied on payrolls has a negative impact on employment which, together with high statutory severance pay, reduces firms' ability to hire in the formal sector. It also encourages tax evasion and perpetuates informality in the labour market. For contributions levied on firms' gross revenues, the cumulative impact on those revenues depresses industrial competitiveness and, again, encourages tax evasion. Such excessive reliance on taxing gross revenues is distortionary and penalises sectors that are labour–intensive, realise low ratios of profit to gross revenue and have high horizontal integration in production. Finally, indirect tax revenues increased at the federal level while direct tax revenues rose at the municipal level.

The fall in inflation after 1994 reversed the downward trend in total tax revenue. The increase in consumption by low–income groups, given the income effect generated by the fall in inflation, contributed to an increase in the GDP share of consumption taxes. Whereas the revenue of the ICMS increased over 20 per cent as a share of GDP between 1993 and 1994, that of the IPI remained stable at about 2.15 per cent (Table 8.7). An increment in real income with the fall in inflation also had a positive impact on the GDP shares of income taxes and social security contributions (Tables 8.6 and 8.7).

Conclusions and Perspectives

Fiscal federalism in Brazil is institutionally very complex, given the volume of resources at the disposal of SNGs, their high degree of autonomy, and the diversity of tax sharing and transfer arrangements, both negotiated and statutory (Shah, 1990, Afonso, 1989). Sizeable regional and personal income disparities, coupled with a long history of macroeconomic instability and chronic inflation, play a part in endowing Brazilian federalism with additional complicating features which provide valuable lessons to other federations. Reforming the structure of intergovernmental relations towards the decentralisation of expenditure assignments in line with the overall fiscal decentralisation effort in recent years and the removal of potential sources of quasi–fiscal imbalances would ensure equity in taxation and the consolidation of macroeconomic stability.

Macroeconomic stability in Brazil poses the additional difficulty of being pursued and consolidated in a context of fiscal decentralisation and complex intra– and intergovernmental relations. Analysis of both fiscal and quasi–fiscal disequilibria helps to solve the paradox of chronic inflation and moderate nonfinancial deficits and domestic debt as a share of GDP, and hence reinforces the fiscal nature of conventional inflationary processes by incorporating the financial components of inflation. An important source of quasi–fiscal imbalances in Brazil is the weak control of the Union over the finances of SNGs, which stems both from institutional arrangements and constitutional provisions and from insufficient market–imposed financial discipline. Both phenomena limit control by market institutions, and/or intergovernmental co–ordination, of solvency and indebtedness of SNGs.

Rather than underestimating the fiscal efforts of the Brazilian government in recent years, the deterioration of the fiscal stance of the Union since 1995 reflects the loss of quasi–fiscal sources of revenue with the fall in inflation (loss in seignorage revenue, convergence of multiple exchange rates, loss in revenue due to non–remunerated compulsory reserves, etc.), coupled with the rise in various types of quasi–fiscal expenditures (costly bail–outs, high real interest rates, expensive sterilisation of capital inflows, etc.). The importance of fiscal policy in macroeconomic adjustment and the need for fiscal consolidation cannot be underestimated, particularly if the costs associated with excessive reliance on monetary policy are to be minimised and growth resumed on self–sustained grounds.

To consolidate the macroeconomic stability and low inflation of the last three years as self–sustaining, the most important policy recommendations are the following. *First,* in view of recent trends in international economic integration and the creation of trade blocs, policies must promote increased harmonisation of indirect taxes across trading nations. Greater economic integration increases the responsiveness of tax structures and revenue in one country to changes in tax regimes in others. Such considerations affect Brazil today, given the progressive opening of the economy and greater integration within MERCOSUR (Dain, 1995). International competitiveness can rise in a system of indirect taxation that discourages selective, essentially cumulative, multistage taxes on sales and firms' gross revenue. *Second,* at lower rates of inflation, the adoption of a new tax regime based on greater progressiveness in direct taxation to promote horizontal equity, is strongly advocated. Such a tax reform could increase tax bases instead of the number of tax brackets (vertical progressiveness). *Third,* an overall simplification of the social security system and a reduction of the payroll tax burden are recommended to reduce incentives for tax evasion and labour–market informality.

A more stable distribution of negotiated transfers over time and across states would reinforce the principle of horizontal equity and promote more continuity in social programmes in less prosperous states and regions. An erratic flow of resources from such transfers makes it more difficult to finance a steady flow of investment into social areas in regions that need it most. Excessive transfers to lower levels of government also discourage fiscal austerity (Afonso and Souza, 1985).

Finally, to eliminate the sources of quasi–fiscal disequilibria with the consolidation of macroeconomic stability, the liquidation of state–owned financial institutions and incentives towards streamlining the private banking sector are also recommended. To reduce the debt of SNGs, more rigid budgetary restrictions and debt–restructuring programmes should be implemented, making subnational finances more transparent to the Union and private financial institutions. Subnational sources of quasi–fiscal imbalances, such as illiquid state banks and the borrowing requirements of SNGs should be more carefully monitored by the central bank (Ter–Minassian, 1997). Due to political short–termism, the ability of SNGs to contract debt with their own banks (currently prohibited in Brazil, but difficult to monitor) should be limited by the monetary authorities, particularly following the electoral cycle. Given political fragmentation in the Brazilian legislature, it is unlikely that such controls, including limits to SNG borrowing requirements, could find easy agreement among different levels of government. The conduct of fiscal policy in large federations requires a more hierarchical and less collegial framework.

Notes

1. The Federal District has a separate legal status in the constitution. It will be considered here as a state.

2. Quasi–fiscal imbalances are related to the non–fiscal costs of financing fiscal disequilibria. See Easterly *et al.* (1994), Tanzi (1995) and McKenzie (1997), for a more detailed discussion on quasi–fiscal deficits and macroeconomic performance.

3. Brazil is one of the most decentralised federations in the developing world (Shah 1990; 1994). In 1990, over 53 per cent of total public spending was controlled by the federal government, against over 80 per cent in Mexico. In 1992, the figure fell to over 45 per cent of total spending, against over 54 per cent in the case of subnational governments.

4. In March 1990, the Collor administration froze about $100 billion worth of private financial assets as part of a non–orthodox stabilisation plan aimed at controlling inflation.

5. In recent years, the most important spending categories in the federal public sector have been payroll and social security (respectively at 5.6 per cent and 5.3 per cent of GDP in 1995). The latter taken together have exceeded investment provisions, which reinforces the strain on the ability of the public sector to finance investment spending. Investment and fixed capital formation nevertheless increased as a share of subnational spending.

6. Ideally, operational, rather than primary, balances would provide a clearer picture of public dissaving. However, subnational operational balance figures are not available for the whole time span under examination.

7. Given widespread financial market restrictions on domestic credit and international capital flows in the 1980s, and price–wage distortionary policy making in the period, it is unlikely that this direct crowding–out would provide strong evidence of Ricardian Equivalence.

8. Evidence from the United States (where the share of subnational debt to GDP has been stable for decades at around 16 per cent of GDP) suggests that stringency in credit markets limits the issue of subnational debt and strengthens market control of subnational finances. Capital market stringency is reinforced by fierce tax and regulatory competition across states, and limited revenue sharing and equalisation payment across subnational governments, McKinnon (1997).

9. See Weingast *et al.* (1981), for further details.

10. See Tanzi (1991) and Easterly *et al.* (1994), for a more detailed discussion on money creation as a source of revenue for the public sector.

11. See Biasoto and Mussi (1997) for further details of the Brazilian experience.

12. See Hausmann and Rojas–Suarez (1996) for further details and an international comparison of the costs of bailout programmes.

13. See de Mello and Carneiro (1997) for a more detailed discussion on the behaviour of parallel market premia in selected Latin American economies, and Dornbusch (1989) for a survey of the literature on exchange rate determination in developing countries.

14. See Fry (1997) for further details and international comparisons.

15. In fact, to my knowledge, the ICMS is the only case in the world of a consumption tax not levied by the central government. See McLure (1997) for an analysis of VAT taxation in Brazil.

16. Net revenue in the case of banking and financial institutions.

17. Since 1980, the share of total tax revenue accruing to the Union has fallen from over 70 per cent to 60 per cent, while the share of the states has risen from 24 per cent to 30 per cent, and that of the municipalities, from 6 per cent to 10 per cent.

18. The composition of the funds is as follows: FPE (21.5 per cent of IPI and ICMS revenue, each), FPM (22.5 per cent of IPI and IR revenue, each), and FPEX (10 per cent of IPI revenue).

19. Widespread indexation affected mainly the income taxes (IRPF and IRPJ) and a reduction in the time of collection affected mainly the federal consumption tax (IPI), the income tax of salaried workers (IRF), and the social security contributions.

20. For a more detailed discussion, see Silva (1991).

Bibliography

AFONSO, J.R.R. (1989), "Despesas Federais com Transferências Intergovernamentais: Uma Revisão de Conceitos e Diagnóstico", IPEA/INPES Working Paper No. 12.

AFONSO, J.R.R. (1996), "Descentralização Fiscal, Efeitos Macroeconômicos e Função de Estabilização: o Caso (Peculiar) do Brasil", VII Seminário Regional de Política Fiscal, CEPAL.

AFONSO, J.R.R. AND J.C. RAMUNDO (1996), *Notas sobre el Estado Actual del Federalismo Fiscal en Brasil*, Seminário Internacional de Descentralización Fiscal y Regímenes de Coparticipación Impositiva, Universidad Nacional de la Plata, Argentina.

AFONSO, J.R.R. AND M.C. SOUZA (1985), "O Sistema de Relações Financeiras e seu Papel no Financiamento de Estados e Municípios", *Revista de Finanças Públicas*, 362.

DE ALMEIDA, S.C.F. AND C.E.G. CAVALCANTI (1995), "As Contribuições Sociais e a Reforma Tributária", in R.B.A. AFFONSO AND P.L.B. SILVA (eds.), *Federalismo no Brasil: Reforma Tributária e Federação*, FUNDAP/UNESP, São Paulo.

BARRERA, A.W. AND M.L.M. ROARELLI (1995), "Relações Fiscais Intergovernamentais", in R.B.A. AFFONSO AND P.L.B. SILVA (eds.), *Federalismo no Brasil: Reforma Tributária e Federação*, FUNDAP/UNESP, São Paulo.

BENNETT, R.J. (1980), *The Geography of Public Finance*, Methuen, London.

BIASOTTO, G. AND C. MUSSI (1997), "Anos Noventa: de Novo o Déficit Quasi–Fiscal", *Proceedings of the IX Fiscal Policy Regional Seminar*, ECLAC.

DAIN, S. (1995), "Experiência Internacional e Especificidade Brasileira", in R.B.A. AFFONSO AND P.L.B. SILVA (eds.), *Federalismo no Brasil: Reforma Tributária e Federação*, FUNDAP/UNESP, São Paulo.

DIKSHIT, R.D. (1976), *The Political Economy of Fiscal Federalism: An Inquiry into Origins and Stability*, Macmillan, Delhi.

DORNBUSCH, R. (1989), "Real Exchange Rates and Macroeconomics: A Selective Survey", *Scandinavian Journal of Economics*, 91.

EASTERLY, W., C.A. RODRIGUEZ AND K. SCHMIDT–HEBBEL (eds.) (1994), *Public Sector Deficits and Macroeconomic Performance*, Oxford University Press, New York.

FRY, M. (1997), "The Fiscal Abuse of Central Banks", in M.I. BLEJER AND T. TER–MINASSIAN (eds.), *Macroeconomic Dimensions of Public Finance: Essays in Honour of Vito Tanzi,* Routledge, London.

HAUSMANN, R. AND L. ROJAS–SUAREZ (eds.) (1996), *Banking Crises in Latin America,* Inter–American Development Bank, Washington, D.C.

INTERNATIONAL MONETARY FUND, *International Financial Statistics,* various issues.

LIVINGSTONE, W.S. (1956), *Federalism and Institutional Change,* Oxford University Press, London.

MCKENZIE, G.A. (1997), "Quasi–Fiscal Activity of Public Financial Institutions", *Proceedings of the IX Fiscal Policy Regional Seminar,* ECLAC.

MCKINNON, R.I. (1997), *EMU as a Device for Collective Fiscal Retrenchment,* Meeting of the American Economic Association.

MCLURE, C.E., JR (1997), "Topics in the Theory of Revenue Assignment" in M.I. BLEJER AND T. TER–MINASSIAN (eds.), *Macroeconomic Dimensions of Public Finance: Essays in Honour of Vito Tanzi,* Routledge, London.

DE MELLO, L.R., JR AND F.G. CARNEIRO (1997), "The Long–Run Behaviour of Exchange Rates in Brazil, Chile and Argentina: A Cointegration Analysis", *International Review of Economics and Finance,* Vol. 6, No. 1.

OATES, W. (1977), *The Political Economy of Fiscal Federalism,* Heath, Lexington, D.C.

SHAH, A. (1990), "The New Fiscal federalism in Brazil", World Bank Discussion Papers No. 124, World Bank, Washington, D.C.

SHAH, A. (1994), "The Reform of Inter–governmental Fiscal Relations in Developing and Emerging Market Economies", *World Bank Policy and Research Series Paper No. 23,* World Bank, Washington, D.C.

SILVA, M.T. (1991), "Casos de Êxito na Política Fiscal Brasileira", *Série Política Fiscal No. 15,* CEPAL/PNUD, Chile.

TANZI, V. (1991), *Public Finance in Developing Countries,* Edward Elgar, London.

TANZI, V. (1995), "Government Role and the Efficiency of Policy Instruments", International Monetary Fund Working Paper No. 95/100, Washington, D.C.

TER–MINASSIAN, T. (1997), "Financial Management of Government Operations: Selected Macroeconomic and Institutional Aspects", *Proceedings of the IX Fiscal Policy Regional Seminar,* ECLAC.

WEINGAST, B., K. SHEPSLE AND C. JOHNSEN (1981), "The Political Economy of Benefits and Costs: A Neo–Classical Approach to Distributive Politics", *Journal of Political Economy,* 89.

Chapter 9

Conditional Transfers to Promote Local Government Participation: the Case of Mexico

Rafael Gamboa

Introduction[1]

By many standards, Mexico is a very centralised country. Compared to other federal countries (including developing countries), subnational governments (SNGs) in Mexico have responsibility for a smaller fraction of government expenditure (Figure 9.1)[2]. This results mainly from the involvement of the federal government (FG) in functions that would be provided more efficiently by SNGs. The concentration of activities at the federal level reflects two features of the Mexican institutional setting — *first,* an unclear legal assignment of expenditure functions across levels of government, which allows the simultaneous provision of services by governments at different levels; and *second,* a larger share of the collected revenue concentrated in the hands of the FG (Figure 9.2).

If this is an inefficient outcome, why does the FG not delegate fiscal responsibilities to SNGs which could provide better service, probably at a cheaper cost? Despite some progress in education, regional development and health, the SNGs' demand for further decentralisation continues. The problem is that a change in control over an expenditure function potentially represents a different allocation of public funds, and decisions taken by SNGs may not satisfy FG preferences.

SNGs have different priorities than the FG in their expenditure patterns. *First,* they would prefer to increase spending on functions that may create local externalities and spend less on those that generate national benefits. Many local functions have a distributive effect because of the impact they have on poverty reduction, but income distribution is a federal concern (according to Musgrave's classic division). As SNGs have to compete for richer tax bases, they tend to decrease expenditure on local services to the poor and spend on activities complementary to capital. The positive benefits that extend to the rest of the country, associated with a better educated and healthier population, also reduce local expenditure on poverty reduction, an effect particularly important in poorer localities where the more productive workers tend to move to wealthier communities. We see the intrusion of the FG in local functions mainly in activities with an impact on living standards. *Second,* SNGs want to attract as large a share of federally collected revenue as they can through intergovernmental transfers, while the FG would like it to be just enough, even though it does not have enough information about SNGs' provision costs.

Figure 9.1. **International Comparison of Centralisation**

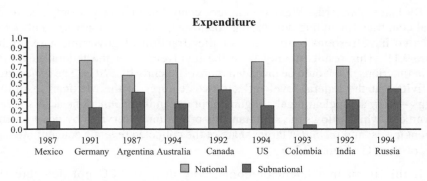

Source: IMF government financial statistics.

In Mexico, most federal transfers resemble block grants. The SNGs may use them for functions the FG wants them to cover; for decreasing local tax collection or for changing the expenditure pattern and thus income distribution. The SNGs benefit from an information asymmetry generated by these multiple objectives. They do not provide information on their expenditures by function, and they demand more transfers to decrease their own taxes despite evidence that they have used part of their proceeds from tax–sharing agreements.

Figure 9.2a. Comparison of Local Expenditures in Education among Selected Countries

Subnational Expenditure in Education in 1990 (per cent)

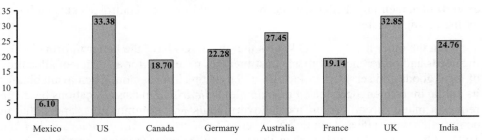

Source: IMF government financial statistics.

Figure 9.2b. Comparison of Local Expenditures in Health among Selected Countries

1990 Health Expenditures by Local Governments (percentage)

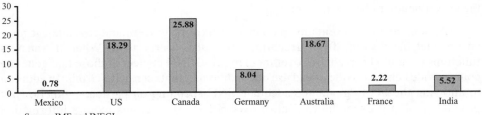

Source: IMF and INEGI.

In the presence of multiple uses of federal transfers, and in the absence of information on the costs of providing SNG services, it has been difficult to determine an adequate level of federal transfers. The tax–sharing grant is divided among the SNGs using an objective formula that can be changed only with the agreement of both parties. In negotiating the level of tax sharing, budget deficits have been used implicitly to determine whether the transfers meet SNG needs. The FG reacted to the appearance of persistent deficits in most states by increasing transfers in 1990, 1994, and 1996, and also by negotiating a change in the formula to include population, along with a timetable to gradually increase its weight. The population factor probably tries to link the transfers to SNG costs. On their side, SNGs have presented their deficits as evidence of the insufficiency of existing transfers, and have requested an increase in transfers instead of asking for a change in the formula to cover their costs. Even poor states, which for other purposes complain that rich ones ought to compensate them for an unequal distribution of federal investment, ask for more money rather than for reformulation. Contrary to information about expenditures by function, SNGs eagerly reveal their budget and debt figures[3]. In this situation, the decentralisation of functions to SNGs could lead to less expenditure on those goods and services whose benefits extend out of their jurisdictions, while the FG could lose fiscal control over expenditures by increasing transfers.

On the other hand, the FG knows that the SNGs have the better information on the needs and preferences of local constituencies necessary for an efficient allocation of local goods and services. In fact, the FG uses this information, when available, for its public investment decisions. For example, *Solidaridad* makes allocations based on requests made directly from local governments and communities, and plans in conjunction with state and municipal governments (*Program Nacional de Solidaridad*, 1994)[4]. Other federal agencies follow this type of planning in their investment decisions. The FG, by decentralising functions in which local information is important, could attain a more efficient allocation of goods and services, as it would *i)* save resources in information–gathering activities; *ii)* assign responsibility for service deficiency and insufficiency (particularly important in the relatively new context of conflicting political parties at different levels of government); and *iii)* satisfy the preferences of the constituency rather than federal agents.

As long as the FG remains in control of most of government revenues, it must ensure that the benefits from decentralisation also accrue to it. When it transfers functions it should keep control over them to avoid SNG neglect of those that generate countrywide benefits. Widespread use of conditional grants can achieve this. In addition to allowing the FG to guarantee adequate SNG spending on particular functions, it provides tools for expenditure control over SNGs. Such grants require information on the expenditures they are conditioned on, which can be used for cost estimation and yardstick competition or other cost–reducing incentive schemes. By separating expenditures, the FG can limit possible revenue insufficiencies to particular functions. The transfers could be matching grants that can increase local tax–collection effort by requiring local contributions, while the problem of dwindling local tax collections can be addressed through the tax–sharing agreement (Gramlich, 1977). Conditional grants could also provide incentives for SNGs to decrease provision costs, e.g. by increasing the matching rate for SNGs with lower costs.

This paper starts by reviewing the current fiscal assignment of expenditure and revenue functions in Mexico. For the former, it shows that Mexico's legal design allows SNGs to take most responsibilities but the assignment is unclear, which leaves the door open for the FG to take part in functions more efficiently provided by local governments. It also shows the bias already noted in the information that SNGs provide: a lack of information on expenditure by function at the state and municipal levels and ample data on their persistent deficits and increasing indebtedness. The description of the division of revenue sources and the system of intergovernmental transfers reveals that the SNGs have access to many small tax bases which generate poor cumulative collections, while the FG controls the broader and richer ones. The FG compensates lower–level governments mainly through the federal block grants programme[5]. The total size of the transfers increased to compensate states that lost out when the sharing formula was changed. The formula started with fixed coefficients. The states' shares then increased twice — once according to their economic activity and again with the federal taxes they collected; recently the formula has incorporated population. The persistence of state deficits is likely to create further changes.

The analysis moves on to evaluate the problem of centralisation as one of reconciling different government preferences. The level of government that controls revenues will keep control over expenditure functions in which preferences are different, even if that is inefficient for the country as a whole. In Mexico, the FG has been able to interfere in SNG activities because of the legal void and because it has more revenue. For decentralisation to proceed, the FG has to make sure that its priorities are satisfied. Therefore, state and municipal governments must devote enough resources to national services and provide good information on their expenditure levels, so that the FG can determine the adequacy of its transfers to meet SNG functions. Using conditional grants as mentioned above would achieve this objective, as is argued in the final policy recommendations.

Mexican Fiscal Expenditure Assignment

The Introduction established in international comparisons two bases on which one can consider Mexico as relatively centralised — its lower share of SNG expenditures in total government outlays and the involvement of the FG in delivering services often provided at lower levels in other federations (see Figures 9.1 and 9.2)[6]. This condition neither depends on nor associates with income or development levels, as can be seen by looking at both OECD and non–OECD countries[7]. To see whether Mexico can gain from decentralisation, the analysis here first determines which functions should be lower–level responsibilities and then compares them with actual assignments.

Mexico has three layers of government: federal, state, and municipal. Because the primary difference among levels of government is their geographical range, the literature has looked at the geographical characteristics of government functions. This type of analysis follows Musgrave's classification (following the incentives at each level for efficient provision), which allocates functions to different levels depending on the spatial characteristics of the public goods. These features are explained in greater detail in Shah (1994). The expenditure functions (services) are taken from Shah (1990, 1994). Table 9.1 assigns each function to a level of government according to the concept of *subsidiarity*. This principle assigns the service to that authority for which externalities are internalised, when it is possible to separate production from provision of the service (see Inman and Rubinfeld, 1993)[8]. The optimal assignment appears in the last column, while the previous column shows the authority that would regulate the activity (the level at which the good is public)[9].

Table 9.1. **Division of Functions**

Public service	Type of public good	Externalities	Economies of scale	Economies of scope	Preferred good	Regulating authority	Providing authority
National defence	F	F	F	F	F	F	F
International relations	F	F	F	F	F	F	F
International trade	F	F	F	F	F	F	F
Monetary policy	F	F	F	F	F	F	F
Interstate trade	F	F	F	F	F	F	F
Natural resources	F	F	F	F	F	F	F
Industrial policy	F	F	F	F	F	F	F
National statistics	F	F	F	F	F	F	F
Post service	F	M	F	F	F	F	F
Border and federal police	F	F	F	F	F	F	F
Special police	F,E	F	F,E	F,E	E	F,E	F,E
Income distribution	F	F	M	M	F	F	F
Regional develop.	F	F	M	F	E,M	F	E,M
Airlines and trains	F,E	F	F	F	E	F	F,E
Ecology	F,E,M	F,E,M	M	F,E	M	F,E	F,E,M
National parks	F	F,E	E	F,E	F,E	F,E	F,E
Ind. and agricult.	F,E	F,E	F	F,E	E	F	F,E,M
Education	M	F,E	F	F,E,M	M	F,E	F,E,M
Health	M	F,E	F,M	F,E,M	M	F,E	F,E,M
Water use	M	F	M	F	F	F	E,M
Housing	M	E	E	E,M	E	F,E	E,M
Hospitals	M	E	F,E	E	E	F,E	E,M
Culture	M	E	E	E	E	E,M	E,M
Water supply	M	M	E	E	M	E,M	E,M
Sewerage	M	M	E	E	M	E,M	E,M
Local transit	M	E,M	E,M	E,M	M	E,M	M
Public libraries	M	E,M	E,M	E,M	M	M	E,M
Firemen	M	M	M	M	M	M	M
Local police	M	M	M	M	M	M	M
Parks	M	M	M	M	M	M	M
Street repair	M	M	M	M	M	M	M
Waste disposal	M	M	M	M	M	M	M
Street lighting	M	M	M	M	M	M	M
Air pollution	M	M	M	M	M	M	M
Slaughterhouses	M	M	M	M	M	M	M
Markets	M	M	M	M	M	M	M
Cemeteries	M	M	M	M	M	M	M
Highways							
Interstate	M	F	E	F,E	F	F	F.E
State	M	E	E	E	E	E	E

Note: (F) means federal level, (E) state and (M) municipal.

162

Mexican legal assignment is clear and coincides with the theoretical framework on the assignment of expenditure functions and tax bases to the federal and municipal levels. It is vague about what belongs to the state level, however, and such a wide scope in assignment actually works to limit the performance of SNGs. The federal level interferes in functions where its responsibility is not explicitly mentioned. SNGs barely participate in functions provided together with the FG, as the National Congress assigns most of the services to the wealthier federal level (Figure 9.2).

Besides thwarting state participation in expenditure functions, this lack of clarity leaves the final assignment subject to the interpretation of the authority distributing revenues or in charge of solving conflicts among levels. This authority hitherto has been the National Congress, which is perceived as following orders from the federal executive[10]. With the recent reform of the judiciary, the Supreme Court could potentially decide the fiscal arrangement based on poorly determined constitutional boundaries. Table 9.2 illustrates the relative importance of the federal level under the present arrangement. The large participation of the federal level in infrastructure expenditures also shows the federal level intervening in state responsibilities[11].

Table 9.2. **Comparison of Expenditures of Government Levels**

Type	Federal government[a]			State governments			Municipal governments		
	A	(type/ A)	(A/A+B+C)	B	(type/B)	(B/A+B+C)	C	(type/C)	(C/A+B+C)
	Billion pesos	% of expense	Fraction by level	Billion pesos	% of expenses	Fraction by level	Billion pesos	% of expenses	Fraction by level
Total[b]	58 381	100	62	26 218	100	28	9 520	100	10
Administrative	33 086	56	65	11 918	45	24	5 761	61	11
Investment[c]	19 638	34	66	7 375	28	25	2 621	28	9

a. Two factors are excluded from federal expenditure for the comparisons. First, federal expenditure on interest payments is much larger than debt payments made by other levels since the FG has greater access to credit markets and it performs the stabilisation function. Second, federal transfers to other levels are larger than those provided by any other level.
b. Expenditures on interest payments by the federal level and transfers by the three levels are excluded to compare resource allocations on similar concepts. Therefore other types of expenditures that are not compatible are not presented explicitly but are included in the total.
c. This comes from *Gasto de capital* for the federal level and *Obras públicas y de fomento* for state and municipal levels.
Source: INEGI, *Finanzas Publicos Estatades y Municipales*; Appendix 2 explains the adjustment made for the comparisons of this table.

Table 9.3 compares the *de facto* and theoretical Mexican expenditure assignments. Information on expenditures by function exists for the federal level but not for the state and municipal levels; the data on services at these levels come from available information on functions for which these governments charge fees[12]. This table shows that municipalities perform only their prescribed functions. SNGs take the functions that the fiscal federalism literature recommends, but the states also participate in areas that Table 9.1 assigns to the municipal level. This could result from the small size of many municipalities, in population, income level or geography. Poor municipalities require state support to provide services, while others are so scarcely populated or have such a small territory that state service provision generates economies of scale[13]. The most important deviation from the theoretical assignment comes at the federal level; the FG is involved in more activities than Table 9.1 prescribes. This interference comes mainly through the National Solidarity Programme because the services provided by the local levels have a strong impact on people's living standards and, as Musgrave argued, the distributive function should be a federal responsibility.

Table 9.3. **Functions Undertaken by Different Levels**

Public Service	Regulatory level	Providing level	According to framework	Public service	Regulatory level	Providing level	According to framework
National defence	F	F	F	Culture	F,E,M	F,E,M	E,M
International relations	F	F	F	Local trade	F,E,M	F,E,M	M[a]
International trade	F	F	F	City planning	F,E,M	F,E,M	M
Monetary policy	F	F	F	Water service	F,E,M	F,E,M	E,M
Interstate trade	F	F	F	Sewerage	F,E,M	F,E,M	E,M
Natural resources	F	F,E	F	Transit	E,M	E,M	M
Industrial policy	F	F	F	Public transportation	E,M	E,M	E,M
National statistics	F	F	F	Libraries	M	M	E,M
Postal service	F	F	F	Firemen	M	M	M
Federal and border police	F	F	F	Local police	E,M	M	M
Special police	F,E	F,E	F,E	Parks	M	M	M
Distribution	F	F	F	Streets	F,M	F,M	M
Regional development	F	F,E,M	F,E,M	Waste disposal and cleaning	M	M	M
Airlines and Trains	F	F,E	F,E	Public lighting	E,M	E,M	M
Ecology	F,E	F,E,M	F,E,M	Air pollution	M	M	M
Industry and agriculture	F,E	F,E,M	F,E,M	Cemeteries	E,M	E,M	M
Education	F,E	F,E,M	F,E,M	Markets	M	M	M
Health	F	F,E,M	F,E,M	Slaughterhouses	M	M	M
Water use	F,E	F,E,M	E,M	Highways			
Housing	F,E	F,E	E,M	Intestate	F	F.E	F,E
Hospitals	F	F	E,M	State	F,E	F,E	E
National parks	F,E	F,E	F,E				

a.   Local trade, zoning, street cleaning and waste disposal only appear in this table as they are the services on which governments collect charges. These are municipal services.

Revenue Sources across Levels of Government

On the revenue side, state and municipal governments have few tax bases they can use efficiently and at low administrative cost; the FG exploits the broadest and richest tax bases. The FG therefore must transfer part of its tax collections to local governments, which makes them heavily dependent on these grants and allows the FG to interfere with local functions. Bird (1992) argues that the tax bases efficient and simple to administer by local governments are few and poor. Local taxation creates several distortions, such as tax exportation and externalities (Inman and Rubinfeld, 1993). This precludes SNGs from imposing ideal–benefit taxation, in which communities face a clear link between service provision and cost.

With high factor mobility, tax externalities could have a sizeable impact, as small changes in rates affect other SNGs. Tax exportation is a major concern for goods produced in few locations around the country, in which case the location of factors would hardly depend on local taxes — hence the prescription to assign to the federal level the taxation of natural resources and other goods with site–specific locations (because of tax exportation) and of factors with elastic supply (because of tax externalities). Additionally, because taxes on people or corporate incomes require information about transactions taking place in several locations within the country, the FG, which has this knowledge, can better assess this tax base. This is also the case with value added taxes, which require cross–referencing of information from different points in the country. Economies of scale also favour assignment to the federal level, because it is essential to handle the information in a single administrative location.

The tax structure also reflects distributive and stabilisation concerns, federal functions according to Musgrave, adding more tax bases to the federal level. Tanzi (1995) stresses the importance of the federal level because the stabilisation problem that most developing countries face is a national rather than regional one; national co–ordination is more important than decentralised policy making. Macroeconomic stability sometimes requires drastic changes in public finances (as in Mexico, at least in 1982, 1988 and 1995). The larger the portion controlled by the FG, the more likely stabilisation is to be successful. Local governments often create fiscal problems for the FG by running deficits they cannot cover (Bomfim and Shah, 1994). All of these considerations have been taken into account in the design of the Mexican revenue structure, which is fairly centralised as a result (Figure 9.1).

To take advantage of decentralised provision, the system must transfer resources from the richer federal tax bases to local governments. Yet a transfer system could itself be inefficient. Federal grants should be large enough, together with local tax revenues, for local governments to perform their functions. To the extent that grants fail to satisfy this objective, they will promote misuse of public funds because resources are wasted, rich communities enjoy lower tax rates, or the funds cannot cover local expenses. Problems associated with inappropriate amounts of transfers could also impose distortions on local government allocation of public resources. The FG may use transfers as instruments to achieve national goals. A well designed distribution formula could eliminate local tax distortions, provide incentives to internalise externalities, improve income distribution, or help to stabilise the economy. Table 9.4 shows the current division of tax bases among levels of government, which, for the most part, is consistent with the theoretical framework. It assigns the richest and broadest tax bases to the federal level. State revenues have remained fairly constant in real terms for the last 15 years, but with an important change in the revenue components. Figure 9.3 shows an increase in federal transfers and a decline in direct, state–collected revenues — but

Table 9.4. **Division of Tax Bases According to Revenue Laws**

Federal tax bases	State tax bases	Municipal tax bases
Income	Shows and entertainment	Property
Firms assets	Lotteries and allowed gambling	Patrimonial transmissions
Special over production and	Motion pictures	Property acquisition, transmission
value added	Payrolls	Zoning
Foreign trade	Wage income	Empty yards
Property acquisition	Professional services	Residential developments
Vehicle possession and use	Honoraria	Property improvements
New cars	Sale of second-hand vehicles	Property establishment
Oil benefits	Sale of second-hand mobile	Shows and entertainment
Accessories	Vehicle possession and use	Lotteries and allowed gambling
Telephone services	Commercial or industrial activities	Commercial or industrial,
Public services provided using	Unclassified outlets	Commercial activities and
	Editorial business	professions
	Benefit of construction materials	Private and decentralised education
	transmission of property over	Non-combustion vehicles
	property	Sale of second-hand vehicles
	Patrimonial transmissions	Advertisements in the public way
	Notary public functions	Assistance to games and shows
	Public instruments and contractual	Public instruments and contractual
	Parking lots	Urban public transportation
	Construction works supervision	Additional
	Residential developments and	Exceptional
	production damages	
	Additional	
	Private education	
	Urban public transport	
	Penalties	

Source: Federal, state and municipal revenue laws for 1994 (compilation made by INDETEC).

Figure 9.3. **Composition of State Revenues**

1993 Pesos (billions)

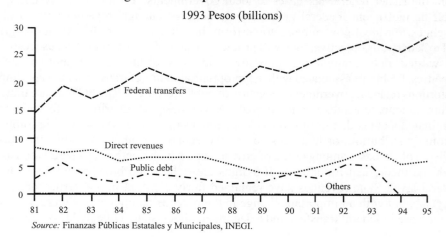

Source: Finanzas Públicas Estatales y Municipales, INEGI.

not all direct revenue components have declined; user charges (*derechos*) show a slight increase (Figure 9.4). In 1990, federal transfers reached 70 per cent of non–debt state revenues, while none of the other sources constituted a significant fraction of the total (Figure 9.5).

By agreement among the three levels of government, the federal level shares its tax collections with local levels. The National System of Fiscal Co–ordination (*Sistema de Coordinación Fiscal*, SCF) took effect in 1980 to expand tax collection and reduce production distortions arising from double taxation. Under this agreement, states exchanged their tax bases over income, production and sales for larger transfers. The SCF attained its objective because total resources available to federal and local governments have increased over the life of the programme by 30 per cent in real terms. Although the fraction of federal revenues transferred to state and local governments has increased, federal revenues as a proportion of total government revenues have remained almost constant.

A major problem emerged from the SCF's failure to provide a link between state needs and revenues, because it extended the federal transfers (the tax–sharing transfers) based on the share of tax collections each state had in 1979. Although the formula has changed to include population size, it still provides larger transfers to states with richer tax bases[14]. Furthermore, in per capita terms, the transfers increase with state income much faster than average wages (a proxy for public service costs). This allows SNGs with richer tax bases to provide better or more services than poor ones, preserving regional disparities and necessitating further participation of the FG in the provision of distributive goods. The loss of connection between transfers and costs presents a problem given the importance of this source of revenue to SNGs. The FG has an implicit obligation to cover SNGs' costs, but it does not know them. SNGs have incentives to overlook possible expenditure–reducing policies because the cost of raising revenues is mainly paid by the FG. The SCF started a process that has benefited the state level; the share states receive from the federal level steadily increased from 18.45 per cent in 1980 to 22.72 per cent in 1994. Table 9.5 describes the evolution of the SCF.

Table 9.5. **Summary of the History of the SCF**

Year	Characteristics	Share of Fund
1980-83	The share is equal to the fraction of state collections in 1979.	18.45
1984-86	The formula considers the economic development and collection efforts by the states. The *Fondo Financiero Complementario* (FFC) increases.	18.85
1987	The FFM becomes a fraction of the fund. Incentives to collect value added taxes.	19.25
1988-89	The contingency reserve guarantees revenues at 1987 levels.	20.51
1990-94	The formula includes the FFC and uses the population factor for sharing. Creates the *Fondo de Reordenamiento Urbano*.	22.72

Source: SHCP.

Figure 9.4. **State Direct Revenues**

1993 Pesos (billions)

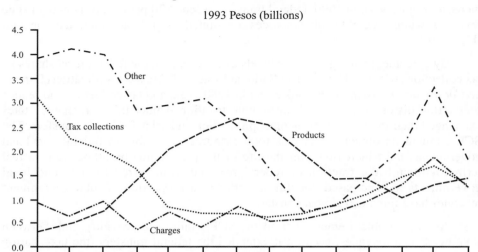

Source: Finanzas Públicas Estatales y Municipales, INEGI.

Figure 9.5. **Composition of State Revenues in 1990**

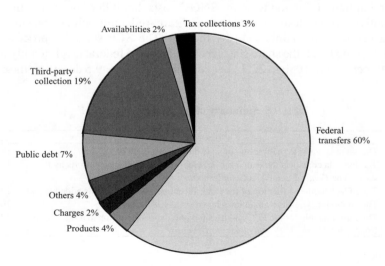

Source: Finanzas Públicas Estatales y Municipales, INEGI.

Under equalisation transfers, federal grants would show a negative correlation with state fiscal capacity, but in Mexico richer states receive larger transfers[15]. Yet poor states do not demand a change, and neither opposition by rich states nor uncertainty about the benefits of a new formula provide strong enough reasons to explain this behaviour. The controversy over the appropriate size of the transfer fund solves this puzzle; states compete for more resources from the federal level rather than dispute among themselves. Disputes arise over the total size of the tax–sharing fund (which as a result has increased constantly for the past 15 years), with little discussion of objective criteria for dividing it. Even so, the transfers have not covered costs and the states have accumulated debt at an unsustainable pace during the past seven years, with commercial banks the major lenders. Since 1988 the debt has grown 62 per cent in real terms (Figure 9.6) to cover the sharp increase in state expenditures (Figure 9.7).

Figure 9.6. **Real State Debt**

1993 Pesos (billions)

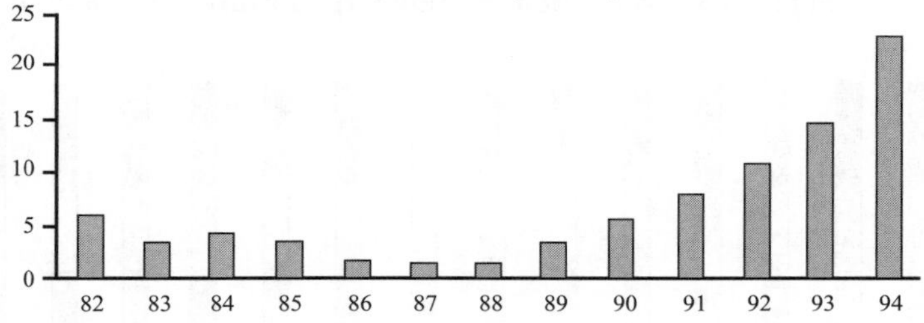

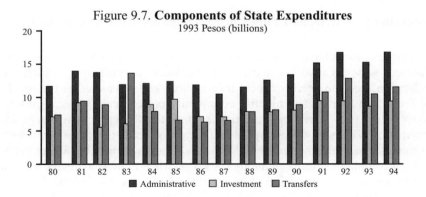

Source: Banxico.

Figure 9.7. **Components of State Expenditures**

1993 Pesos (billions)

The constitution authorises states to accumulate debt only to finance productive investments. Yet the data show that increased debt has not raised state revenues. Perhaps borrowing has covered higher costs of providing services or made up for decreased revenues. Due to the lack of data on expenditure by function, and because the available information does not show a change in any particular type of expenditure (Figure 9.8), one cannot determine if cost increases have caused these persistent deficits. Furthermore, debt accumulation is not correlated with the sources of state revenues (federal or direct); overborrowing is not exclusive to states with less revenue[16]. One simply cannot establish responsibility in this debt accumulation episode. A structural solution cannot be based on trend projections of current expenditures and revenues. It is necessary to clarify the functions performed by the different levels to determine responsibility. If the deficits arise from higher costs, higher transfers are in order; if they derive from poor or deceitful administrations, higher transfers will simply increase an already inefficient allocation of resources.

Figure 9.8. **Proportion of State Expenditure Components**

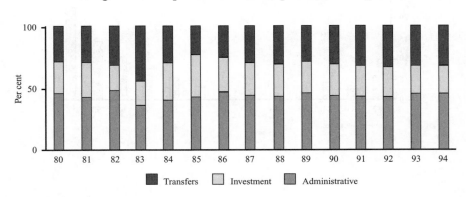

Transferring Functions and Funds in Exchange for Cost Information

Different levels have different abilities to absorb allocated functions. Providing government services involves a trade–off between co–ordination, which requires centralisation, and the need for local information, better handled at the local level. Local levels can more easily identify community preferences for local goods. They can react faster to new needs and save higher authorities from processing large amounts of information. The basis for taking subsidiarity into account is: favour state and local governments when information about local conditions is important. Where the actions of an SNG complement those of another SNG — when there is a greater need for co–ordination because the provision affects many states — prefer federal direction. For many functions the separation among levels becomes difficult, as Table 9.1 shows. Which level should take charge of these functions? The variation across countries demonstrates that no obvious answer exists. The particular conditions each level faces

170

translate into different preferences for the provision of these functions; public allocation of funds varies depending on the level that provides the function. As the need for co–ordination increases, these preferences tend to diverge. Local authorities tend to ignore complementarities and externalities, while it becomes more expensive for federal agents to acquire local demand information.

The assignment of functions depends on who decides the assignment. The FG, the SNGs, and a benevolent central planner would hold different opinions. Table 9.1 presented the central planner's allocation. The current Mexican division, because of its revenue centralisation, perhaps reveals the FG's preferences[17]. When a function is not legally assigned to a specific level, the level with the richer tax base will keep it to meet its own priorities. The history of the fiscal structure determines the possible reforms (Bird, 1992; Quigley, 1993). In Mexico, the evolution of institutional arrangements has benefited the FG at the expense of the SNGs. As the preferences of the two levels diverge, the FG tends to keep the function rather than delegate it (Armstrong, 1994). This explains the high degree of centralisation in Mexico and the division of expenditure functions. Yet having control over a function and providing the service are two different things. Mechanisms exist to transfer functions without relinquishing control, but first it is important to see where such transfers benefit the FG.

The advantages of delegation are, *first,* that provision could accord with local market information, and, *second,* that separating responsibilities could facilitate more powerful incentive schemes. The advantage of decentralisation over integrated provision is a better match between local preferences and services provided, with savings on gathering and processing information. In its allocation decisions, the Mexican FG recognises the superiority of the SNGs in providing local information because it does investment planning together with them, but the final outcome is a federal responsibility. The mechanism creates distortions because local governments negotiate for funds while trying to satisfy federal preferences over expenditures in SNG–preferred activities. At the bargaining table, these governments overstate the needs which reflect federal concerns to attract more resources, attempting to shape federal programmes according to their own priorities.

The federal level attempts to overcome this difficulty in two ways. *First,* each federal agency negotiates separately on behalf of the federal level. *Second,* the FG encourages the states to provide part of the funding for state activities, in order to evaluate their need for federal funds. The discretion involved in these procedures does not align the preferences of the two levels or extract all states' private information. Instead, negotiation costs multiply, the SNGs receive weak incentives to search for better investment projects for which they do not pay the costs and the states end up encouraging their preferred activities in any case.

Many problems of decentralisation can be solved by using conditional grants, where the funds are allocated to the function favoured by the FG on the basis of an objective formula. Decentralising responsibilities through such an objective system of transfers conditioned on service delivery could use private information to elicit better performance. In functions which involve simultaneous provision by federal and state governments (and local advantage), the additional benefit of a clear assignment of responsibility in case of service deficiency or insufficiency could emerge. This would allow strong incentive schemes. The benefit of a clear assignment is frequently neglected by those who blame lack of accountability on the absence of locally generated revenues. In Mexico, several thousand demands for local services were addressed directly to the federal level, through Solidarity. The blame for local community demands not met could go to any of the three levels. The clear assignment of responsibilities becomes particularly important now that different political parties are running different levels of government and politics may start to jeopardise local service provision.

Concluding Remarks and Policy Recommendation

Mexico is relatively centralised. State and local levels decide over a lower share of government expenditure than in other federal countries. The federal level intervenes in many functions that could be efficiently provided at the state or local level. On the revenue side, state and local levels depend heavily on federal grants, which limits their ability to adjust revenues to expenditure needs.

Created in 1980, the SCF transfers federally collected revenues to local governments. The system has successfully increased total government revenues, but tax sharing among different levels of government has created other problems. *First,* revenues are not distributed according to government needs and seem insufficient to cover provision costs. *Second,* by giving up part of their tax bases, the states became particularly dependent on these transfers. Because the division of expenditure functions is not clearly determined, the assignment of most expenditure functions has gone to the FG, the level with enough resources to finance these activities. Under these conditions, improvements toward decentralisation depend on the advantages that the FG sees in delegating functions to other levels. When local levels have access to information on community needs and preferences, local governments can make a more efficient allocation of public funds. For the FG, collecting this information is costlier and the problems of processing all the information even greater. Therefore, the FG would gain from transferring functions that require large amounts of local information.

The FG has two concerns with SNG provision. *First,* for some services the interests of the SNG and the FG do not coincide. The FG interferes with lower levels in those functions with some nationwide characteristics. FG participation allows it to impose its preferences on public allocations for these services. The *second* concern is more specific to the Mexican context. States have accumulated large debts which cannot be traced to any specific cause as there is no good information to assess the origin of their recurrent deficits. Because of their dependence on federal transfers, the FG has reacted by increasing the fraction of its revenues it transfers to the states (with, recently, some effort to link transfers and costs). The FG suspects that by transferring more functions it will lose all its control over revenues, as local functions would also be financed through the SCF.

Decentralisation of more functions does not have to proceed along these lines. Other types of transfer could finance local service provision and align local preferences with national interests. The current system of transfers covers only local functions (those currently under the control of states and municipalities), using a formula that closes the gap between local revenues and service costs by taking into account local tax bases as indicators of revenue capacity and population as an indicator of need[18]. To finance functions with externalities or those that improve income distribution, conditional grants should be used. For national goods, those with a distributive character, a per capita transfer that guarantees a minimum level would be appropriate, while a matching grant could guarantee that externalities are internalised. If transfers are made conditional on acceptable provision by the local government, the FG would guarantee its interests and receive the relevant information. If transfers are made conditional on expenditure by function, lower levels would have to provide information on such expenditure. State and municipal governments must improve their accounting practices and their release of financial information.

A federalist structure in which local governments act independently requires revenue and cost projections as well as transparent information about the use of public funds. This is important to improve accountability and, as the recent indebtedness problem of the states shows, to define whether more transfers are required. Transfers should not be discretionary but proceed from an objective formula that matches nationally adequate levels of provision with the states' capacity to raise revenues for each function. Currently in Mexico, federal agencies use local information for their planning, but in negotiations between the FG and SNGs the SNGs provide biased information to obtain more funds. Because the responsibility is not completely theirs, these governments have weak incentives to gather information relevant to proper decisions.

The following tables are mentioned in notes 14, 15 and 16.

Table 9.6. **Federal Transfer Funds**

Fund	Sharing Formula
General de Participaciones (General Transfers Fund)	45.17 per cent according to the number of inhabitants.
	45.17 per cent according to the increase in federal tax collections over vehicles and special bases multiplied by the share received during the previous year.
	9.66 per cent in inverse proportion to what was collected in per capita terms according to the other two criteria.
De Fomento Municipal (Municipal Development Fund)	Increase in property taxes and water user charges collections multiplied by the share received during the previous year.
Reserva de Contingencia (Contingency Reserve)	Guarantees that states receive the equivalent of their previous year's grant.

For this system to work better, it must have a clear assignment of responsibilities, with local public services provided exclusively by local governments. The FG should concentrate on other functions without interfering in municipal and state responsibilities. It should persist and even increase its participation in the distribution function; but it also should restrict itself to progressive taxation and fund transfers that allow all regions to provide optimal services with national characteristics, leaving expenditure decisions to the states and allowing them to take responsibility for their decisions.

Table 9.7. **Federal Transfers Distribution and Direct State Revenues**

Year	Dependent Variable	Independent Variables	Coefficient	t-statistic
1980	log of per capita federal transfers	Constant	-4.856	-6.664
		log of per capita state GNP	1.378	4.913
1985	log of per capita federal transfers	Constant	-2.712	-5.505
		log of per capita state GNP	0.632	3.111
1992	log of per capita federal transfers	Constant	-2.359	-9.086
		log of per capita state GNP	0.589	5.383
1980	log of per capita direct revenues	Constant	-4.983	-4.563
		log of per capita state GNP	1.369	2.800
		log of per capita federal transfers	-0.184	-1.182
1992	log of per capita direct revenues	Constant	-4.288	-6.027
		log of per capita state GNP	0.9263	4.255
		log of per capita federal transfers	0.27107	0.767

Note: Results from OLS regressions using the White heteroskedastic robust procedure.

Table 9.8. **Regressions on State Debt**

Dependent variable	Independent variable	Coefficient in 1	t-statistic in 1	Coefficient in 2	t-statistic in 2
Outstanding debt	Constant	0.045	1.598	-0.019	-0.844
	Federal transfers	-0.016	-0.147	-0.063	-0.926
	Direct revenues	0.100	1.356	0.118	2.183
	GNP	0.000	-0.675	1.829	1.338
Change in real	Constant	0.084	1.208	0.022	-1.024
direct revenues	Own revenues (-1)	0.700	1.387	0.202	2.172
	Debt (-1)	-119.05	-1.571	-24.26	-1.271
	Debt (-2)	-100.94	-1.237	-14.97	-0.616
	Debt (-3)	12.74	-0.166	-197.15	-2.180

Note: Coefficient in 1 means 1991 data, and in 2 1992 data for the dependent variable and those for which a lag is not specified.
The number in parenthesis shows the number of lags that the independent variable has with respect to the dependent one.

174

Notes

1. Thanks are due to Raul Livas, John Quigley and Daniel Rubinfeld for helpful suggestions.

2. In this paper, unless otherwise specified, the term *subnational governments* (SNGs) represents all the governments not at the federal level, which is the highest level in the country. The government at this level is called the *federal government* (FG).

3. This was the case when the FG proposed to change Article 9 of the *Ley de Coordinación Fiscal*, which requires SNGs to provide debt information.

4. *Solidaridad* is the name of the federal programme for poverty reduction and regional development that operated between 1989 and 1994. Previous and existing federal programmes use SNG information in similar ways (SPP, 1988). Starting in 1996, half of the funds for regional development are provided as block grants.

5. These grants constitute the *Sistema de Coordinación Fiscal*, a tax sharing agreement between the FG and SNGs, and are called federal transfers.

6. Military expenditures are excluded from these numbers. This is a federal expenditure that varies with factors unrelated to the division of functions among levels of government.

7. In Mexico, local governments have more expenditure decision power than under unitary governments. For example, in Chile the central government is in charge of 91.62 per cent of total expenditures, while in Spain it has control over 88 per cent. The latter case is particularly striking, because the degree of political independence of the provincial governments is not matched by their economic responsibilities.

8. In those cases in which the separation is impossible, the table uses the criterion coming from the decentralisation theorem of Oates (1972) which assigns the service to the lowest level for which there are no externalities, at which the benefits of the good are exhausted, and which can produce the service without incurring higher costs.

9. Provided that the existent fiscal gap regulation could be implemented through pecuniary incentives, the regulatory authority should be involved in the financing of the function.

10. *The Economist* in its 28 October 1995 issue calls it a "rubber–stamp congress".

11. Investment expenditure by SNGs in centralised, developed countries amounts to 68 per cent of the total in France and 55 per cent in the United Kingdom; in federal, developing countries it is 60 per cent in India, 65 per cent in Brazil and 49 per cent in Argentina. On the other hand, Mexico is ahead of centralist developing countries like Chile where it is ten per cent.

12. This information is taken from the 1993 revenue laws of the states and the 1994 revenue laws of municipalities. It is based on the revenue concepts extracted by INDETEC (1994). The functions of the federal government are taken from the "Sexto Informe de Gobierno de Carlos Salinas de Gortari" and the "Informe sobre el Programa Nacional de Solidaridad". It is worth mentioning that the existence of a fee does not show the degree of participation of the level in the function. On the other hand, it is possible for a government to provide a service for no fee.

13. The extreme example is the State of Oaxaca, which divides its 36 275 square miles among 570 municipalities.

14. Table 9.6 describes the sharing formula.

15. Table 9.7 shows that federal transfers have a significant and positive correlation with State GDP and that direct revenues also present this type of correlation.

16. Table 9.8 presents regressions of debt accumulation with several variables.

17. The SNGs' opinion was presented in the 1995 meeting of state secretaries of finance. Five central states of Mexico, which constitute Fiscal Zone 5, suggested that the federal level would only keep international matters and national defence.

18. This indicator has the advantage of being objective, reduces rent–seeking activities, and is available annually, which makes it flexible.

Bibliography

ARMSTRONG, M. (1994), "Delegation and Discretion". Discussion Papers in Economics and Econometrics, No. 9421, University of Southampton.

BIRD, R. (1992), *Tax Policy and Economic Development,* Johns Hopkins University Press, Baltimore.

BOMFIM, A. AND A. SHAH, (1994), "Macroeconomic Management and the Division of Powers in Brazil: Perspectives for the 1990s", *World Development*, 22.

GRAMLICH, E.M. (1977), "Inter–governmental Grants: A Review of The Empirical Literature", in W. OATES (ed.), *The Political Economy of Fiscal Federalism*, Lexington, MA.

IMF, *Government Financial Statistics*, various issues.

INDETEC (1994), *Revista Hacienda Municipal*. No. 49, December.

INMAN, R.P. AND D.L. RUBINFELD (1993), "Designing Tax Policy in Federalist Economies: An Overview", mimeo, Stanford University.

OATES, W. (1972), *Fiscal Federalism*, Harcourt, Brace, Jovanovich, Inc., New York.

QUIGLEY, J.M. (1993), "Fiscal Federalism and Economic Development: A Theoretical Review", mimeo. University of California, Berkeley.

SHAH, A. (1990), "The New Fiscal Federalism in Brazil", World Bank Working Papers 557, Washington, D.C.

SHAH, A. (1994), "The Reform of Inter–governmental Fiscal Relations in Developing and Emerging Market Economies", World Bank Policy and Research Series, No. 23, Washington, D.C.

TUANZI, V. (1995), "Fiscal Federalism and Decentralisation: A Review of Some Efficiency and Macroeconomic Aspects", Annual Bank Conference on Development Economics, World Bank, Washington, D.C.

Bibliography

A Comment

by Rui Affonso

Federalism and decentralisation must be differentiated if we are to grasp the full spectrum of the Latin American outlook, especially in countries such as Brazil, Argentina, Mexico, Venezuela and Colombia. Federalism and decentralisation are both ways in which the state attempts to take into account the many and varied requirements of the country, to make national and local levels compatible in terms of managing public finances. Broadly speaking, decentralisation consists of reallocating resources, decision–making spheres, skills and responsibilities — in short, political and economic power — between the central government and lower levels of government.

Federalism is characterised by the distribution of powers among several centres, whose authority stems not from decentralisation/delegation of powers by the central government, but from voters. The fundamental difference is that several sovereignties co–exist within federalism; unity and diversity cohabit within a single nation. Accordingly, decentralisation does not necessarily involve the creation of a federation. In contrast, federation presupposes a certain degree of existing decentralisation. One of the main characteristics of federalism is an ongoing process of pragmatic exchanges, or "federal pacts", which take the form of institutional arrangements[1]. Historical configurations show a diversity of situations[2]: for example, Colombia is a unitary, highly decentralised country; Venezuela is a federal and highly centralised country; Brazil has a sufficiently decentralised, yet dislocated structure.

Federations are by nature diverse. In Brazil, this diversity reflects social and economic heterogeneity, a fundamental obstacle to development. In addition, the Brazilian federation is encumbered with a complex state apparatus, several components of which — direct government, public enterprises, public finance system — are found at all three levels of government (Union, states and municipalities) in very different forms[3]. These two structural factors mean that the federative pact is materialised through a complex and blurred mechanism of exchanges between spheres of government and between regions. Flows of private trade, labour and financial resources have failed to reduce social and economic heterogeneity; instead, they tend to accentuate it.

In addition to fiscal and similar transfers, viewed as inter–regional compensation mechanisms, direct spending by the Union in the regions has to be taken into account, along with implicit transfer payments to public and federal enterprises, the public

179

finance system and social security spending. The leading public enterprises play such an important role in some regions that they can be compared to regional development agencies[4]. The separation between economic and political power, as reflected by the disproportionate representation of regions in Congress, should also be considered from this angle, that of implicit compensation within a heterogeneous structure. What should be stressed is that the process of redefining the state's role, combined with international trends such as privatisation, the opening of economies and globalisation, is dismantling a federative co–ordination model within which fiscal federalism in its strictest sense was only a small part of the federative pact.

Throughout the 1980s, Brazil underwent a major budget decentralisation process that, in conjunction with the above–mentioned trends, eroded the ability of the federal government to play a federative role. Decentralisation in Brazil did not stem from a particular plan or initiative on the part of the central government; taken in combination with the increasing heterogeneity of and within the regions over the past few years, it merely served further to uncouple the distribution of revenues and spending, or responsibility on the one hand and overlapping tasks on the other. This is the "present participle" to which Tanzi refers in his paper. The past is fusing with the present and there are no new solutions in sight that would ensure federative co–ordination on the national political stage.

Examination of the federative problem from the point of view of taxes and the budget has done little to resolve or alleviate some paradoxes arising from decentralisation: for example, the outbreak of state budget crises even when the resources made available to state governments are increasing[5]. In other words, the federative budget structure must encompass a larger field of study: the Federation as a structure conveying an inter–regional pact, overdetermined and overtaken by a thorough dismantling.

The third aspect to highlight is one that has been addressed by Lopez Murphy and Luiz de Mello on a number of occasions: the relationship between decentralisation and macroeconomic stability. Their studies show the links between stabilisation policy — based on the appreciation of the real against the dollar and high interest rates — and deteriorating public finances, in particular those of governments below national level. The significant increase in interest rates and slowed economic growth negatively affected both the spending and revenues of states and municipalities. However, the sharp drop in inflation revealed hidden deficits that had been fuelled by the inflation–indexing binomial. Other factors that should be mentioned include:

— the fact that governments cannot finance their deficits by devices such as delaying payments to suppliers, enterprises and civil servants, etc.;

— the inability of governments to reduce spending on civil service salaries and benefits; such expenditures climbed significantly in the final year of the terms of the President and the state governments;

—   the difficulty experienced by governments in financing themselves by delaying payments to suppliers and public works companies, not just because this method is less used, but also because of the higher interest rates prevailing in the private sector;

—   the structural shakiness of the financial system in general and the public sector in particular.

The sudden and significant drop in inflation also curbed the ability of the executive branch of the three levels of government to slow or curb self–awarded salary hikes by the judiciary and legislative branches by limiting Treasury spending. State expenditures specifically linked to the salaries of these two branches rose by 94 per cent in real terms between 1988 and 1994, far outstripping the growth in state and municipal resources. This illustrates the importance of distinguishing between the three branches of power — executive, legislative and judiciary — when studying governments below national level. This is rarely the case in studies on Brazilian federalism, despite the very different trajectories of the three branches in terms of expenditures and institutional behaviour alike. In addition, the linkage among these powers, increased centralisation of executive powers below the national level, and decentralisation of other powers are key factors in understanding the macroeconomic and institutional responsibilities of the different spheres of government.

Two institutional aspects in particular complicate federative co–ordination in Brazil. *First,* the electoral structure — members of Congress are elected at state level, resulting in disproportionate representation of municipalities — and the fragility of political parties mean that elected representatives are heavily dependent on federal resources allocated on a piecemeal political basis. This does not facilitate the introduction of national standards, and frequently creates considerable friction between the executive and the legislature. Congress then resembles a "national town hall". In contrast, the Union needs skills and resources (negotiated transfer payments, non–allocated direct government spending and spending by state enterprises) to be able to forge national alliances and offset the political predominance of regions/states.

Second, Brazil has no exclusively federal institution. This role could be assumed by the federal Senate. This body does not represent the federation's member states, but stands over the House of Representatives as an institution representing the electorate. It is an assembly that revises legislation, rather than a federative body. Finally, the many federative structures presuppose authorities with equal, albeit diversified, powers; this necessitates more decentralised co–ordination — or very heterogeneous federated authorities, which usually entails a more centralised, sometimes even authoritarian, federal organisation. Brazil must reconcile decentralised co–ordination in a democratic context with increasing socio–economic disparity among regions. This disparity is linked to the profound transformations being wrought by globalisation, outward opening, privatisation and market regulation, among others.

Notes

1. See Fiori (1995) and Ricker (1987).

2. See Ernesto Rezk's article.

3. See Affonso (1997).

4. Affonso (1995*c*).

5. This analysis is similar to the approach taken by Luiz de Mello in his paper on the effects of "quasi–fiscal" imbalances.

A Comment

by Fábio Giambiagi

Feedback from decentralisation over the past few years has shown what types of problems can arise with regard to economic policy management, chiefly because the various public sector bodies do not necessarily have the same economic policy objectives. More concretely, the federal government is pursuing economic stabilisation, which requires strict budget controls. At the same time, governments below national level find it to their advantage to increase spending, which brings them political benefits. These diverging objectives are evident in Table 9.1, which shows that the central government and public enterprises saw their budget deficits rise by around 1 per cent of GDP between 1991–92 and 1995–96, compared with 2.1 per cent for states and municipalities.

Tables 9.2 and 9.3 which cover the progress of decentralisation, illustrate the problems inherent in remedying this situation. The national accounts show that non–financial public spending rose from 22 to 31 per cent of GDP between 1981–85 and 1991–95; however, most of this growth can be attributed to spending by states and municipalities. In other words, the federal government must keep inflation down — sooner or later, this will entail a budget adjustment — since its margin with regard to public spending has gradually been whittled away. At present, half the spending undertaken is not under federal control.

The number of Brazilian municipalities has increased substantially over the past few years. This is understandable when seen from the viewpoint of municipalities, which are struggling for their emancipation. However, it results in much less efficiency for government as a whole: public bodies proliferate, leading to a higher public spending/GDP ratio. This poses problems not only for the federal government, but also for states, since the share of state VAT (ICMS) paid to municipalities — 25 per cent of the total amount — will have to be divided by a greater number of units. Although there are some exceptions to the rule, it is not by chance that the two states best managed over the past few years — Bahia and Ceará — have seen a zero or negligible increase in the number of their municipalities. This reflects the stance taken by the two state governments.

Nonetheless, the budget crisis of the last three years has yielded two important lessons. *First,* there is no viable way out of the crisis in a federal country such as Brazil unless the federal government and the states make a concerted effort. *Second,* the federal government shares some of the blame for what is happening in the states: even though the latter are self–governing, they are bound by constraints linked to financing. In other words, states can decide how and where their money will be spent, but the federal government can set limits on their financing possibilities, and thus upon their margin for manoeuvre.

In this regard, the federal government has learned much from the relationship between the various spheres of government at national and state level over the past few years. It has gradually come to keep a tighter rein on the financing sources to which states turned previously. For example, it has banned the practice whereby public banks' resources were used to finance deficits; it has privatised public utilities for electricity distribution — most of which were poorly managed, did not repay what they owed to the federal authorities and had become a further source of public deficit; it has almost completely eliminated the expedient of spending forecast tax revenues (ARO); it has prohibited spurious debt resulting from the so–called "letters rogatory scandal". More recently, it concluded debt negotiation accords with the states whereby the latter will have to agree to a "Tabela Price" repayment scheme and pay outstanding interest, which had previously been capitalised in full. These are all parts of a process which we hope will gradually improve budget control and foster greater transparency of flows among the various levels of government. Once the "federation" (i.e. partial socialisation) of losses incurred as a result of past bad habits has gained acceptance, all that will remain is to ensure that these habits do not crop up again and create further debt. This is probably one of the main issues that monetary and fiscal authorities will have to deal with in years to come.

PART THREE

CASE STUDIES: ASIAN PERSPECTIVES

Chapter 10

Fiscal Decentralisation and Macroeconomic Governance: Asian Perspectives

Kiichiro Fukasaku

Introduction

Reforming the fiscal system, including intergovernmental fiscal relations, has become one of the most important policy issues in many Asian developing countries. As they become increasingly open and market–oriented, it is natural that they reconsider the fiscal role of government in economic development — a particularly fundamental issue for three largest developing countries of the region, China, India and Indonesia, because of sheer size and regional diversity and for political and historical reasons. The key goal is to design and develop a system of public finance that can provide local public services effectively and efficiently while at the same time maintaining macroeconomic stability. How much fiscal decentralisation should there be? How should intergovernmental fiscal relations be managed both to satisfy the growing need for local public services and to preserve national integrity and fiscal discipline?[1]

The issue of fiscal decentralisation has also become important for public policy debates in several outward–oriented East Asian economies with traditionally highly centralised fiscal systems. Some of these economies have rising concerns over the continued existence of pockets of poverty and marked regional inequality, particularly growing gaps between wealthier metropolitan areas and poorer rural areas. Thailand is a case in point, as its rapid industrial development has brought an exceptionally high spatial concentration in the Bangkok metropolitan area. The economic advantages of such industrial agglomeration have now turned into disadvantages by aggravating infrastructure strains and pollution to almost intolerable levels, and by worsening regional inequality[2]. In a similar vein, Hill (1996) argues in favour of fiscal decentralisation by referring to the recent experience of Indonesia in which the central government no longer has the capacity to finance large–scale regional development programmes and regional–local factors have become much more important as determinants of provincial economic performance.

The very complex relationship between fiscal decentralisation and macroeconomic governance deserves special attention in developing countries[3]. This paper addresses some of the problems related to fiscal decentralisation from Asian perspectives, although a full treatment lies beyond its scope[4]. Macroeconomic stability and human resource development continue as critically important policy goals for Asian developing countries to sustain outward–oriented growth. To promote human resource development, more active participation by localities is desirable because lower–level governments are largely responsible for providing primary education, health care and other social services. On the other hand, the principles of fiscal federalism assign the task of macroeconomic stabilisation to the central government. This dilemma remains a major challenge for many Asian developing countries.

Openness, Public Finance and Macroeconomic Stability

Policy makers in outward–oriented East Asian economies hold to a general consensus that a stable macroeconomic framework[5] is a necessary although not sufficient condition for sustained long–run growth. Low and predictable inflation is a *sine qua non* for such stability, a cornerstone of East Asia's "miracle" stories (World Bank, 1993)[6]. High inflation is inconsistent with outward–oriented development policy because it leads to real exchange–rate appreciation under a fixed or quasi–fixed exchange–rate regime and a corresponding loss of international competitiveness. High inflation also hurts private investment and productivity growth by distorting price information required for an efficient allocation of resources and by raising uncertainty about future inflation and risk[7].

East Asia differs from other developing regions by its sustained growth and relatively low inflation during the 1980s and 1990s. Table 10.1 presents both growth and inflation performance of selected Asian economies between 1980 and 1996. Despite major disturbances on the world economic scene, most East Asian economies (except the Philippines) have achieved remarkable growth performance and at the same time managed to bring high inflation of the 1970s down to below 10 per cent in the 1980s and 1990s[8]. Chinese Taipei, Korea, Malaysia, Singapore and Thailand especially have proven more "inflation–averse" than others, keeping annual rates of inflation within a 5–6 per cent range. China, India, Indonesia, Pakistan, the Philippines, Sri Lanka and Viet Nam registered much higher rates of inflation, although their recent inflation episodes (with the notable exception of Viet Nam in the 1980s) are mild by developing–country standards and certainly more moderate than Dornbusch and Fischer's (1993) case of "moderate inflation" (15–30 per cent). Viet Nam has also managed to bring three–digit inflation down to a moderate level in the 1990s.

Table 10.1. **Openness, Growth and Inflation in Selected Asian Economies**

	Trade openness[a] 1994	Average annual percentage change in real GDP[b]			Average annual percentage change in CPI[c]		
		1980-90	1990-95	1996	1980-90	1990-95	1996
Hong Kong	238.3	6.5	5.5	4.7	8.1	9.4	6.0
Singapore	286.9	7.3	8.5	7.0	2.3	2.6	1.4
Korea	50.6	9.2	7.5	7.0	6.3	6.2	5.0
Chinese Taipei	73.9	7.9	6.6	5.7	3.1	3.8	3.1
Malaysia	167.2	6.0	8.7	8.8	3.2	4.3	3.5
Philippines	55.9	1.6	2.2	5.5	14.0	10.4	8.4
Thailand	69.6	7.9	8.4	6.7	4.4	4.8	5.9
Indonesia	41.0	5.5	7.1	7.8	8.6	8.9	7.9
India	17.2	5.9	4.4	6.8	8.9	10.5	8.9
Pakistan	31.2	6.2	4.7	6.1	7.0	11.2	10.8
Sri Lanka	68.2	2.0	4.5	3.8	12.2	10.3	15.9
Viet Nam	52.7	7.1	8.2	9.5	191.2	21.7	6.0
China	43.8	8.9	12.3	9.7	6.8	11.8	6.1

a.   Trade openness is defined as merchandise imports plus exports as a percentage of GDP.
b.   For India, Sri Lanka and China, the source used for the calculation of the last period is the *World Development Indicators 1997* of the World Bank.
c.   Consumer price index, except for China and Viet Nam in which retail price index was used.
Sources: IMF, *IFS 1997 and* World Bank, *WDI 1997*. Except for Chinese Taipei: *Taiwan Statistics Data Book 1996* and for Real GDP of Hong Kong: *Quarterly Report of GDP Estimates 1996*. Figures for 1996 are taken from ADB, *Asian Development Outlook 1997 and 1998*.

Two common characteristics underlie the stable macroeconomic environment in East Asia: economic openness and fiscal conservatism. On the relationship between them, it has been argued that economic openness can serve as an effective incentive for national governments to stick to sound macroeconomic policies — because maintaining price stability is a prerequisite for sustaining outward–oriented development policy for countries with large tradable sectors (see Table 10.1, column 1). Moreno (1994) argues that price stability in East Asia has more to do with the region's high degree of openness and thereby the low incentive to inflate than the degree of central bank independence as such[9]. While macroeconomic risks associated with large capital inflows and sudden outflows should not be overlooked, these risks can best be accommodated by a combination of appropriate policies, including fiscal restraint and realistic exchange–rate policy (Fukasaku and Hellvin, 1996; Fukasaku, 1997)[10].

A recent study by the World Bank (1996a) also points out that economic globalisation — the increased integration of world markets for goods, services and capital — places a high premium on sound macroeconomic policies, allowing outward–oriented developing countries to have better access to foreign markets, capital and technology. The study also suggests that the positive effect of freer trade and foreign direct investment on growth is one of the most critical factors underlying strong growth performance in East Asian economies. Petri (1995) also argues that the emergence of a "trade–investment nexus" is a key feature of East Asia's outward–oriented growth. Liberalisation of trade and investment regimes unilaterally by many East Asian economies has improved the policy environment for expanding both trade and investment flows, while strong trade and investment performance has encouraged governments to sustain outward–oriented policies, thereby integrating their economies more closely into the global market. Such a positive relationship between policy initiatives and strong trade and investment performance works in favour of outward–oriented East Asian economies within a relatively stable macroeconomic framework.

Figure 10.1. **Central Government Fiscal Surplus/Deficit 1980-84, 1990-94 Average**
(As a percentage of GDP)

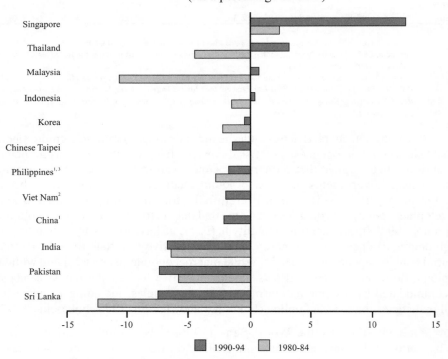

Note: 1. Budgetary central government.
2. General government.
3. 1990-93 average.
Source: GFS tape, IFS CD-rom, World Bank (Viet Nam).

190

Fiscal conservatism constitutes another pillar of macroeconomic stability in East Asia. While some countries such as Malaysia and Thailand ran substantial fiscal deficits in the early 1980s, they have managed to keep them within limits that can avoid destabilising the economy. As Figure 10.1 shows, the fiscal performance of central governments in East Asia has improved substantially over the past decade, in sharp contrast with mediocre performance in three South Asian countries, India, Pakistan and Sri Lanka. Despite recent efforts to cut back public expenditures in these countries, central government fiscal deficits remain high. This divergence between East and South Asia requires a closer look at the size and structure of government expenditures and experience with fiscal adjustment since the late 1980s.

Size and Structure of Government Expenditures

It is not easy to make a cross–country comparison of the size and structure of government expenditures, given limited comparable financial data on the public sector, including all levels of government[11]. This applies particularly to developing and transition economies in which government–directed expenditures of public enterprises play an important role in economic activities. Figure 10.2 compares the size of (consolidated) central government expenditures expressed as percentages of GDP among selected Asian economies. Perhaps most striking from the international perspective, such expenditures tend to be far smaller in Asian developing countries than in several European Member countries of the OECD[12]. Among the latter, central government expenditures in Belgium, Italy and the Netherlands reach 50 per cent of GDP. Higher government spending in these countries reflects a substantial expansion, notably in the 1960s and 1970s, of the government role in providing a variety of public goods and services, including education, health care, pensions and social assistance. Based on historical experiences in OECD countries, Tanzi and Schuknecht (1997) argue that many of the potential social gains from government expenditures could have been realised with smaller governments spending 30 to 40 per cent of GDP[13].

For developing countries, it is even more difficult to grapple with the idea of the optimum size of government expenditure, because local public services are in chronic short supply in most countries. Casual observation of Figure 10.2, however, suggests a clear divergence between East and South Asian economies; the former (with the exception of Malaysia) tend to have smaller governments than the latter.

Such inter–regional differences become even sharper when one compares government expenditures at the state/local level. With the notable exception of China, the fiscal systems of East Asian economies are highly centralised. Despite its geographical diversity as an archipelago nation with a population of more than 190 million, Indonesia has developed a unitary system of public finance in which local governments have little administrative or judicial power and thus rely heavily on financial transfers from the central government (Hill, 1996). Even in Malaysia, which has a federal political system, the fiscal powers of the states are very limited (Asher, 1989). On the other hand, China provides a unique case of fiscal decentralisation in Asia. Two federations in South Asia, India and Pakistan, fall in between.

Figure 10.2. **Size of Central Government**
1980-84, 1990-94 Average
(As a percentage of GDP)

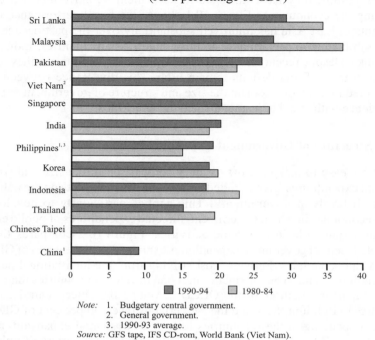

Note: 1. Budgetary central government.
2. General government.
3. 1990-93 average.
Source: GFS tape, IFS CD-rom, World Bank (Viet Nam).

Table 10.2 compares relevant fiscal indicators at two levels of governments for five Asian developing countries, India, Indonesia, Malaysia, the Philippines and Thailand. Although available data are very limited, the table reveals some salient features of Asian fiscal systems. *First,* state/local government expenditures relative to GDP are much smaller in the four ASEAN countries than in India — 10 to 20 per cent of central government expenditures, as against roughly 65 to 75 per cent for India.

Second, the relative importance of revenue transfers from central to state/local governments varies widely from country to country. At one extreme, under Indonesia's unitary fiscal system, transfers from the central government account for more than 70 per cent of state governments' revenues. At the other, the comparable figure for Malaysia is roughly 20 per cent. The federal government of Malaysia bears a much larger burden of providing public services such as primary education and health care than do the central governments of Indonesia, the Philippines and Thailand.

Third, in these five Asian developing countries the central government rather than state/local governments represents the primary source of overall fiscal imbalances, although fiscal deficits at state level remain substantial in India (Table 10.2). Malaysia and Thailand illustrate this point. As Figure 10.1 shows, a remarkable improvement occurred in their central governments' fiscal positions between 1980–84 and 1990–94

192

Table 10.2. **Fiscal Indicators for Central and State/Local Governments
in Selected Asian Countries**

		1980-84	1985-89	1990-94[a]
India	Consolidated central government			
	Overall deficit/surplus/GDP	-6.4	-8.4	-6.7
	Total revenus and grants/GDP	12.6	14.4	13.7
	Total exp. & lend-repay/GDP	19.0	22.9	20.5
	Transfers to other levels of nat. govt./total exp.	(33.5)	(32.7)	(35.1)
	State, region or province governments			
	Overall deficit/surplus/GDP	-3.0	-3.1	-2.9
	Total revenus and grants/GDP	10.9	11.9	12.2
	Grants from other levels of nat. govt./total rev	(42.6)	(43.5)	(44.0)
	Total exp. & lend-repay/GDP	13.8	14.9	15.1
Indonesia	Consolidated central government			
	Overall deficit/surplus/GDP	-1.5	-2.1	0.4
	Total revenus and grants/GDP	21.6	19.2	18.7
	Total exp. & lend-repay/GDP	23.1	21.3	18.3
	Transfers to other levels of nat. govt./total exp.	(15.6)	(16.7)	(20.1)
	State, region or province governments			
	Overall deficit/surplus/GDP	0.1	0.0	0.0
	Total revenus and grants/GDP	3.0	2.4	2.5
	Grants from other levels of nat. govt./total rev.	(81.5)	(77.7)	(72.9)
	Total exp. & lend-repay/GDP	2.9	2.3	2.5
Malaysia	Consolidated central government			
	Overall deficit/surplus/GDP	-10.6	-3.8	0.7
	Total revenus and grants/GDP	26.6	27.4	28.3
	Total exp. & lend-repay/GDP	37.2	31.2	27.6
	Transfers to other levels of nat. govt./total exp.	(2.5)	(5.8)	(4.0)
	State, region or province governments			
	Overall deficit/surplus/GDP	-1.5	-0.3	-0.9
	Total revenus and grants/GDP	5.7	6.0	4.7
	Grants from other levels of nat. govt./total rev.	(21.4)	(23.1)	(19.7)
	Total exp. & lend-repay/GDP	7.2	6.3	5.6
Philippines	Budgetary central government			
	Overall deficit/surplus/GDP	-2.8	-2.9	-2.1
	Total revenus and grants/GDP	12.4	14.2	17.5
	Total exp. & lend-repay/GDP	15.2	17.0	19.6
	Transfers to other levels of nat. govt./total exp.	(4.2)	(3.5)	(6.9)
	Local governments			
	Overall deficit/surplus/GDP	0.1	0.1	0.2
	Total revenus and grants/GDP	1.8	1.5	1.8
	Grants from other levels of nat. govt./total rev.	(39.3)	(38.0)	(45.6)
	Total exp. & lend-repay/GDP	1.7	1.4	1.7
Thailand	Consolidated central government			
	Overall deficit/surplus/GDP	-4.4	-1.6	3.2
	Total revenus and grants/GDP	15.3	16.2	18.5
	Total exp. & lend-repay/GDP	19.6	17.8	15.3
	Transfers to other levels of nat. govt./total exp	(5.9)	(2.9)	(2.3)
	Local governments			
	Overall deficit/surplus/GDP	0.1	0.1	0.1
	Total revenus and grants/GDP	2.1	1.4	1.4
	Grants from other levels of nat. govt./total rev.	(52.2)	(36.6)	(25.4)
	Total exp. & lend-repay/GDP	1.8	1.4	1.5

a.   India 93 (State Governments); Indonesia 93 (State Governments); Philippines 93/92 (Budget Central Govt./Local
      Governments).
Source: GFS Tape, IFS CD-Rom.

193

— a turnaround certainly facilitated by buoyant tax revenues associated with strong economic growth since the mid–1980s, but also reflecting government efforts to curb both operational and development expenditures (Salleh and Meyanathan, 1993; Robinson *et al.*, 1991; World Bank, 1992). More importantly, this shift to fiscal conservatism took place in the context of economic globalisation and these countries' policy responses to increased private capital flows in the 1990s.

Fiscal Adjustment in the 1990s

Recent episodes in Malaysia, Thailand and other emerging economies in Asia suggest fiscal tightening as an effective instrument for responding to heavy capital inflows, as it helps to reduce aggregate demand, lower interest rates, and thus discourage such inflows[14]. More recently, in reaction to capital outflows in the aftermath of the Mexico crisis in late 1994, the Philippines' government tightened public expenditure promptly to counterbalance a heavy loss of foreign reserves during the first and third quarters of 1995 (Kuroyanagi and Hayakawa, 1996). It aimed to pre–empt a balance–of–payments crisis following heavy capital flight, by reducing domestic absorption and limiting adverse effects of credit squeezes on private investment. Given this "asymmetry" in fiscal policy responses to heavy capital inflows and sudden outflows, Heller (1997) argues that "... the expected value of the appropriate fiscal stance in an open capital regime is more conservative than when capital is immobile" (p. 31).

Recent trends in central–government revenues, expenditures and fiscal balances suggest that fiscal conservatism has been put firmly in place in Malaysia and Thailand, and to a lesser extent in the Philippines (Figure 10.3). In Indonesia, the government since 1966 has adopted the "balanced budget" rule as the core principle of macroeconomic management. As Figure 10.3 shows, the Indonesian central government has run fiscal deficits in a conventional economic sense but has managed to keep them within a small range. To be sure, the "balanced budget" rule can be maintained only because the items financing budget deficits, such as aid and external borrowings, are counted as revenues. Nonetheless, this rule has effectively kept the lid on political pressures demanding an extravagant expansion of public expenditures (Hill, 1996).

On the other hand, India's fiscal adjustment has been inadequate at both central and state levels. While the central government managed to reduce its fiscal deficit from 8.4 per cent in 1985–89 to 6.7 per cent in 1990–94, the state governments slashed theirs only marginally, despite the centre's power to control their borrowing (Table 10.2). Joshi and Little (1994) state that "... India's fiscal problem is not irresolvable. The extent of soft budgets and hidden subsidies is so large that the required adjustment could be achieved quite rapidly *without compromising efficiency and equity*. Of course, the political constraints are severe. But unless they are overcome, the reform process could grind to a halt" (p. 43; italics are added.).

Figure 10.3. **Recent Trends in Consolidated Central Government's Revenue, Expenditure and Fiscal Balance in Selected Asian Countries, 1980-95**
(As a percentage of GDP)

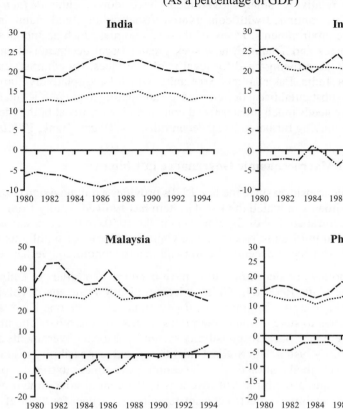

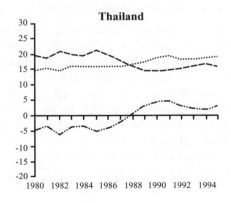

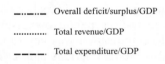

Overall deficit/surplus/GDP

Total revenue/GDP

Total expenditure/GDP

Note: * Budgetary central government.
Source: GFS tape, IFS CD-rom, World Bank (Viet Nam).

In sum, the past ten years witnessed divergent trends in fiscal performance among both unitary and federal Asian developing countries. Several outward–oriented East Asian economies with relatively "small" governments have adopted either *de facto* or *de jure* unitary systems, continued with conservative fiscal policies and maintained stable macroeconomic environments. Many of these economies, such as Indonesia, Malaysia, the Philippines and Thailand, now seek greater fiscal decentralisation to meet more effectively the growing need for local public services. By contrast, three South Asian countries, India, Pakistan and Sri Lanka, which have relatively "large" governments, still run substantial fiscal deficits and are attempting to put public finance in order. India urgently needs much greater fiscal consolidation efforts at both federal and state levels before moving further to fiscal decentralisation (World Bank, 1996*b*)[15].

Decentralisation and Macroeconomic Governance in China

China's economic transition since the late 1970s provides a unique Asian case of decentralisation experiments in which the fiscal system has evolved fitfully from one extreme of complete central control of fiscal powers in the 1950s to the other extreme of fiscal decentralisation until quite recently. The Chinese experience highlights the complexity of problems of fiscal decentralisation and macroeconomic governance[16].

An open–door policy and decentralisation have been the two pillars of China's economic reform since late 1978[17]. In China "decentralisation" means devolving decision–making power from the central to local governments on the one hand, and from planning authorities to state–owned enterprises (SOEs) on the other. The main instruments for this were the "fiscal responsibility system" for local governments and the "contract responsibility system" for SOEs. Under the "fiscal responsibility system", provincial governments signed contracts with the central government to transfer pre–fixed amounts (or a certain growth rate) of revenues to the central government over specified periods, while retaining rights to keep any remaining revenues for themselves. Similarly, under the "contract responsibility system", SOEs agreed to transfer pre–fixed amounts of taxes and profits to the state annually and retain the rest.

"Decentralisation" differs conceptually from "liberalisation", which implies the removal of government intervention to economic activity *at all levels*, although these two initiatives often link in reality. China since the mid–1980s has seen the emergence of a "decentralised public–ownership economy", a terminology used by Fan Gang. While decentralisation was key to China's economic dynamism in the post–reform era, it also brought serious side effects in persisting budget deficits and excessive monetary expansion at local levels. Beijing was losing control of public finance; central budget revenue fell from over 60 per cent of total government budgetary revenue in the 1970s to 37 per cent in 1993. At the same time, the total also dropped from 31 per cent of GDP in 1978 to about 12 per cent in 1994 (Fan, 1996).

The principal problem for fiscal decentralisation in China has been the "free–rider" behaviour of provincial/local governments, which seek to take advantage of fiscal powers granted to them without much helping to fund central budgetary revenues (Laffont and Senik–Leygonie, 1997)[18]. Under the fiscal responsibility system, it was difficult to control this "free–rider" behaviour because the central government had insufficient access to information on local SOEs. The upshot of fiscal decentralisation was thus a sharp decline of financial resources under central government control. The decline of the centre's power to collect taxes and allocate financial resources seriously damaged its ability to redress regional disparity between the wealthier coastal and poorer interior provinces[19].

Given worsening income distribution among regions, the central government has taken new steps to increase its revenue share by recentralising resources. Under the new revenue–sharing system announced in 1994, it took over the administrative function of collecting shared taxes and retaining a larger share of tax revenues; for example, 75 per cent of value added tax now goes to the central government, which can decide how much should be transferred to local governments. Doubts have been raised over the effectiveness of this fiscal recentralisation in the power struggle between different levels of government (Laffont and Senik–Leygonie, 1997). Ma (1995) argues that the 1994 revenue–sharing system still suffers from weak institutional arrangements for the division of tax bases between central and local governments based on the ownership of SOEs. Moreover, a decentralised monetary system provides no effective mechanism for the monetary authorities to check money supply at local levels, because the banking sector must continue to provide funds to save loss–making SOEs and finance both central and local infrastructure projects.

The movement towards fiscal recentralisation also fails to recognise the new development of local economies and the responsibility of local governments to provide public goods and services to local communities. Fan (1996) points to the increasing importance of "non–standard" revenues in local economies; he also calls them "extra–extra–budgetary revenues", since they are not recorded officially. These are "funds raised from local sources by local governments and spent on local projects or used to cover local governments' current expenditures". The full scale of "non–standard" revenues has yet to be grasped, although some sample surveys show that these funds account for an important share of local government revenues[20]. It has also been argued that the growing demand for fiscal autonomy by provinces and municipalities has much bearing on local democracy as well as the problem of corruption (Fan, 1996)[21].

In short, recent fiscal developments at the local level pose a fundamental question about macroeconomic governance in China, in the apparent conflict of interests between different levels of government over the control of financial resources in an extremely decentralised economy. How to design intergovernmental fiscal transfers remains an open question in China.

Concluding Remarks

This paper has discussed some of the problems related to fiscal decentralisation and macroeconomic stability by drawing on recent experiences of Asian developing countries. Given other examples from large federations such as Brazil and India, this issue poses a new challenge for outward–oriented East Asian countries that have traditionally developed highly centralised fiscal systems. Decentralisation policies have attracted strong interest in many East Asian economies as a way to improve allocative efficiency of pubic expenditures, and as both budgetary pressures and economic and political forces for greater democratisation continue to develop.

Recent studies of Indonesia indicate that such policy initiatives remain in the early stages, with the reform agenda long and wide–ranging (Shah and Qureshi 1994; Crane, 1995; Smoke and Lewis, 1996). As Table 10.2 indicates, the share of intergovernmental fiscal transfers in central government expenditures has increased substantially over the past decade, and these transfers represent the main source of local financing for infrastructure, although local authorities have attempted to reduce their financial dependence on the centre. Ideally, greater local participation in the national planning process would improve co–ordination between central and local authorities for effective decentralisation. Some observers note, however, that "[t]he most binding constraint in many cases has been the fragmentation of responsibility at the *central* level and the inability or unwillingness of the central government to improve co–ordination" (Smoke and Lewis, 1996; italics are added).

The foregoing highlights the importance of political–economy considerations in designing and implementing decentralisation policies, including intergovernmental fiscal transfers. China's fiscal decentralisation without substantial central control and oversight has weakened tremendously the capability of the central government to manage financial resources for infrastructure investment and develop an effective system of macroeconomic management. Decentralisation policies must also move carefully in tandem with fiscal consolidation efforts in large federations such as India and Pakistan, where fiscal deficits remain substantial.

Finally, the political and economic landscape in Asia has changed dramatically over the past year, almost beyond recognition. In the wake of financial and currency crises in 1997, Asian countries have grappled with the daunting task of putting their economies on a sound footing. The immediate effects of the crises are a substantial decline in real income, a hike in unemployment and a drop in public services. Thus, many crisis–affected economies in the region will have to strengthen their public finances in order to meet new challenges in coming years.

Notes

1.	There is a large body of literature on this topic in the context of developing countries. As regards Asian developing countries, see, *inter alia*, Agarwala (1992); Asher (1989, 1992); Boadway, Roberts and Shah (1994); Crane (1995); ESCAP(1991); Kohli (1991); Laffont and Senik–Leygonie (1997); Ma (1995); Manasan (1990); Roy (1995); Shah and Qureshi (1994); Tanzi (1987, 1995); Tanzi and Shome (1992); and Xavier (1996).

2.	In 1991, the per capita GDP in the Bangkok Metropolitan region was about $5 600, or 5.6 times that for the rest of the country, and the income gap between the two has also widened over the last decade or so (Sussangkarn and Chalamwong, 1996)

3.	See Boadway, Roberts and Shah (1994) and Tanzi (1995).

4.	See, for example, Wildasin (1996) for a concise overview of problems of fiscal decentralisation and macroeconomic governance in a broader context.

5.	Stanley Fischer defines the macroeconomic framework to be stable "when inflation is low and predictable, real interests are appropriate, fiscal policy is stable and sustainable, the real exchange rate is competitive and predictable, and the balance of payments situation is perceived as viable" (Fischer 1993).

6.	See also Sachs and Bajpai (1996).

7.	For example, a pooled cross–country regression study by Hiemenz (1995) supports the view that macroeconomic instability and policy–induced distortions of goods and capital markets tend to reduce the locational advantage of a recipient country in international competition for investable funds.

8.	Recent macroeconomic data and short–term projections by ADB (1997) suggest that the Philippine economy is picking up at an annual rate of 5–6 per cent, while simultaneously bringing down inflation to a single digit level.

9.	According to the index of central bank independence compiled by Cukierman *et al.* (1992), the Philippine central bank has the highest index for legal independence within East Asia, while Chinese Taipei's index is among the lowest.

10.	Mismanagement of exhange–rate policy has been identified as one of the major causes of the Asian financial and currency crisis in 1997, together with financial sector weaknesses (IMF, 1998).

11. The government can also affect private economic activities through non–financial measures, such as formal and informal regulations, including so–called administrative guidance. This makes international comparison even more difficult.

12. Non–European Member countries of OECD (e.g. Australia, Canada, Japan and the United States) tend to have much smaller central government expenditures than the European ones.

13. This measure refers to the size of general government.

14. See Fukasaku (1997) and Fukasaku and Hellvin (1996) for a detailed account of policy responses by Asian and other emerging economies to increased private capital inflows in the 1990s.

15. See also the chapter by P. Shome in this volume for a detailed discussion of fiscal federalism in India.

16. See also the chapter by Fan Gang in this volume.

17. See Fukasaku and Wall (1994) for a detailed account of China's open–economy reform.

18. The "free–rider" behaviour of provincial/local governments is often referred to as "whipping the fast buffaloes" in Chinese: the fast buffaloes (the fast–growing provinces) tend to be whipped (taxed) most; in other words, the better they perform, the worse they are treated (Laffont and Senik–Leygonie, 1997).

19. For example, a recent paper by Jian, Sachs and Warner (1996) shows that regional incomes in China have begun to diverge since 1990 following a convergent trend between 1978 and 1989. They argue that regional convergence in the 1980s was associated with rural reforms and was particularly strong within the coastal regions as a result of foreign trade and investment liberalisation. They also argue that the tendency for divergence since 1990 will probably continue between fast–growing coastal provinces and poorer interior provinces if current policies remain unchanged.

20. According to Fan (1995), the relative importance of "non–standard" revenues varies widely across provinces and townships, for example from more than 90 per cent of total revenue in some townships of Guangdong to about 40 per cent in Hunan province. See, however, the comment by Bert Hofman.

21. See also the chapter by Fan Gang in this volume.

Bibliography

AGARWALA R. (1992), "China, Reforming Inter–governmental Fiscal Relations", *World Bank Discussion Papers* 178, Washington, D.C.

ASHER, M.G. (1989), "A Comparative Overview of ASEAN Fiscal Systems and Practices", in M.G. ASHER (ed.), *Fiscal Systems and Practices in ASEAN: Trends, Impact and Evaluation*, Institute of Southeast Asian Studies, Singapore.

ASHER, M.G. (1992), "Lessons from Tax Reforms in the Asia–Pacific Region", *Asian Development Review*, Vol. 10, No. 2.

ASIAN DEVELOPMENT BANK (1997), *Asian Development Outlook, 1997 and 1998*, Oxford University Press, Hong Kong.

BOADWAY, R., S. ROBERTS AND A. SHAH (1994), "The Reform of Fiscal Systems in Developing and Emerging Market Economies: A Federalism Perspective", *Policy Research Working Paper* No. 1259, World Bank, Washington, D.C., February.

CHINESE TAIPEI (1996), *Taiwan Statistics Data Book 1996*, Taipei.

CRANE, R. (1995), "The Practice of Regional Development in Indonesia: Resolving Central–Local Co–ordination Issues in Planning and Finance", *Public Administration and Development*, Vol. 15, No. 12.

CUKIERMAN, A., S.B. WEBB, AND B. NEYAPTI (1992), "Measuring the Independence of Central Banks and its Effects on Policy Outcomes", *World Bank Economic Review*, Vol. 6.

DORNBUSCH, R. AND S. FISCHER (1993), "Moderate Inflation", *World Bank Economic Review*, Vol. 7.

ESCAP (1991), "Fiscal Decentralisation and the Mobilization and Use of National Resources for Development: Issues, Experience and Policies in the ESCAP Region", *Development Papers* No. 11, Bangkok.

FAN, G. (1995), "On New Rules of Public Finance" (in Chinese), mimeo.

FAN, G. (1996), "Growth of 'Off–budget Revenue' and Evolution of Local Governance in China", China Reform Foundation, National Economic Research Institute, mimeo, Beijing.

FISCHER, S. (1993), "The Role of Macroeconomic Factors in Growth", *NBER Working Paper Series,* No. 4565.

FUKASAKU, K. (1997), "Macroeconomic Framework for Sustaining ASEAN's Outward–oriented Growth", in S.Y. CHIA AND J. TAN (eds.) (1997), *ASEAN and the EU: Forging New Linkages and Strategic Alliances*, Institute of Southeast Asian Studies, Singapore.

FUKASAKU K. AND D.WALL (1994), *China's Long March to an Open Economy*, Development Centre Studies, OECD Development Centre, Paris.

FUKASAKU, K. AND L. HELLVIN (1996), "Stabilisation with Growth: Implications for Emerging Economies", Paper prepared for a joint OECD–KDI–ICEG Conference on *Growth and Competition in the New Global Economy*, Shilla Hotel, Seoul, 27–28 June.

HELLER, P.S. (1997), "Fiscal Policy Management in an Open Capital Regime", *IMF Working Paper,* WP/97/20, International Monetary Fund, Washington, D.C.

HIEMENZ, U. (1995), "Determinants of Private Investment in the Asia–Pacific Region", in B.K. KAPUR (eds.), *Development, Trade and the Asia–Pacific: Essays in Honour of Professor Lim Chong Yah*, Prentice Hall, Singapore

HILL, H. (1996), *The Indonesian Economy Since 1966*, Cambridge University Press, Cambridge.

HONG KONG (1996), *Quarterly Report of GDP Estimates*, Hong Kong.

IMF (1997), *International Financial Statistics*, Washington, D.C.

IMF (1998), *World Economic Outlook*, Washington, D.C., May.

JIAN, T., J. SACHS AND A. WARNER (1996), "Trends in Regional Inequality in China", *China Economic Review*, vol. 7, No. 1.

JOSHI V. AND I.M.D.LITTLE (1994), *India, Macroeconomics and Political Economy, 1964–1991*, Oxford University Press, Oxford.

KOHLI, K.N. (1991), "The Role of Fiscal Policy in Asian Economic Development", *Asian Development Review*, Vol. 9, No.1.

KUROYANAGI, M. AND M. HAYAKAWA (1996), "Macroeconomic Policy and Capital Movements in Four ASEAN Countries: Indonesia, Malaysia, Philippines and Thailand", *Journal of Research Institute for International Investment and Development (Kaigai–Toshi–Kenkyusho–Ho)*, Vol. 22, No. 4 (in Japanese).

LAFFONT, J.–J. AND C. SENIK–LEYGONIE (1997), *Price Controls and the Economics of Institution in China*, Development Centre Studies, OECD Development Centre, Paris.

MA, J. (1995), "The Reform of Inter–governmental Fiscal Relations in China", *Asian Economic Journal*, Vol. 9, No. 3.

MANASAN, R.G. (1990), "A Review of Fiscal Policy Reforms in the ASEAN Countries in the 1980s", Philippine Institute for Development Studies *Working Paper* No. 90–14, Manila.

MORENO, R. (1994), "Explaining Asia's Low Inflation", *FRBSF Weekly Letter*, No. 94–38.

PETRI, P. (1995), "The Interdependence of Trade and Investment in the Pacific", in E.K.Y. CHEN and P. DRYSDALE (eds.), (1995), *Corporate Links and Foreign Direct Investment in Asia and the Pacific*, Harper Educational.

ROBINSON, D. *et al.* (1991), "Thailand: Adjusting to Successs – Current Policy Issues", *IMF Occasional Paper* No. 85, International Monetary Fund, Washington, D.C., August.

ROY, J. (ed.) (1995), *Macroeconomic Management and Fiscal Decentralisation*, EDI Seminar Series, World Bank, Washington, D.C.

SACHS J.D. AND N. BAJPAI (1996), *India's Economic Reforms: Some Lessons from East Asia*, Development Discussion Paper No. 532a, Harvard Institute for International Development, July.

SALLEH, I.M. AND S.D. MEYANATHAN (1993), *The Lessons of East Asia: Malaysia – Growth, Equity and Structural Transformation*, World Bank, Washington, D.C.

SHAH A. AND Z. QURESHI (1994), "Inter–governmental Fiscal Relations in Indonesia, Issues and Reform, Options", *World Bank Discussion Papers* 239, Washington, D.C.

SMOKE, P. AND B.D. LEWIS (1996), "Fiscal Decentralisation in Indonesia: A New Approach to an Old Idea", *World Development*, Vol. 24, No. 8.

SUSSANGKARN, C. AND Y. CHALAMWONG (1996), "Thailand: Development Strategies and their Impacts on Labour Markets and Migration", in D. O'CONNOR AND L. FARSAKH (eds.), *Development Strategy, Unemployment and Migration: Country Experiences*, OECD Development Centre, Paris.

TANZI, V. (1987), "The Public Sector in the Market Economies of Developing Asia", *Asian Development Review*, Vol. 5, No. 2

TANZI, V. (1995), "Fiscal Federalism and Decentralisation: a Review of Some Efficiency and Macroeconomic Aspects", Annual Bank Conference on Development Economics, World Bank, Washington, D.C., May.

TANZI, V. AND L. SCHUKNECHT (1997), "Reconsidering the Fiscal Role of Government: the International Perspective", paper presented at AEA Session on *Reconsidering the Fiscal Role of Government*, 6 January.

TANZI, V. AND P. SHOME (1992), "The Role of Taxation in the Development of East Asian Economies", in, T. ITO AND A.O. KRUEGER (eds.) (1992), *The Political Economy of Tax Reform*, University of Chicago Press, Chicago.

XAVIER, J.A. (1996), "Budget Reform – the Malaysian Experience", *Public Administration and Development*, Vol. 16.

WILDASIN D. (1996), "Introduction: Fiscal Aspects of Evolving Federations", *International Tax and Public Finance*, 3.

WORLD BANK (1992), *Malaysia: Fiscal Reform for Stable Growth*, Washington, D.C.

WORLD BANK (1993), *The East Asian Miracle: Economic Growth and Public Policy*, World Bank, Oxford University Press.

WORLD BANK (1996*a*), *Global Economic Prospects and the Developing Countries*, Washington, D.C.

WORLD BANK (1996*b*), *India, Country Economic Memorandum, Five Years of Stabilization and Reform: The Challenges Ahead,* Washington, D.C.

WORLD BANK (1997), *World Development Indicators*, Washington, D.C.

Chapter 11

Fiscal Federalism in India: Experience and Future Directions

Parthasarathi Shome

Introduction[1]

The rationalisation and harmonisation of revenue sharing and tax assignment, as well as the allocation of expenditure responsibilities among different tiers of government, comprise important elements in the many economic functions of government. These fiscal federalism rules include allocative and distributive considerations as well as, increasingly, of macroeconomic stabilisation.

The *allocative* issue relates to the extent of decentralisation most suitable for a particular federal state; which taxes are best collected and retained by the central or local government; what autonomy local governments should have in structuring their own taxes versus parameters laid down by the central government for local taxation; which taxes are most suitable for revenue sharing; and whether local governments could "piggy–back" on centrally levied taxes. On the expenditure side, the questions focus on the best division of expenditure responsibilities of the various tiers of government for efficient provision of public services: whether the central government should provide education; should primary education be the responsibility of local government with higher education left to the central government; and whether local authorities should maintain roads, with highways a joint responsibility of different tiers of government.

The *distributive* issue focuses on how the resources are divided among different levels of government to achieve income redistribution or development goals, either through revenue–sharing formulas that recognise such criteria, or through expenditure assignment rules that directly affect those concerns. For example, revenue–sharing formulas could include the inverse of per capita GDP, population or other such criteria. On the expenditure side, the question would focus on how a particular expenditure assignment across levels of government or an expenditure allocation within a particular tier of government affects different income or expenditure classes. For example, would central or local responsibility for university education be better for low income groups?

Finally, it has become increasingly apparent that macroeconomic management and economic stabilisation are intricately affected by fiscal federalism rules and practices. In a relatively loose federal arrangement, if local governments can borrow freely and without constraint from the central government, the impact is bound to affect the overall fiscal position of the economy and consequently fiscal stabilisation. Similarly, with heavy use of revenue sharing rather than assignment of particular taxes to individual tiers of government, a tendency is likely that every time a central government raises tax revenue to reduce its own fiscal deficit, local government would receive a corresponding revenue benefit which it can spend. This would tend to inhibit the potential for reducing the overall fiscal deficit. Thus, the design of fiscal federalism structures on both the tax and expenditure sides has important ramifications for macroeconomic management (Tanzi, 1995).

The Indian Context

An Historical Perspective

Fiscal arrangements of the British Raj between the centre and provinces (as states were called then) in India trace back to the Montague–Chelmsford reforms of 1919 (Bagchi, 1995) which separated central and provincial subjects or responsibilities as well as revenue sources. The provinces received land revenue, excises and an income tax share. As a result they often had surpluses, and subsequently a contributory system from the provinces to the centre was devised. In 1935 a Government of India Act sought to correct the imbalance. It assigned the revenue–productive personal income tax, corporation income tax and customs duties to the centre. At the same time, because the provinces had responsibility for the delivery of important public services, a system of devolution — the Nieneyer Awards, after the expert who designed them — was devised to ensure a workable financial footing for the provinces.

At the formation of independent India in 1947, as "princely states" and provinces opted or were persuaded to join the "Union", the Constitution provided for a federalist arrangement to reassure states, yet with a central focus to ensure cohesion within the newly formed country. An appreciation of modern fiscal federalism in India calls for a comprehensive understanding of the administrative structure — one of central cohesion yet with multiple centrifugal forces — from ancient times. To quote Akbar (1985), "a separate accession treaty had to be obtained from each one of the 565 princely states on this subcontinent at the time of independence" (p. 18). Thus, it is chastening yet expectable that, as India's democratic political structure matures, fiscal federalist tendencies will increasingly tug at the centre in the quest for greater decentralisation. This is already happening. Its manifestations appear through increasing pressures to pass on more tax instruments to state purview even as the centre tends to send more social–expenditure responsibility to the states (see Shome, 1997a). Decentralisation assumes special importance because the consolidated fiscal deficit of general government might become larger as increased fiscal independence of the states gives them further opportunities to increase their fiscal deficits[2].

The forces of decentralisation face challenge from factors particular to the Indian economy: the vastness in its size, requiring careful co–ordination of policies; interstate competition, most recently manifested through interstate tax competition and increasingly calling for more co–ordination among states (perhaps at the centre's behest); and severe inter–regional income differences and infrastructural disparities, giving rise to arguments that the centre should take an active rather than merely catalytic role in development. This is clearly evident in both the deterministic role of the Finance Commission and the multilevel framework of the Planning Commission.

Overall Constitutional Framework

Since independence, fiscal federalism arrangements in India have been guided by constitutional directions concerning tax assignment among central and state governments as well as by the recommendations of stipulated Finance Commissions regarding revenue sharing and intergovernmental transfers. Recently, constitutional amendments have gone beyond the specification of centre–state relations to include appropriate functions for and relations with local government, both urban (municipalities) and rural (*Panchayats*). Today, a composite framework delineates fiscal functions among central, state and local governments.

The constitution defines in some detail the domains of various taxes. Indeed, some experts consider them so specific as to have led to inflexibility in the use of tax instruments by different levels of government (sometimes referred to as the principle of separation). Further, such details have also resulted in complexity and overt dependence on the judiciary for interpretation — an approach somewhat different from that of the United States where different levels of government may generally tax the same base, for example, income (the principle of concurrence). Some critiques from Indian experts also assert that the criteria used for transfers have not necessarily been consistent. Similarly, the revenue–sharing formulas have changed over time without sufficient rationale. Discussions have often centred on how different Finance Commissions have used rather different criteria for the disbursement of central funds.

While central–state fiscal relations and a delivery mechanism in place developed long ago, no separate provisions existed for local government until the recent changes, even though local self–government has functioned for millennia. The constitution defined local–government functions only recently through the 73rd and 74th Amendments, which designate 27 functions for *Panchayats* and 18 for municipalities. These amendments have given impetus to drawing up local government powers and responsibilities and requiring states to pass associated legislation. State–level finance commissions have been formed to recommend the best ways to identify resources for carrying out these functions, i.e. own tax effort and/or transfers from upper–level government. Some reports have already been submitted but the task remains awesome.

Implementation will follow consideration of the reports of the states' finance commissions. In general, the recommendations favour removing the prevailing "octroi" tax, an entry tax levied by municipalities and considered distortionary, and stepping up use of the property tax, as well as improving the design of charges and cost recovery from public utilities. The process faces several remaining impediments because the judiciary usually has been unsympathetic to levying property tax based on market value of a property (Mathur, 1997). Despite the critiques, anomalies and sometimes even apparent lack of rationale, the overall system of fiscal federalism seems to have a robust institutional framework which has recently been extended from the central–state to the state–local level. This holds in comparison with the disequilibria associated with other, perhaps comparable federal countries such as Argentina or Brazil, which often adhered to no perceptible rule for any length of time and redesigned the framework itself to suit the exigency of the moment (Shome, 1994).

Centre–State Fiscal Relations

Tax and Expenditure Divisions

The Union List and the States List of the Seventh Schedule of the Indian Constitution (1950) delineate the functions and fiscal powers of the centre and the states. The centre has overriding powers in an auxiliary Concurrent List, plus any residuary powers. The Union List comprises defence, armed forces, foreign affairs, and all–India services such as the railways, posts and telecommunication, national highways, shipping, navigation on inland waterways, and air transport. In addition, currency, coinage, foreign exchange, foreign loans, the central bank, external trade, interstate trade and commerce, corporate matters spanning more than one state, banking, insurance, bills of exchange, cheques, promissory notes, stock exchanges, control of industries declared by Parliament to be of public interest, and oil fields and mines in the public interest are included. The States List includes police and public order, public health, agriculture, irrigation, land rights, fisheries, non–Union List industries and some others.

Among taxes, the centre is assigned personal and corporate income taxes, excises other than on alcoholic beverages and customs duties. States are assigned taxes on the sale and purchase of goods, land revenue and agricultural income tax, taxes on land and buildings, excises on alcoholic beverages, vehicles and goods and passengers carried by road or inland waterways, luxuries and entertainment, stamp duty, and taxes on trade, professions and callings. Institutional provisions for tax sharing and grants from the centre address any mismatch between revenue sources and expenditure responsibilities of states. The personal income tax is constitutionally shared while excise duties are shared subject to parliamentary approval. Further, revenue from particular taxes, mainly estate or related duties and taxes on passengers and goods by rail, sea or air transport, on rail fares and freight, on sale or purchase of newspapers and advertisements, on interstate sales and on stock exchange transactions must be passed on totally to the states after being collected by the centre.

The tenth Finance Commission has proposed to make all central taxes sharable, albeit at 29 per cent for the first fifteen years. Economists debate this. It would cut back the discretionary powers of a five–member quinquennial body and render the division of resources permanent and predictable; but not all favour it because they fear that the measure could "blur the distinction between tax sharing and grants as instruments of federal transfer, constrict the centre's manoeuvrability for macroeconomic management and ... impose a rigid rule of devolution that would pre–empt any radical reform in an area that cries out for restructuring" (Bagchi, 1996).

The centre makes grants to states in need as provided in Article 275 of the Constitution. The Finance Commissions also cover these matters. More generally, through Article 282, the centre or the states can make grants for any public purpose. Since the institution of the Planning Commission in the 1950s, transfers from the centre to the states have taken place as "Plan grants" and, over time, the "Plan exercise" has taken on significant importance. It focuses not only on "vertical" centre–state transfers but also on "horizontal" interstate imbalances[3].

Role and Experience of Finance Commissions

Intergovernmental transfers take place through the Finance Commission and the Planning Commission, and by means of discretionary grants from institutional agencies such as the Life Insurance Corporation or the Unit Trust of India to support Plan expenditure (Rao and Chelliah, 1991).

Arrangements and Implementation

The constitution requires a Finance Commission to be set up every five years by the head of state, the president, to determine: (1) the revenue from each tax to be shared by the centre and the share each state will receive; (2) the principles for grants–in–aid for states in need; and (3) any other matter as referred by the president for buttressing state finances. Some consider this semi–judicial arrangement to redress fiscal imbalances with precision and regularity quite unique (Lakdawala, 1967). Under item (3), the various Finance Commissions have covered several tasks, as follows: i) the states gave up their power to tax the sale of sugar, textiles and tobacco to the centre in a "tax rental arrangement" in 1956, and appropriate revenue distribution formulas were devised for them; ii) the tax on railway passenger fares was repealed, and compensatory grants were identified; iii) distribution of estate duty proceeds (other than on agricultural land) was carried out until repeal of the tax in 1986; iv) compensatory grants to states after abolition of the wealth tax on agriculture property were identified; v) recommendations were made for reducing state debt as well as on ways to control state overdrafts with the central bank; vi) suggestions were made for provisioning of state expenditures for natural calamities; and vii) attempts were made to identify new revenue–raising measures from unused taxes and duties (Article 269)[4].

Nevertheless, as a Plan–based economic philosophy emerged during the 1960s, Plan expenditures came strictly under the purview of the Planning Commission, and such expenditures[5] were de–emphasised from the purview of the Finance Commission. Indeed, with the third Finance Commission the focus shifted mainly to revenue expenditures even though the constitution does not prohibit grants for capital expenditures. Thus a self–propelled division between the spheres of influence of the Planning Commission and the Finance Commissions grew over time. Finance Commissions have on the whole adopted a practice of assessing the revenue needs of states and their own sources of revenue, and attempting to fill the gap between them, while maintaining some comparability among states towards the achievement of fiscal balance among them. Thus they have varied the distribution of sharable taxes between the centre and the states. For example, for the individual income tax and excises, while economic indicators have been used for devolution, the centre's resource constraints played only a limited role. The Finance Commissions also raised the distribution across states. Once tax shares were determined, filling the remaining gaps seemed to have had an important objective of "assigning" those taxes for which the centre acted as a collection agency even though the distribution was based *prima facie* on what each state would have collected had they collected the tax themselves.

The states have often expressed dissatisfaction over the centre's role as collection agency under the tax rental arrangement (additional excise duty), because the central government has not delivered the promised tax revenue based on the goods "cleared" (recorded) from these sources. Any proposed reform in this area has met resistance from states, however, because of either their general dissatisfaction with the arrangement itself or the apprehension of some states that they would not garner the same revenue were they to themselves collect the tax. States have also complained about a lack of enthusiasm at the centre to explore possibilities of expanding their tax base. Indeed, little likelihood exists that the states would prefer taxing selected services such as advertising or radio and television since the centre has itself revealed a tendency to tax such services recently.

Both the terms of reference and the methodologies adopted by the many Finance Commissions in making recommendations for transfers have varied. While the earlier ones were required in their terms of reference to recommend estate duty devolutions, later ones were absolved from doing so when the duty was repealed, giving rise to a perceptible change of focus in their operations. When the tax on railway passenger movement was repealed, subsequent Finance Commissions had to look for compensatory grants. When a separate income tax on corporations was introduced in 1959, revenue from this source disappeared from the divisible pool, thereby affecting the way income taxes are shared[6].

These differences become all the more apparent for shared taxes where changing economic indicators have been used for devolution. Until the seventh Finance Commission, the indicators used to devolve the individual income tax differed from those for excise duties. The argument ran that the former had to be compulsorily shared while the latter's distribution depended on parliamentary approval under Article 272 of the Constitution. Apart from different indicators for different taxes,

Finance Commissions have also used different economic indicators for the same tax. This may have led individual states to argue in favour of criteria ostensibly beneficial to them.

Some of the criteria used for tax sharing have been controversial. Although most Finance Commissions have used a 10–20 per cent "contribution" factor for income tax sharing, economists have disagreed over whether this factor should be used at all. Many have questioned backwardness as a factor for excise tax sharing, while others have questioned the efficacy of the singular use of population as a factor. Nevertheless, the seventh Finance Commission handled criticism of lack of progressivity by increasing the weight of the backwardness factor even as the pool of excise revenue to be devolved increased from 20 per cent to 40 per cent. The use of particular indices for backwardness has also been controversial. The fifth Finance Commission assigned equal weights to selected socio–economic variables. The sixth used per capita state GDP. The seventh used relative levels of poverty but not differential poverty lines among states. The first report of the ninth Finance Commission used the poverty ratio and encountered severe criticism (Bagchi, 1988).

Finance Commissions have recommended grants to fill gaps in states' non–Plan revenue expenditures and to enable the provision of specific public services (Article 275). Such grants also have encountered criticism, either as general grants or because few links could be deciphered between the allocations and the services they were supposed to finance. Rao and Chelliah (1991) have succinctly summarised the main critiques of the approach of the earlier Finance Commissions, based on Lakdawala (1967), Sastry (1966), Gulati (1973), Chelliah *et al.* (1981) and others.

To summarise: *first,* even though the various Finance Commissions' terms of reference required them to consider the resource position of the centre on an objective basis, this has not typically occurred. Indeed, while the centre's resource needs have not received sufficient attention, the increase in shared percentage of tax collection presumed that the centre typically collects more than its needs. *Second,* the objective of unconditional transfers, ameliorating interstate fiscal imbalances, was not met. Instead, economic indicators rather than the criterion of fiscal disadvantage alone, were used. *Third,* filling budgetary gaps with grants has been criticised as clearly detrimental to tax effort and not amenable to budgetary improvements or improved public services (because the gaps were usually calculated at a given level of provision). The cumulated result might very well have been iniquitous since, ultimately, population became the most important scale variable and the emphasis on budgetary needs made it difficult for the poorer states with low expenditure levels to be allocated high levels of grants[7].

The more recent Finance Commissions (perhaps since the sixth) have addressed the criticisms in the following ways. They have used more comprehensive methods to forecast revenues and expenditures by assuming selective norms, interest rates on government loans, dividends on government investment, etc. They also recommended "upgradation" grants to equalise public service standards across states for particular services such as primary education and communications (even though the objective might have existed even in the earlier Finance Commissions). Whether this was achieved, however, remains a bone of contention. The ninth Finance Commission reverted to linking transfers mainly to fiscal disadvantage, but that concept — based on indices of economic development, tax effort, revenue capacity and fiscal potential — has remained difficult to define and measure, reflecting a degree of arbitrariness in the sub–variables of the indices (Bagchi, 1977; Gupta, 1978). Finally, only the ninth Finance Commission was not required to distinguish Plan from non–Plan in assessing receipts and expenditures of the centre and states. It also worked out "fiscal capacity" and "needs" for the first time, although the emphasis on tax devolution as a principle and economic backwardness as the focal criterion continued to prevail.

Relative Roles of the Finance and Planning Commissions

Considerable duplication and dichotomy certainly have existed between these two Commissions that convey intergovernmental transfers. Some have criticised the diminished role of the constitutional Finance Commissions with the emergence of a political Planning Commission, arguing that it may have led to the commonly recognised "capital account" problem of the states — their dearth of funds for capital expenditure which could come only through the planning process until the ninth Finance Commission's terms of reference were eased (Thimmaiah, 1977).

Plan transfers as loans and grants were discretionary in the early years. Since 1969, however, they have been based on the so–called Gadgil formula (after the economist who designed it); the formula was modified in 1990. It earmarks assistance to "special category" (poorer/minor) states and the residual is transferred to the other (major) states based on a weighted formula that assigns 55 per cent to population, 25 per cent to per capita state GDP, 5 per cent to fiscal management and 15 per cent to particular state problems. The "special category" states receive loans and grants in a ratio of 10:90 while for major states the ratio is 70:30. Thus transfers to states for Plan purposes — as well as the loan–to–grant proportion — occur irrespective of matching fund availability, performance or relative state capacities. These criteria are independent from those used by the Finance Commissions in distributing non–Plan resources. On its face, this is difficult to rationalise.

Various recommendations have been made to co–ordinate and reform the institutional arrangements. Many focus on making the Finance Commission permanent. Others would have the Planning Commission itself undertake appropriate studies in federal finance on a continuing basis. Still others have argued in favour of making both institutions permanent. Much of the debate has rested on an institutional focus rather than on efficiency. The very fact that Finance Commissions have had finite lives has given them a stamp of approval and their recommendations — made within specified deadlines — have largely been accepted by government. In contrast, the permanent Planning Commission has become a cumbersome and overstaffed bureaucracy whose projections are seldom realised.

Some rationale exists for merging the two commissions, with no distinction between Plan or non–Plan expenditures and with finite time limits well defined for every task. This does not imply that the role of planning has vanished in the prevailing environment of liberalisation. Much can be achieved through "indicative planning" of, for example, infrastructure, health and other public services. A complementary approach encompassing project design, capital expenditure and current expenditure for operations and maintenance could be achieved through a consolidated commission.

The Macroeconomic Scenario and Borrowing Capacity of States

In recent years, the states have collected approximately 30 per cent of total government revenues and incurred 55 per cent of total expenditures. They generate 43 per cent of their expenditures from taxes assigned to them, depending on central transfers for the rest. This proportion has steadily fallen from 54 per cent in 1975–76, mainly reflecting higher growth in current expenditures than in revenues (Rao and Vaillancourt, 1994). From this perspective, what is their ability to borrow?

Relative restraint on their capacity to borrow has probably helped contain the consolidated general government fiscal deficit, even though general government finances have not been salutary in recent years. Between 1974–75 and 1990–91, per capita government expenditures in constant prices grew at about 6 per cent per annum, whereas per capita revenues in constant prices rose at only 4.6 per cent a year (Rao, Sen and Ghosh, 1995). Thus the fiscal deficit of the country as a whole has tended upward with a constant struggle to keep it within limits. An obvious outcome is recourse to net borrowing, both domestic and foreign (and/or deficit financing). Table 11.1 provides the relevant figures (Shome, Sen and Gopalakrishnan, 1996)[8].

Rising domestic borrowing has had two effects on growth prospects[9]. It has pushed up interest rates, making the cost of capital higher (Table 11.2), and this in turn has meant that fewer investment projects at the margin are profitable, which reduces the demand for investment. On the supply side, government demand for the investible surplus has tended to crowd out private demand. Because the rate of capital formation is lower in government (Table 11.2), the level of investment in the economy suffered as a result, with obvious, unenviable growth implications. Unbounded independence for states to borrow would exacerbate the dearth in private sector credit availability, in addition to its possible adverse ramifications for the fiscal deficit. Article 292 of the Constitution forbids a state to borrow without the centre's permission if it is indebted to the centre. Because all states are so indebted, the centre allocates market loans to them in consultation with the central bank[10]. Old loans tend to get paid with new loans, although the margins remaining after repayment have been higher for the poorer states.

Table 11.1. **Aggregate Budgetary Trends in India, Per Capita**
(in Rs)

Item	1974–75	1980–81	1990–91	1991–92	1992–93	1993–94	1994–95 (R.E.)
Per capita (in Rs)							
A. Total expenditure[a]	249.07	532.93	1 892.63	2 114.63	2 322.41	2 534.34	2 885.94
of which: States[b]	122.46	292.06	991.95	1 157.71	1 263.73	1 353.74	1 619.23
B. Revenue receipts	183.89	348.66	1 195.78	1 432.22	1 562.70	1 630.54	1 926.53
C. Gap (a–b)	65.18	184.27	696.87	682.41	759.69	903.80	959.41
D. Domestic borrowings	23.39	91.20	460.53	409.72	461.95	674.00	404.28
E. External borrowings	11.29	18.59	37.87	62.42	59.26	55.45	36.08
F. Overall surplus/deficit	−12.65	−51.97	−140.12	−84.60	−146.72	−140.01	−66.65
As percentage of GDP							
A. Total expenditure[a]	20.19	26.01	28.97	28.70	28.14	31.39	30.87
of which: States[b]	9.93	14.26	15.18	15.71	15.31	16.77	17.32
B. Revenue receipts	14.91	17.02	18.30	19.44	18.94	20.20	20.60
C. Gap (a–b)	5.29	8.99	10.67	9.26	9.21	0.00	10.26
D. Domestic borrowings	1.90	4.45	7.05	5.56	5.60	8.35	4.32
E. External borrowings	0.92	0.91	0.58	0.85	0.72	0.69	0.39
F. Overall surplus/deficit	−1.03	−2.54	−2.14	−1.15	−1.78	−1.73	−0.71

a.   Excludes inter–governmental transactions.
b.   Includes inter–governmental transactions.
Source: *Indian Public Finance Statistics* and *Economic Survey,* various issues.

Table 11.2. **Cost of Capital and Rate of Capital Formation in India**

Year	Prime lending rate of IFCI	Rate of gross capital formation (aggregate)	Rate of gross capital formation (public sector)
1970–71	9	17.10	6.51
1975–76	12	20.83	9.63
1980–81	14	20.92	8.65
1985–86	14	24.19	11.22
1990–91	14–15	25.66	9.74
1991–92	18–20	22.87	9.17
1992–93	17–19	23.30	8.87
1993–94	17–19	21.35	8.58

Source: *Report on Currency and Finance* (various issues), Reserve Bank of India and *National Income Statistics*, Central Statistical Organisation.

The highest proportion of loans from the centre to the states goes for Plan purposes. Since incorporation of the Gadgil formula in 1969, 70 per cent of Plan assistance to the major states takes the form of loans, which have risen with the growth of plan expenditure, creating non–Plan capital gaps in the states. To avoid adverse effects on plan implementation, Finance commissions have sometimes been asked to design appropriate debt relief. The sixth, seventh and eighth Finance Commissions did this through such measures as writing off and rescheduling loans and revising interest rates downward.

The ninth Finance Commission took a different view. It did not favour write–offs but did favour making the terms and conditions more reflective of prevailing conditions. For example, if the centre floated 20–year securities in the market, it should also lend on similar terms to the states, and the first five years could comprise a grace period. Other measures also made loan structures less stringent. Despite them, the overall state indebtedness problem remains significant. It is unlikely, therefore, that direct market borrowing by states irrespective of their debt position vis–à–vis the centre would be a sound macroeconomic step now. Many of the smaller or poorer states seem unable fully to use available funds transferred from the centre, obviating any need for them to possess independent powers to borrow.

State–Local Fiscal Relations

As indicated earlier, the 73rd and 74th Amendments to the Indian Constitution stipulate devolution of 29 expenditure categories to *Panchayats* and 18 to municipalities. Higher level governments have mandates to do their best to hand over charge for these expenditure responsibilities to their local counterparts. Such expenditure devolution requires commensurate revenue sources. Accordingly, articles of the same amendments address revenue sharing and grants — devolution of taxes and the functions of state finance commissions, already formed by most states. Although some reports have been completed, progress varies, partly reflecting very little experience in this nascent area of policy formulation in India.

Even international experience is sparse, however. Few developing countries have seriously addressed fiscal federalism at the state–to–local level, with most experience confined to the centre–to–state level. One may argue that the efficiency argument for fiscal decentralisation[11] is more persuasive for developed than developing countries because it relates to democratic environments where service provision by local government can increase consumer/voter satisfaction. India's democratic tradition fits this reasoning, but this may not necessarily be so in newly emerging market economies of the former Soviet Union or even some Latin American countries without long–run democratic traditions, and where voter preferences may not get reflected in the public sector budget all that easily. In short, unfortunately, not many relevant models in developing countries offer useful lessons for India.

First, India has to make specific assignments from the rather long lists of *Panchayat* and urban expenditure responsibilities. Laws are not sufficient; devolution of both tax and expenditure responsibilities must be taken through the implementation stage successfully. Expenditure assignment should have priority, with decisions on *a)* what proportion of expenditure responsibilities a state will retain and how much will pass on to local governments; and *b)* once this is decided, the responsibility must be divided among the three tiers of local government.

Second, and only when expenditure assignment is clear, the devolution of revenues could take place with a matching of expenditure responsibilities and revenue needs. Revenue–sharing formulas of various degrees of complexity might be emulated from abroad (centre–state sharing formulas exist abundantly), appropriately modified to suit particular state needs.

Third, the post–arrangement, consolidated public sector deficit will need monitoring, at least in the initial stages. Macroeconomic stability cannot be sacrificed in the process of devolution of fiscal functions. Brazil's experience reveals that with macroeconomic instability federal fiscal arrangements can be easily ignored if not abrogated.

Fourth, the rules of the game should be kept as simple and flexible as possible, although fundamental changes may require constitutional amendments. The United States provides a good example of flexibility relative to the formula–laden Australian case. In India, the formulas should be both optimal and usable in terms of availability and timeliness of information. Flexibility would allow states to maintain better control over their own budgets

Fifth, legislating a federal fiscal arrangement at any level of government does not ensure successful implementation. That requires an efficient workforce to administer both taxes and expenditures. Budgeting for personnel, other operating costs and infrastructure has prime importance at all three levels of local government.

The expected impact on local finances as a result of the 73rd and 74th Amendments to the Constitution likely will worsen the consolidated fiscal deficit of general government. While the amendments list various functions that could be passed on to lower levels of government, the primary concern so far has stressed the types of resources to devolve downwards and appropriate resource–sharing mechanisms. International experience, although sparse, underlines the danger in passing down revenue sources without commensurate expenditure responsibilities. Even when parallel transfers of both revenues and expenditures have been legislated, experience reveals that implementation could fall behind. The central or state governments or both may have to spend on local expenditure responsibilities to ensure a minimum social safety net, despite passing down revenue to local bodies, thereby fuelling fiscal pressures on consolidated general government.

Concluding Observations

The importance and role of fiscal federalism in macroeconomic management emerge from the size, scope, and need for control of public debt in India. They favour support for fiscal consolidation through central control — but maturing democracies face strong pressures to decentralise fiscal powers down along the chain from the centre to the states, municipalities and *Panchayats*. A balance has to be struck, therefore, between appropriate decentralisation and effective policies for fiscal consolidation.

More tax bases may be passed to the states but their borrowing powers might remain circumscribed. Local governments might be given strong taxing powers, but borrowing powers, if any, might be confined to those with extraordinary credit ratings, and that only on an experimental basis — in order not to constrain efficient local governments unnecessarily and because their borrowing might not have immediate deleterious effects on a national scale[12]. All this calls for a well designed strategy rather than a piecemeal approach aimed at satisfying too many objectives and too many interests.

The states have continued to compete in eroding their tax bases, although some have begun to rationalise their sales tax rates. Disharmony in federal tax relations bears heavily upon the behaviour of the predominant sales tax. It reflects both competition in rates and an erosion of the base through incentives for new investments. In December 1995, state finance ministers met and declared that they would not grant tax incentives after April 1997 which undercut one another's tax bases. Yet they have continued to grant incentives. In December 1996, they met again to re–emphasise their original intentions.

Currently, states levy the sales tax on the basis of the origin principle; the state of origin (as opposed to consumption) of the taxed item keeps the revenue from it. For revenue reasons, states tax not only final goods but also raw materials, intermediate goods, and capital goods. The tax is levied at the manufacturer–importer stage. Thus, the more a state produces, it not only receives more revenue but also "exports" higher retail prices to states that import its goods.

India now stands at a crossroads regarding the reform of consumption and production taxation. It needs to replace its present cascading consumption and production taxes with a well co–ordinated VAT. This has already happened at the central level with the excise structure. A comparable base for separate state and central VATs would be desirable in a "concurrent" VAT system. Because important administrative and political realities cannot be ignored, a dual system in which the VAT is levied by the two levels of government independently may also be considered.

In practical terms, this should amount first to conversion of the present Union MODVAT into a manufacturers' VAT, with extension to selected services; rationalisation of rates, with eventually only one rate, would be determined by revenue needs. Second should come adoption of destination–based VATs on goods (and some services) by the states on a harmonised base with few exemptions, in place of their existing sales taxes, with two or three rates within specified bands. While this would represent a big stride in the right direction, a few cautionary notes must intrude. If a well structured intergovernmental VAT emerges from the current debate, there are some good reasons for keeping excises on sumptuary items separate. Not the least of these is to relieve pressure for multiple VAT rates. Much of the potential economic benefit of a VAT system comes from operating on a large tax base with services taxed broadly. Agreement on the base for services might be easier to achieve if the discussions and negotiations focus on what should be explicitly excluded rather than what new items should be covered.

India needs a well conceived strategy for progress towards a co–ordinated system with salient effects for general government fiscal consolidation. A group of experts and officials, under the chairmanship of this author, has examined the issue of inter–state sales tax (called Central Sales Tax) to explore the feasibility of moving from the origin principle to the destination principle. State finance ministers met in July 1997 to discuss these proposals. Shome (1997*b*) has reported in some detail the progress of VAT reform in India at both the central and state levels. The same concern applies to local government tax reform. While several state finance commissions have submitted their reports, many must still complete their work. More important is the likely role of the judiciary in rendering it impossible to make property tax bases reflective of their market values and to rationalise tax rates (see Shome, 1997*c*, Chapter 7). Unless the executive and legislative branches develop a strategy in co–operation with the judiciary, large–scale improvement is unlikely to occur in local government finance. The revenue side of general government will then continue to remain shaky if not worsen.

The expenditure side also needs a reform strategy. While the Minister of Finance announced in his 1996/97 budget speech that a national commission would be formed to examine and report on expenditure control within four months, that time has almost elapsed with no commission named. Perhaps it can be accomplished by the next budget. Bagchi (1997) has delineated in his treatise the major prevailing shortcomings of public expenditure management under fiscal federalism. Unless these matters are faced squarely and as quickly as they deserve, the expenditures of general government will exacerbate the precarious overall fiscal position, with concomitant ramifications for public debt and the debt burden of future generations.

Notes

1. The paper was written when the author was Director, National Institute of Public Finance and Policy, New Delhi, India. The opinions expressed are those of the author and not necessarily of any other individual or institution unless otherwise mentioned.

2. Professor Oates once, in a comment at a seminar presentation by this author in the University of Maryland at College Park, expressed an opinion that increased independence should give lower level government more responsibility and, therefore, they would be more prudent. The same argument is made for local government in India, by selected researchers who favour allowing municipalities with good credit ratings to borrow from the capital market. One problem is that in their credit-rating exercise, the rating agencies include distortionary sources of revenue such as the "octroi" (an entry tax levied by municipalities) as a positive factor, thereby vitiating confidence in ratings (see CRISIL, 1996). Another problem is that it is difficult to foresee how, in terms of equity, only selected municipalities could be given borrowing powers, with other municipalities being excluded. In a democratic environment, such selectivity is unlikely to last long.

3. The states are, however, limited in their borrowing capacity as long as they have debt with the central government, as is usually the case. There is also a ceiling to the debt that states can incur with the central bank.

4. Even though, as indicated below, there has been criticism by some states that this has been inadequately carried out.

5. Broadly, in the Indian taxonomy, the "revenue account" includes on the receipts side, tax and non-tax revenue, the latter including interest receipts and dividends. On the expenditure side figure interest payments, wages and salaries and subsidies. Capital account receipts comprise recovery of loans, disinvestment and borrowings. In the Plan-Non-Plan nomenclature, Plan expenditures would relate to capital expenditure on programmes and schemes included in the Central Plan, plus Plan-driven "revenue" expenditure on operations and maintenance. Non-Plan expenditure, on the other hand, in addition to defence, interest payments and subsidies, includes expenditures on maintaining assets created in previous Plans.

6.   Thus, the shares of the divisible taxes to be devolved to the states were increasingly recommended to be increased by successive Finance Commissions. For example, the eighth and ninth Finance Commissions recommended that 85 percent of the personal income tax and 45 percent of excise duties be passed on to the states.

7.   In any event, Gopalakrishnan and Rangamannar (1996) have shown that the poorer states have also been relatively less successful in implementing programmes financed by central transfers than have the richer states. Bagchi (1997) also presents a detailed account of growing differences in fiscal federal indicators among states.

8.   Note, however, that central government expenditure as a percentage of GDP has declined on average in the 1990s compared to the 1980s, while figures for the states have increased. At least at the level of the central government, contrary to popular views, it seems that the tax revenue to GDP ratio needs redoubled attention; it declined by approximately one per cent of GDP during the 1990s.

9.   See *Economic Survey*, 1996, for a discussion of the components of total internal and external government liabilities, which have now reached 67 per cent of GDP.

10. The principles behind such allocations are not, however, spelt out. They could be merely procedural. Every year, a fixed proportion seems to be added to the state's repayment liability to the centre to determine that year's allocation.

11. The efficiency argument says that local governments can better respond than higher level governments to the preferences of inhabitants for quality and quantity of local services, and their commensurate willingness to pay for such services.

12. This would meet the objective of allowing local governments to focus on redressing the remarkable breakdown in urban (and rural) health and infrastructure. This has affected even large urban centres which have been hit with health epidemics from diseases that had earlier remained controlled for decades.

Bibliography

AKBAR, M.J. (1985), *India – The Siege Within: Challenges to a Nation's Unity*, Penguin, Suffolk.

BAGCHI, A. (1988), "First Award of the Ninth Finance Commission – An Appraisal", *Economic and Political Weekly*, 3 December.

BAGCHI, A. (1995), "Inter–governmental Fiscal Relations: The Cases of India and Indonesia", in J. ROY (ed.), *Macroeconomic Management and Fiscal Decentralisation*, EDI Seminar Series, Economic Development Institute of The World Bank, Washington, D.C., December.

BAGCHI, A. (1996), "Pooling Union Taxes for Devolution", *Economic Times*, 30 August.

BAGCHI, A. (1997), "Fiscal Management — The Federal Dimension", in P. SHOME (ed.), *Fiscal Policy, Public Policy and Governance*, Centax Publications Pvt. Ltd., New Delhi.

CHELLIAH, R.J., P.K. AGGARWAL, R. GUPTA AND M.G. RAO (1981), *Trends and Issues in Indian Federal Finance*, Allied Publishers Private Ltd, New Delhi.

GOPALAKRISHNAN, S. AND T.S. RANGAMANNAR (1996), "Shortfalls in States' Plan Outlays: An Analysis", *NIPFP Working Paper,* No. 6, New Delhi.

CRISIL (The Credit Rating Information Services of India Ltd.) (1996), "Credit Rating of Municipal Bonds", mimeo, presented at a seminar on "Property Tax Innovations in India", FIRE Project, New Delhi, 29–30 August.

GULATI, I.S. (1973), "Approach of the Finance Commissions", *Economic and Political Weekly*, June and July 21. Reprinted in I.S. GULATI (ed.) (1987), *Centre–State Budgetary Transfers*, Oxford University Press.

GUPTA, S.P. (1978), "A Note on Relative Roles of the Planning Commission and the Finance Commission", paper presented at a seminar on "Major Issues in Indian Federal Finance", National Institute of Public Finance and Policy, New Delhi, July 1–2.

INDIA, CENTRAL STATISTICAL ORGANISATION, *National Income Statistics*, various issues.

LAKDAWALA, D.T. (1967), *Union–State Financial Relations*, Lalvani Publishing House, Bombay.

MATHUR, O.P. (1997), "Property Tax Policy and Local Government", in P. SHOME (ed.) *Fiscal Policy, Public Policy and Governance*, Centax Publications Pvt. Ltd., New Delhi

RAO, M.G. AND R.J. CHELLIAH (1991), *Survey of Research on Fiscal Federalism in India,* National Institute of Public Finance and Policy, New Delhi.

RAO, M.G. AND F. VAILLANCOURT (1994), "Sub–national Tax Disharmony in India: A Comparative Perspective", *NIPFP Working Paper,* No. 4, New Delhi.

RAO, M.G., T. K. SEN AND M. GHOSH (1995), "Uneven Growth of Government Expenditure in India: An Analysis of the Trends Between 1974–75 and 1990–91", *Journal of Indian School of Political Economy*, 7.

RESERVE BANK OF INDIA, *Report on Currency and Finance*, various issues.

SASTRY, K.V.S. (1966), *Federal–State Fiscal Relations in India*, Oxford University Press, Oxford.

SHOME, P. (1994), "Fiscal Federal Relations and Macro Economic Management: Selected Latin American Experiences", Inaugural Address, Sixth Regional Conference, UN Commission for Latin America and the Caribbean (ECLAC), Santiago de Chile.

SHOME, P. (ed.) (1997*a*), *India: Tax Policy for the Ninth Five Year Plan (1997–98 to 2001–02)*, Centax Publications Pvt. Ltd., New Delhi.

SHOME, P. (ed.) (1997*b*), *Fiscal Policy, Public Policy & Governance*, Centax Publications Pvt. Ltd., New Delhi.

SHOME, P. (ed.) (1997*c*), *Value Added Tax in India: A Progress Report,* Centax Publications Pvt. Ltd., New Delhi.

SHOME, P., T.K. SEN AND S. GOPALAKRISHNAN (1996), "Public Expenditure Policy and Management in India: A Consideration of the Issues", *National Institute of Public Finance and Policy Working Paper* No. 8, New Delhi.

TANZI, V. (1995), "Fiscal Federalism and Decentralization: A Review of Some Efficiency and Macroeconomic Aspects", *Annual Bank Conference on Development Economics*, World Bank, Washington, D.C., May.

THIMMAIAH, G. (1977), *Burden of Union Loans on the States,* Sterling Publications, New Delhi.

Chapter 12

Transition to Fiscal Federalism: Market–Oriented Reform and Redefinition of Central–Local Relations in China

Fan Gang

Introduction

China's market–oriented economic reform since the late 1970s has resulted not only in the decentralisation of decision–making powers from the government to individuals and from the centre to the localities, but also in dramatic changes in the fiscal system. Along with the further development of the market system, intergovernmental relations continuously show gradual but dynamic evolution. Confusion, difficulties and conflicts have arisen in the process and more problems will emerge in the future, as this is a fundamental transformation for China on its way towards a modern market economy.

The basic goal is a common one: how to make the fiscal system more efficient and effective in the allocation of resources and provision of local and national public goods, while maintaining macroeconomic stability and social equality. The country–specific characteristics of the system and its manner of implementation remain in question. What will be the special Chinese features in the relationships between the central and local governments? What special path of transition will China take, with its long history of over 2 000 years of centralised political control and a unitary fiscal regime, not to mention the past 40 years of experience in central planning?

This paper will not explore all the related issues, but it will focus on changes in the Chinese fiscal system over the past 18 years, the current state of central–local relations, and new developments in local public finance. Market–oriented reform must lead to changes in the role of government and in intergovernmental fiscal relations, but they may be incremental and gradual and involve many steps or phases. China is not reforming according to some "well–designed, comprehensive, and perfect theoretical model", or any "country model"; it is experiencing a real political evolution in its institutions. This transformation is unique in human history, with fiscal decentralisation taking place in a big country in terms of both space and population, with a long history of centralisation.

The Evolution of China's Fiscal System

China had a centrally planned economy and a unitary fiscal system in its "Soviet–type socialism" period between 1953 and 1978. During this period, the profits of all state–owned enterprises (SOEs) were counted as part of state revenue and had to be submitted to the central government, which then appropriated investment funds to firms to keep them running and/or to develop their production capacity. In addition to the national production plan, the central government controlled the distribution of goods and set wages. It not only decided the number of staff and workers employed by SOEs and government institutions but also strongly influenced income distribution among citizens. Thus it was both the largest collector and the most powerful distributor of income.

Although fiscal administrations existed at the provincial, municipal and county levels, the central government enjoyed the absolute authority of allocating fiscal resources and taking control over both central and local expenditure. Provincial and local governments acted only as its local agents. The centrally set, consolidated budget included the budgets of provincial and local governments. The provincial expenditure plan had to be reported to and supervised by the centre; provincial governments in turn controlled the lower–level local budgets approved by the centre. Neither provincial nor local governments had real, decisive power over the provision and financing of local public goods. The centre not only provided national public goods but also enjoyed a monopoly in supplying local public goods. It even controlled expenditure on administrative services and the salaries of officials and clerks of the provincial and local bureaucracies.

This unitary system was considered as partly a convenient continuation of the Chinese tradition of governance and partly a mechanism to maintain central control over national resources and speed up capital accumulation for industrialisation. The system (together with the central planning system which was new in Chinese history) was inefficient and unsustainable. It ended up with shortages of not only private consumer goods but also all public goods. Expenditures on education, health and cultural facilities, for instance, declined from 10.5 per cent of total fiscal expenditure in 1960 to 8.7 per cent in 1975. Reform was deemed inevitable.

Fiscal reform since the early 1980s has experienced two phases: the first, between 1984 and 1993, featured the so–called "fiscal responsibility system", and the second, since 1994, introduced the "tax–sharing system". Fiscal reform came under consideration at the very beginning of the economic reform because in its absence other reforms would not have been possible. After some experiments with decentralisation during 1978–83, the process formally started nationwide in 1984 with introduction of the fiscal responsibility system.

In the basic framework of the fiscal responsibility system, the central authority allowed local governments to retain revenues after remitting a sum fixed for a certain period to the central government; this gave them an incentive to expand their revenue bases. Revenue transfers to the central government were preset by contracts established in one–to–one bargaining between the two sides (provincial governments signed contracts with cities and counties in the second round of contracting). The local government could retain revenues after meeting its contracted target remittances to the central budget. The contracts could be renegotiated and revised after three to five years. Fearing a "ratchet effect", local governments tried to slow the growth of budgetary revenue by giving local enterprises more incentives and resources, such as various tax exemptions[1] to achieve higher growth in the local economy. This contributed to a fall of budgetary revenue as a share of GDP. Such "local favouritism" continues today under the tax–sharing system but in other forms, such as delay of payment of central taxes.

In most cases, the contracted rates of increase in local revenue remittances were lower than the growth rates of the local economy. In Guangdong province, for example, the contracted annual growth of remittances was zero per cent for 1981–84 and 9 per cent for 1985–93, while the province's annual average GDP growth exceeded 16 per cent during 1980–93. As a result, central government revenues and expenditures did not increase along with the growth of local economies. All these changes contributed to a dramatic fall in government budgetary revenue as a proportion of GDP. Total revenues dropped from 31 per cent of GDP in 1978 to 11 per cent in 1995 (Figure 12.1). At the same time, central budgetary expenditures fell as a share of total government budgetary expenditures from over 60 per cent in the 1970s to 30 per cent in 1993. One might argue that such development should have led to an improvement in the efficiency of resource allocation and incentives to enterprises, individuals and local governments for higher growth. Yet the decline in central revenues significantly weakened the government's ability to conduct effective fiscal policy and redress income inequality.

To stop these trends, the government took a major step at the beginning of 1994 to end the fiscal responsibility system and implement further reforms in taxation and the fiscal system in general. The key points of this reform were *i)* introduction of value added tax as the major revenue source; and *ii)* setting up the tax–sharing system to replace the previous fixed–amount remittance scheme.

Currently, China's fiscal system features "two–level" budgets: provincial (as "local") and central. Tax sharing between the two occurs as follows. *First,* 70 per cent of value added taxes is allotted to the central budget while 30 per cent goes to the local one. *Second,* corporate taxes from centrally controlled enterprises, mainly the large SOEs, are included in the central budget, while corporate taxes from all other firms, including locally controlled SOEs and non–state enterprises, are in the local budget. While the central government collects tariffs, local governments collect other "small items" such as the land–transaction tax. The central taxation bureau has been separated from newly established local taxation bureaus. *Third,* tax exemptions arranged by local governments are prohibited.

Figure 12.1. **Budgetary Revenue in China**
(as a percentage of GDP)

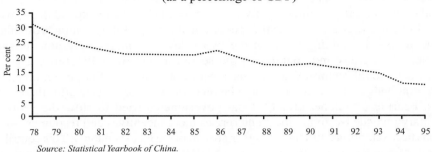

Source: Statistical Yearbook of China.

The 1994 reform had two main objectives: to increase the centre's share of total budget revenue, and to increase the share of total fiscal revenue in national income. The first goal is feasible; the centre's share increased immediately after the reform, from 33 per cent in 1993 to 56 per cent in 1994, although it fell back to 52 per cent in 1995[2]. Achieving the second goal may not be so easy, however. Total budgetary revenue has continued to decline as a share of GDP (Figure 12.1).

The reform seems far from completed, as the following problems remain. *First,* a fiscal transfer system still must be developed to deal with regional disparities in public service provision. *Second,* the definition of functions and accountability at different levels of government remains unclear. *Third,* central government's ability to carry out macroeconomic policy through fiscal instruments remains weak. *Fourth,* while formal budgetary revenue remains low as a share of GDP, so–called "off–budget revenue" continues to grow as a part of local and sectional (ministries') public finance at all levels of government. *Fifth,* due to complications in enforcement the collection of value added taxes has faced difficulties since its introduction. In some regions, fixed lump–sum collections actually replace the VAT. *Sixth,* collection of income taxes, especially the individual income tax, remains very weak, and a lack of income or property taxes aiming at social equality persists.

Perhaps the most important issue involves how to develop a new pattern of intergovernmental relations in the new decentralised market environment. The ineffectiveness of the current system in dealing with problems like "off–budget" revenue indicates that fiscal reform still has a long way to go. The recent recentralisation attempt reveals the central government's failure to recognise positive aspects of local autonomy in improving the allocation of fiscal resources. It also does not take into account the recent development of local economies and local accountability in providing local public goods. The legacy of the centrally planned economy prevents people from realising that in a big country like China any stabilising fiscal mechanism should include the participation of local governments. Moreover, in a social environment without personal income tax, an effective taxation system, especially that of a private market economy, would hardly develop if local people continue to be alienated from the centralised fiscal system. The current system seems still to suffer the conventional dilemma of "decentralisation versus recentralisation."

The Growth of "Off–Budget" Revenues

In addition to *formal* budgetary revenues, other, crucial revenues do not appear in official statistics. These are "extra–budgetary" and "off–budget" revenues (the latter sometimes called "extra–extra–budgetary"). They have become increasingly important in recent years and may already exceed formal budgetary revenues.

Budgetary revenues refer to various taxes and part of remitted profit from SOEs. They constitute the formal government budgets (both local and central), have declined as a share of GDP ("national tax ratio") for the reasons analysed above and have been subject to reforms since 1984.

Previously, in the state fiscal accounting system, "extra–budgetary" revenues included the following main items: *i)* SOEs' retained earnings; *ii)* government departments' revenues (from SOEs), used mainly for the management of SOEs and by the industrial ministries or "bureaus", the supervisory bodies of SOEs; *iii)* revenues from provision of services by governmental agencies and various "fees", including fines; and *iv)* in recent years, part of the revenue from land sales. In 1992, total extra–budgetary revenue reached about 93 per cent of formal budgetary revenue (Table 12.1).

Table 12.1. **Extra-budgetary Revenue**

Year	Extra-budgetary revenue (EBR) (billion yuan)	Total EBR[a] as equivalent of budgetary revenue (per cent)	Public EBR as equivalent of budgetary revenue (per cent)
1978	34.7	31.0	8.4
1979	45.3	41.1	9.9
1980	55.7	51.3	12.4
1981	60.1	55.1	11.6
1982	80.3	71.4	13.1
1983	96.8	77.5	13.1
1984	118.8	79.1	13.1
1985	153.0	82.0	14.8
1986	173.7	76.9	14.9
1987	202.9	85.7	17.0
1988	227.0	86.4	17.5
1989	265.9	90.2	18.8
1990	270.9	81.8	19.3
1991	324.3	89.8	21.2
1992	385.5	92.8	23.5
1993	143.3[b]	28.2	28.2
1994	186.2	35.7	35.7

a.   Including local extra fiscal revenue by bureaux of public finance, extra-budgetary revenues by public institutions and SOE and industrial bureaux' retained funds.

b.   Since 1993, the SOE revenue and government industrial bureaux' revenue are no longer included in the EBR.

Source: *Statistical Yearbook of China.*

Since 1993, SOEs' earnings and government–department revenues are no longer counted as fiscal revenue (either budgetary or extra–budgetary); this changed statistical definition of fiscal revenue now includes only the other extra–budgetary revenue items, which equalled only roughly 30 per cent of formal budgetary revenue in 1993. The change made clearer the exact amount of funds available for providing public goods and services.

Extra–budgetary revenue is not a new category, but it has new features: *i)* it has increased more rapidly than budgetary revenue since decentralisation started; and *ii)* the local share of total extra–budgetary revenue has risen constantly in the past 14 years. These trends reflect both the expansion of local government autonomy and the shift of fiscal resources since the beginning of reforms.

Despite their name, extra–budgetary revenues are, in fact, "budgetary" because they are planned to be collected and spent. The central government sets or approves regulations for the definition and management of various revenue items. Local governments must report their extra–budgetary revenue to the central government and a national budget exists for extra–budgetary revenues and expenditures. In regulation, accounting and auditing, extra–budgetary revenue is treated in the same way as budgetary revenue.

"Off–budget" revenue represents an innovation since the beginning of market–oriented reforms. It includes funds raised from various local sources by local governments and spent on local public projects or used for current expenses not covered in any formal budget at any level. It remains "informal" so far, but is part of total government revenue and indeed is used for projects ranging from infrastructure to public services[3]. It has registered the highest increase both in absolute terms and relative to revenues, although admittedly measurement problems plague this kind of informal, unreported activity.

The sources of off–budget revenue include the following items:

Public contributions by individuals and enterprises to specific public projects, such as roads, bridges, airports, schools, hospitals, local public security forces, etc. In some coastal regions, such as Guangdong and Fujian, a significant part of such donations comes from returned overseas Chinese who invest in their ancestral hometowns. Funds raised from these informal resources finance many public projects managed by township governments. This kind of revenue involves a particular way of fund–raising: local government initiates public projects and then calls for contributions. Usually, some democratic procedure is involved in the decision making process.

Profits of township–owned enterprises. In some regions, especially Jiangsu province and some areas of Guangdong province where township and village enterprises (TVEs) have developed since the 1980s, profits of TVEs represent the "big pocket" of township governments. Besides contributions to public projects, most townships rely on TVEs' profits as a regular resource for all kinds of public services including administration, public security and school expenses. In terms of fiscal relations, these township economies closely resemble the pre–reform, centrally planned economy in which enterprises' profits formed part of the government's budget — with the difference that these revenues and related expenditures now all lie outside the formal budgetary system and belong to local governments.

Fees and Fines. Government agencies now charge fees for services rendered and levy fines. Some categories of fees and fines are regulated by the central or provincial government and included in extra–budgetary revenue because they are regulated. Local governments still define and manage many others. Local regulations on fees and fines serve the interests of local communities, but sometimes local governments may abuse their taxing power.

Revenue from sales (leasing) of land. In recent years, the real estate market has grown in more developed regions. What is "sold" in the market is not the ownership of land, but its lease for a certain period of time, usually 50 to 70 years. After paying the land–transaction tax to the centre, local governments retain the lease revenue. Such revenues have financed many local public infrastructure projects. Local governments may not actually collect the money but put the infrastructure project as a "tax in kind" into the overall deal with the land buyers; the lease price may be low but the buyers become responsible for developing infrastructure on or around the land traded.

Sufficient data is not yet available permit an accurate estimate of how much off–budget revenue local governments receive every year. Broad observation indicates, however, that it accounts for an increasingly larger part of local government revenue. In recent years, many towns and cities have rapidly developed their infrastructure and urban public utilities. Most of funds used were not part of the state budget.

Table 12.2 is calculated from survey data from Township E[4] in Hubei province, which has kept fairly complete revenue records. This township is quite typical in terms of the increase in the share of off–budget revenue in total government disposable revenue in recent years. Off–budget revenue is more important at the township level than at higher levels. Some surveys of township–level public finance indicate that it equals 100–300 per cent of budgetary revenue[5]. Table 12.3 is calculated from several different surveys and case studies in various regions.

Table 12.2. **Change of Off-Budget Revenue as Share of Total Disposable Revenue Township E in Hubei Province**

Year	Budgetary revenue (million yuan)	Off-budget revenue (million yuan)	Total disposable revenue (million yuan)	Share of off-budget revenue (per cent)
1989	9.92	7.76	17.68	43.9
1990	10.72	11.00	21.72	50.6
1991	12.58	11.45	24.03	47.6
1992	17.12	25.33	42.45	59.7

Source: Survey data by Institute of Economics, Chinese Academy of Social Sciences, 1994.

Table 12.3. **Off-Budget Revenues (OBR) of Townships and Villages**

Locality (Towns and villages)	OBR as percentage of total government	Year	Source
National Average	19.0	1990	Xiang
A village in north China	50.0	1992	Huang
A village in Beijing	77.0	1989	Sun
A town in Zhejiang	72.5	1989	Sun
A town in Guang zhou	91.6	1991	Sun
A town in Dalian	74.6	1991	Sun
A village in Shanghai	67.0	1991	Sun
An agricultural town in Zhejiang	41.7	1991	Sun
A town in Ijangmen, Guangdong	85.7	1991	Fan
A town in Leping City,	63.2	1993	Fan
Zhejiang	87.0	1993	Fan
A town in Yongjia City, Zhejiang	69.7	1994	Fan
A town in Yicheng City, Hubei	59.7	1992	Fan

Sources: Sun *at al.* (1993); Huang (1994); Xiang (1992); Fan Gang *et al.*, 1994, data from case studies in various provinces on local public finance, sponsored by Ministry of Finance and the State Council Development Research Centre.

Off–budget revenue, more easily identified at lower levels of government such as township and county, can also be found at higher levels. All government departments at all levels up to the central ministries receive some form of it. Various service fees, land–leasing revenue, and enterprises' profits are the three major sources. For city governments, land–leasing revenue is an important resource in financing urban infrastructure and other public facilities. For government departments, such as industrial bureaus at local levels or ministries at the central level, enterprise profit is the most important source, filling the gap between the formal budget and actual financial needs. Government departments usually set up some typical activity for their own enterprises to generate off–budget revenues — this is one of the reasons for the boom in "officially–run" businesses in recent years. Surveys in several southern cities, notably Guangdong and Zhejiang, provide some evidence that budgetary revenue accounts for only about one–third of total government expenditures. Another third comes from regulated extra–budgetary revenue and the rest is off–budget, used mostly to finance "bonuses" and housing for government officials, office expenses (including building construction) and other administrative expenses. Off–budget revenues often finance projects for technology upgrading, environmental protection and infrastructure investment.

The lack of data on off–budget revenue at upper levels of the government is due mainly to the greater complexity of their bureaucratic structures, which makes it difficult to aggregate "total revenues" even by city governments. Table 12.4 provides an illustration of how significant off–budget expenditure is for local administration.

Table 12.4. **Off-Budget Administrative Expenditure (OBAE),**
Departments of J City, Guangdong Province, 1994
(percentage)

Department	OBAE as percentage of total disposable revenue	Staff covered by OBAE as percentage of total staff
Industry Bureau	59.8	50.0
Construction Committee	85.5	77.9
Education Bureau	79.2	63.2
Public Health Bureau	91.6	57.3

Source: Interview with the officials concerned in J city, 1994.

Available case studies highlight several trends in the sources and structure of off–budget revenues. *First,* the more developed the region, the higher such revenue as a percentage of total government revenue. *Second,* in regions where TVEs are more developed, more off–budget revenue is available from their profits. By contrast, in the regions where the private sector has more prominence, off–budget revenue depends more on individuals' contributions. *Third,* where agriculture remains the chief source of income, with TVEs again less developed, a higher share of off–budget revenue comes from "fees" and goes for administrative spending. This contrasts with more developed regions, which use higher percentages of off–budget revenue for public projects.

Most current debate on China's fiscal reform refers only to issues related to formal budgetary revenue. One can now see how inadequately this measures "public revenue" in China's economy today, because it neglects both extra–budgetary and significant off–budget revenues. From the public finance perspective, off–budget revenues form an integral part of public revenues. Local governments manage and use them for local public purposes. Therefore, to measure the actual size of government properly requires a more adequate measure which includes all important categories of formal and informal public revenues[6].

Political Economy Considerations in "Off–Budget" Revenues

The legitimacy of local off–budget revenue has been controversial. Under formal state regulations, local government has no right to levy extra taxes without a permit from higher authority or the central government. Yet in many cases it has long relied on the extra revenue for administrative functions. For a long time, township governments had to remit all formal tax revenue upward and then received allotments from superior–level budgets. These fiscal allocations were insufficient nationwide, especially as local governments' responsibilities became much broader and more sophisticated as local economies developed rapidly. The allocations cannot even pay the salaries of local officials. Without extra revenues, they would earn only a half or a third of the local average salary, or government offices would have to close down. In regions where TVEs are more developed, local government may rely on their profits; in other areas, they have to find other ways. Local fees and fines are among the options used to cover formal state budget deficits. Indeed, off–budget revenue may well be justifiable under the current fiscal arrangement, given that the demand for local public goods has increased with economic growth and development of the market–oriented system.

The negative side of the current state of the off–budget revenue lies in its randomness, non–transparency and lack of regulation. In many cases, local government officials have decided on extra taxation without following any open democratic procedure; fund–raising is randomly arranged for specific projects or purposes, with no clear regulations for management and auditing of their use. As a result, three major problems have attracted attention in some regions.

i)   *Overtaxation burden.* Most complaints by local taxpayers concern the extra tax burden levied by local governments. Such complaints are heard mostly in relatively poor regions. In regions with higher income levels and rapid growth, people are more willing to pay for public goods and they are more affordable. Moreover, in such richer regions local governments may get more budgetary allotments[7], which reduce the need for extra taxation. In less developed regions, however, even a small extra tax may cause a significant reduction in personal income and cut into people's subsistence wages. It is not surprising that complaints against overtaxation come mainly from the less developed regions of interior provinces.

ii) *Irregularity of fund–raising.* The largest share of off–budget revenues is collected irregularly in terms of the magnitude, timing and means of collection. There are no explicit regulations or rules on how to collect funds.

iii) *Corruption.* Without proper regulation and auditing, corruption in the management of off–budget revenues by local officials occurs. The situation becomes more complicated when extra tax revenue is used to compensate local officials for their low wages. Part of such compensation might be justified by the need to maintain administrative functions, but part of it might not if it gets too high.

In response to complaints against extra local taxes, the centre has taken some measures to reduce local off–budget revenue in recent years. It started a nationwide campaign of "clearing extra fees and extra taxes" (clearing "luan shou fei" and "luan tanpai", in Chinese) to reduce their number and lower the total tax payments of local people, especially those in rural regions. The rules include two major restrictions. *First,* local governments may not use administrative power to raise funds from individuals or households for public projects. *Second,* the total payment of extra fees or taxes by a household should not exceed 5 per cent of average household income per year. The rules also require local governments to reduce the number of tax categories or combine them.

Implementation of these policies has been difficult for many reasons, however. Some case studies show that off–budget revenues continued to grow even after the restrictions on local government revenues were announced in 1992. Fundamentally, the policies overlook the growing need for local public goods. When the demand for public goods is high and people are willing to pay for them, off–budget revenues and expenditures will continue to grow. At a minimum, as long as local government must maintain public order and implement central policies, it should have the necessary resources. If the central government cannot provide funding, the local government has no choice but off–budget revenues. Local government officials also complain that the centre has asked them to take more responsibilities and fulfil greater financial requirements, including higher expenditures for central programmes and an increase of salaries for local civil servants, without any additional budget. They claim that the central government actually forces them to look for off–budget resources.

The new rules have also caused some confusion and dilemmas in the provision of local public goods. In a recent example publicised nationwide, county governments in parts of Anhui province arranged for a series of artificial precipitation efforts to improve the harvest. They then launched a fund–raising programme which required all rural households in the rain region to contribute to the operation. This directly violated the central government restriction, however, and was stopped. Then the majority of the local population started to complain about the halt of the beneficial artificial–rain operation, which had been more effective and cheaper than other attempts. They argued that they were willing to pay and wanted the local government to organise such an operation.

The dilemma here is that to ban off–budget revenue without providing other funds renders the provision of public goods insufficient; but to allow off–budget revenue with no regulation or appropriate procedures invites the abuse of taxation power and overtaxation of the local economy. This dilemma points to the need for a better substitute for the current informal system. The real question is how to turn "off–budget" into "budgetary" revenue, thereby making it more transparent, better–regulated and better–monitored, in a well informed, democratic procedure in which taxpayers participate.

A New Type of Local Governance: Broader Participation by Taxpayers

Finding ways to improve the fiscal system involves identifying the fundamental causes of current problems. The shortcomings of the current fiscal system in fact cause shortfalls in local budgetary revenues and the problems related to their management. Yet, at the same time, the growth of off–budget revenues and expenditures also highlights the evolution of new systems and mechanisms of public finance, and indeed a new type of local governance.

Compared with the conventional, centralised fiscal system, the current arrangement for off–budget revenue works as a better form of public finance in terms of allocative efficiency. Even with its problems, "fund raising" for local public projects has established direct links between tax payments by local people and the provision of local public services and facilities — and therefore enhanced local taxpayers' awareness, long absent in China. Financing local projects directly with local off–budget revenues reduces the "distance" between supply and demand for local public goods, and therefore improves the efficient use of fiscal resources. This is in fact the only way that local people can finance local needs under the conventional, centralised fiscal system. To centralise or prohibit off–budget revenue would merely bring local public finance back into the less efficient conventional regime.

A real challenge, therefore, is to develop a new type of local governance. Case studies in various regions show that in most places where off–budget revenue makes up a large share of local public revenues, some kind of democratic mechanism has emerged spontaneously. For example, people have started to use the local People's Assembly as the mechanism for decision making and monitoring of local public finance. Qingde town of Zhejiang province established three years ago an Assembly subcommittee, a "Financial Committee", as the decision making body for local public finance. Almost 30 per cent of the Assembly delegates joined the committee, whose main task is to discuss and decide whether public projects should be initiated, how they should be financed, how the resources should be mobilised and how the revenues (mainly off–budget revenues) should be distributed and used. The local administration must report to the committee on project implementation and the use of public expenditures. if necessary, the committee would set up an auditing group to check its accounts.

In places where such subcommittees do not exist, local administrations report public–project budgets and use of local fiscal resources to the local Congress. Although such reporting systems remain quite loose, local taxpayers are increasingly better informed of the allocation and use of their money. In places where off–budget revenues become a major source of local public expenditures, the delegates of the local Congress now spend more time in their sessions to discuss, debate, or complain about local public revenue and expenditure issues. "Formal" taxes remain beyond their purview, but local off–budget finance and projects are definitely within it. The growth of off–budget revenues thus promotes the democratic development of local Congress systems.

While the improvements described above represent reforms of the existing system, a new development has occurred as well. In Shahe town of Shantou city in Guangdong province, the local people set up three years ago a special local "Board of Directors for Public Projects". It functions as the decision making (legislative) and administrative body for local public projects, mainly physical projects for infrastructure, including roads, schools and hospitals. The board consists of most of the "elite" of the town, elected by the local people, but includes no current local government officials. it not only makes decisions on projects and fund–raising but also takes responsibility for project implementation and fund expenditures. in some sense, the board functions like a "parallel government" in charge of special fields of local public affairs. Meanwhile, the local administration plays the role of an outside monitor: it still carries out other government duties and at the same time monitors the work of the board and reinforces the formal government policies which need to be taken into consideration.

In both cases described above, we can see the development of democratic mechanisms and a new type of local governance. Such new mechanisms minimise the problems that have arisen with off–budget revenues. As it develops spontaneously, based on solid economic motivations, this local democracy holds promise, with an obviously far–reaching impact on local governance.

Policy Implications

The increase of local governments' off–budget revenues through direct fund raising and extra taxation has already changed not only the structure of local public finance but also the entire fiscal system. What should be done in the next stage of fiscal reform?

Current informal arrangements in local public finance, involving off–budget revenue and locally financed public projects, play a positive and encouraging role in the development of public finance and a new type of governance. Further reform in local public finance should not simply ban these local initiatives or move off–budget revenues into the centrally controlled formal budget, which is what current policies in fact attempt. It should introduce a more transparent, more democratic, more autonomous and more regulated system, with all local revenues integrated into one unified budget. The following recommendations to the central government relate to this task:

— Give more emphasis to clearer definition or redefinition of the responsibilities of the central, provincial and lower–level governments. Decisions on expenditures should be made by those who control the sources of funds. The central government should stop "asking the locals to pay for the centre's party" (translated from a Chinese saying).

— Beginning with experiments, the central government should give local communities (township, county, etc.) legislative power over local taxation and expenditures, conditioned on the establishment of democratic procedure and systems for decision making, regulation, monitoring, and auditing. Popular participation in local public finance should be encouraged as part of the development of local governance at township and county levels.

— Continue experimentation to develop a unified and autonomous budgetary system at local level. This would involve integrating all local public revenues into a single balance sheet subject to unified rules and regulations. The local government should be made responsible for the balance of its overall budget.

— To speed up political reform at local level, the real significance of local elections should be enhanced and the local People's Assembly should be reformed to play a more active role in local governance.

The focus of reform should not be cutting down off–budget revenue under the current system, but helping to develop a new system in which local public finance is brought under more transparent and democratic regulation. It should go in the direction not of re–establishing central control, but of tax payer participation.

Two other, related issues need further exploration:

First, regional inequality. In a situation of enlarging regional disparity, inequality would become more and more frustrating if local public revenue increases take mainly the form of off–budget revenue. It is essential to balance the growth of local revenues in different regions with that of central and local fiscal revenue. The reform of the revenue transfer system should take on urgent priority in the near future.

Second, reforming the political system. The enhancement of local fiscal autonomy will significantly reshape the fiscal and governance relationship between the central and provincial governments, and between provincial and lower level governments. In a country with a history of more than 2 000 years of centralised, unitary regimes (not necessarily without *de facto* local autonomy), changes in local public finance and local governance will have significant ramifications for China's political and institutional arrangements in the future.

Notes

1. According to the author's recent survey in Guangdong province, the aggregate of exempted tax revenues account for about 15 per cent of total tax revenues in some localities (it may be even higher in other places) in recent years.

2. The central government had to return most of the increase in revenue to the local government to prevent local expenditure from falling. As a result, the expenditure share of the central government fell again in spite of the increase in revenue share. The new system still needs time to function fully.

3. There are reports about corruption of government officials involving abuse of off-budget revenues (see the next section).

4. In accordance with the agreement with the officials of the township where the survey was conducted, we should publish the findings without mentioning the name of the township. Such an agreement is also reached in some of other places we went. The agreement itself indicates the nature of the off-budget revenue.

5. That is, the local government is allocated 100 yuan as "budgetary revenue", and receives another 100 to 300 yuan as "off-budget revenue", for a total disposable revenue of 200 to 400 yuan.

6. Under certain realistic assumptions and using survey data, estimated total government revenue was 612.2 billion yuan in 1992, roughly 1 1/2 times the official budgetary revenue of 415.3 billion yuan. In 1993, total government revenue was estimated at 764.8 billion yuan, compared with 508.8 billion yuan of formal budgetary revenue. Total government revenue was estimated at 24.5 per cent of GDP in 1992, instead of 16.6 per cent as measured only by budgetary revenue. Similarly, total government revenue accounted for 22.7 per cent of GDP in 1993, while budgetary revenue alone was approximately 15 per cent. As a result, central government revenue as a proportion of total government revenues dropped from 52 per cent in 1978 to 29.6 per cent in 1992, even more sharply than budgetary revenue (from 54 per cent to 41.4 per cent).

7. There is a reward system for taxation. When a local government remits tax revenue to the state budget exceeding its target, it will be rewarded with an extra revenue allotment proportional to the extra remittance.

Bibliography

HUANG, P. (1994), "Fiscal Reform and Local Public Finance under Province", *Economic and Social System Comparison* (in Chinese), 5.

SUN, T. AND G. ZHU (1993), "Analysis of China's Out–of–System Budgetary Revenues", *Journal of Economic Research (Jingji Yanjiu),* 9.

XIANG, C. (1992), "Fiscal Reform and Public Finance at Under–Province Levels", *Public Finance,* 5.

A Comment

by Isaías Coelho

Kiichiro Fukasaku, Fan Gang and Parthasarathi Shome have provided us with an excellent introduction to the theme of intergovernmental fiscal relations in East Asia, China, and India. It occurred to me that this audience would profit more from my intervention if, instead of commenting in detail on the studies just delivered, I supplemented these three perspectives with my observations about the progress made on this issue in the nations that became independent with the fragmentation of the Soviet Union. In this brief intervention, I will emphasise the transition economies of Central Asia.

The dismembering of the Soviet Union at the beginning of this decade was a relatively quick process which resulted in the emergence of 15 independent nations. As a result, a sudden decentralisation of all state functions took place, including diplomacy, full fiscal responsibility and monetary policy. A framework for macroeconomic policies and institutions, such as central banks, had to be established without adequate preparations. In such circumstances, it came as no surprise that these countries went through a period of high inflation and instability.

At the time of its collapse, the Soviet Union had initiated a process of economic liberalisation and was preparing to adopt market institutions, including a tax system based on the experience of Western countries. Given the short time available to prepare their own tax laws, the independent states adopted almost without changes the tax code which had been proposed to the Supreme Soviet of the USSR. Only gradually did they introduce the changes necessary for each specific country. Even today, the tax and budget laws of these countries exhibit great similarity.

With its gigantic size, the Russian Federation has the more acute problems of intergovernmental relations. It contains 21 autonomous republics, *oblasts* and *krays* (regions), *rayons* (districts), and two metropolitan areas under special administration (Moscow and St. Petersburg). There are some 90 administrative areas for state budget management. As a first approximation, however, one can consider the execution of fiscal policies as taking place in Russia at three levels of government: central, regional, and local.

In Russia, as well as in Kazakhstan and the countries of Central Asia — the Kyrgyz Republic, Tajikistan, Turkmenistan, and Uzbekistan — independence did not bring about a significant change in the distribution of functions between the central and subnational governments. To finance activities old and new, however, a system of tax revenue sharing was introduced along the following lines:

— Taxes assigned to each level of government, without revenue sharing. For example, excises collected by the central government, and municipal charges levied by local powers;

— Taxes shared on the basis of a fixed formula. For example, individual income taxes levied by the central government, with proceeds fully transferred to the local level; and taxes on enterprise profits, with proceeds shared between the central government and the regions;

— Taxes — usually the VAT — shared in negotiated amounts, to cover regional budget deficits after allowance for redistribution to minimise strong regional imbalances.

One of the most difficult points of the reform has involved the transfer to local governments of responsibility for such urban services as street paving, trash collection, and child care and other social services, which very often had been provided or financially supported by state enterprises. With privatisation, these firms tend to cease providing communal services.

Other problems new to the government authorities of Central Asia include unemployment benefits and assistance to the elderly and others unable to fit in the transformation process. In an attempt to limit the cost of such assistance when the economy was contracting and the tax revenue/GDP ratio dwindling, government has resorted to limiting social benefits only to those most in need. The participation of local councils (successors to the former local soviets) and non–governmental organisations has been important in identifying the more needy families and individuals. In some of these countries, the growth of religious (Islamic) organisations has provided a capillary network; it has proved useful in identifying poor families and conveying to them both government assistance and food and other goods donated by international agencies.

Although the redesign of functions among levels of government generally pointed toward decentralisation, these countries soon realised that regional interdependence a number of fields required supranational co–ordination. For instance, the efficient use of irrigation networks and the distribution of electricity, based on large grids stretching over several countries, demands consensus and co–ordination. Another case in point is the disappearing Aral Sea; four countries, with the help of international organisations, are trying to reverse its environmental degradation, caused by many years of excessive irrigation and other unsustainable practices. The development of petroleum resources in the Caspian Sea and the construction of pipelines to transport the oil to international markets also require international agreements and co–operation. The same applies to rail transport, where goods can reach ports for shipment to world markets only after transiting several countries.

A Comment

by Bert Hofman

Fan Gang's paper is a fascinating account of what has become a key feature of China's fiscal system: the ever–rising share of extra–budgetary funds. I have very little disagreement with the paper, except for the numbers quoted.

Size of Extra–budgetary Funds: while big, the extra–budgetary and off–budget funds likely are smaller than Fan Gang says. A 1996 nationwide audit of all extra–budgetary and off–budget funds conducted by the Ministry of Finance, the People's Bank, The National Audit Authorities, the Ministry of Supervision, and the State Tax Administration found that the total of these funds amounted to an estimated Y380 billion, or 6.5 per cent of GDP — little over half of budgetary expenditure and net lending. In addition, social security funds added another Y55 billion to the fiscal envelope, with policy lending by the state banks contributing an estimated additional Y200 billion (Figure 12.2)[1].

Figure 12.2. **China's Fiscal Expenditures and Net Lending**

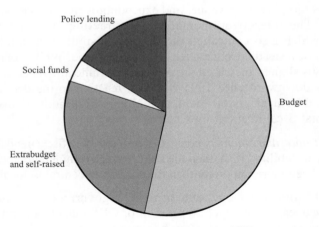

Total 1 404 billion yuan or 24 per cent of GDP

Source: MOF, PBC, IMF.

241

Fiscal Decline and Decentralisation: the question of this conference is the relationship between decentralisation and macroeconomic instability. Extra–budgetary funds are unlikely to be responsible for the macroeconomic instability China has experienced since 1978[2]. The extra–budgetary funds and even the social security funds usually run a small surplus; but the context in which they came about may have been responsible for the loss of macroeconomic control.

The reforms initiated a major shift of the tax base away from the sources traditionally tapped by the tax system, and government revenues declined from over 34 per cent of GNP in 1978 to less than 12 per cent in 1996. Government expenditures followed suit, keeping the budget deficit modest at 2–2.5 per cent of GDP, except in 1979 (Figure 12.3).

Figure 12.3. **Revenue and Expenditure Decline**

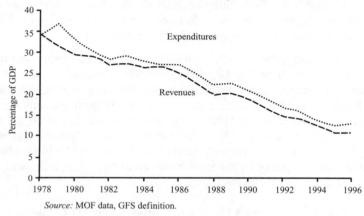

Source: MOF data, GFS definition.

Over the reform period, revenues and expenditures shifted to local governments (Figure 12.4). The intergovernmental tax–contracting system favoured local governments, which also controlled the tax administration. Central government expenditures show a steady decline over the reform period. While tax reassignments in the early 1980s slightly increased the central government revenue share, the trend from 1984 was downward until 1994 when, in reaction to the declining share of government and central government, a major realignment of tax policy and intergovernmental fiscal relations took place.

Decentralisation and Macroeconomic Control: did these fiscal trends cause China's macroeconomic instability? If so, then the shift from government to non–government has most likely been more important than the shift from central to local government.

Decentralisation from government to non–government, or the decline in government revenues, moved over 20 per cent of GDP outside government control. In addition, increases in available income added enormously to the stock of financial assets, which grew from under 20 per cent of GDP in 1978 to over 100 per cent in 1996. At the same time, financial sector reforms lagged, and the administered interest

Figure 12.4. **Revenue and Expenditure Shares
over the Reform Period**

Revenue Share (per cent)

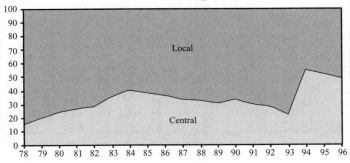

Expenditure Share (per cent)

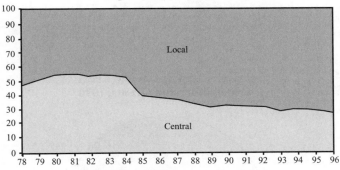

Source: World Bank (1997), *China: Public Expenditure Management.*

rates did not take over the role of managing aggregate demand. Whereas in developed market economies interest rates rise if aggregate demand exceeds supply, in China this requires an administrative decision by the State Council (the cabinet). In both 1988 and 1993, years in which inflationary bouts started, this decision was postponed until inflation started to hurt.

Decentralisation from central to local government could contribute in two ways to macroeconomic instability[3]: local government could spend more on nontradeable goods than central government; and local government could be less concerned with macroeconomic stability and therefore show a procyclical spending pattern. Because expenditure assignments are ill–defined in China, spending patterns of central and local government are very similar[4].

In addition, central and local governments are almost equally likely to spend procyclically. China's budget system allows spending of all extra revenues collected during the year. In boom years, this leads to additional spending which could add over 15 per cent of planned spending (Figure 12.5). In slack years, additional revenues are much less and, accordingly, expenditures decline. This mechanism works at both the

Figure 12.5. **Expenditures in Excess of Budget**

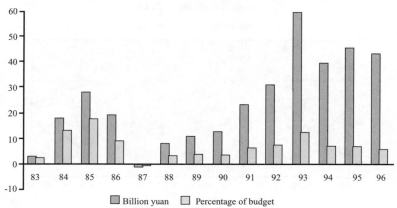

Billion yuan ☐ Percentage of budget

Source: World Bank (1997), *China: Public Expenditure Management.*

Figure 12.6. **Central and Local Expenditure and Grants, 1996**

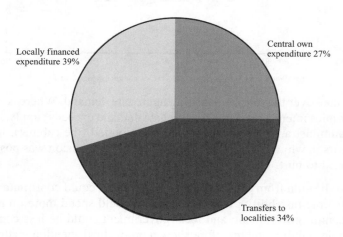

Locally financed expenditure 39%

Central own expenditure 27%

Transfers to localities 34%

Source: 1996 budget speech.

central and local government levels. In short, China does not use its budget for managing aggregate demand. Rather, expenditures are made such that the actual deficits exactly match the budgeted deficits.

Recent reforms: the sweeping 1994 fiscal reforms are unlikely to change this situation. The 1994 budget law did not much change the budgetary mechanism. The budget remains a tool for financing expenditures, not for managing aggregate demand.

Whereas the new intergovernmental fiscal relations increased central government's revenue share (Figure 12.4), the new transfer mechanism does not provide central government with increased macroeconomic control. Central–local transfers rose from virtually nil to about one–third of total government expenditures, and they now finance over 40 per cent of local government expenditures (Figure 12.6). Most of these transfers, however, are so–called tax refund transfers. For a particular province, they consist of the 1993 revenues from taxes reassigned to central government, plus half of the additional revenues from those taxes since 1993. The system boils down to a derivation–based tax sharing. This neither helps macroeconomic stability nor alleviates the ever–growing regional disparities.

Notes

1. Elsewhere, I have argued that policy lending and the *consolidated* government deficit were the causes of China's repeated overheating. I still believe so, but this is not the topic of the conference. See "Fiscal Decline and Quasi–Fiscal Response: China's Fiscal Policy and Fiscal System 1978–1994", Bouin, O., F. Coricelli and F. Lemoine (1998), "Different Paths to a Market Economy: China and European Economies in Transition", OECD, CEPR and CEPII, Paris.

2. Macroeconomic instability in China is of a different magnitude than that in Brazil: Whereas the latter experienced inflation rates of 30 per cent *per month* briefly before stabilization, China's peak inflation during 1992–95 was 30 per cent *per year*.

3. See the contribution of Ter Minassian in this volume.

4. *China: Budgetary Policy and Inter–governmental Fiscal Relations*, World Bank, 1993.

OECD PUBLICATIONS, 2, rue André-Pascal, 75775 PARIS CEDEX 16
PRINTED IN FRANCE
(41 1999 06 1 P) ISBN 92-64-17046-4 – No. 50617 1999